The Complete IDIOT'S Next Step with WINDOWS

by Paul McFedries

alpha books

A Division of Macmillan Computer Publishing
A Prentice Hall Macmillan Company
201 W. 103rd Street, Indianapolis, Indiana 46290 USA

 For information, address Alpha Books, 201 W. 103rd Street, Indianapolis, IN 46290.

International Standard Book Number:1-56761-525-2
Library of Congress Catalog Card Number: 94-72614

96 95 94 8 7 6 5 4 3 2 1

Interpretation of the printing code: the rightmost number of the first series of numbers is the year of the book's printing; the rightmost number of the second series of numbers is the number of the book's printing. For example, a printing code of 94-1 shows that the first printing of the book occurred in 1994.

Screen reproductions in this book were created by means of the program Collage Plus from Inner Media, Inc., Hollis, NH.

Printed in the United States of America

Publisher
Marie Butler-Knight

Acquisitions Editor
Barry Pruett

Managing Editor
Elizabeth Keaffaber

Product Development Manager
Faithe Wempen

Development Editor
Heather Stith

Production Editor
Mark Enochs

Copy Editor
Audra Gable

Cover Designer
Karen Ruggles

Designer
Barbara Webster

Illustrations
Steve Vanderbosch

Indexer
Chris Cleveland

Production Team
Gary Adair, Dan Caparo, Brad Chinn, Kim Cofer, Lisa Daugherty, David Dean, Cynthia Drouin, Jennifer Eberhardt, Erika Millen, Angel Perez, Beth Rago, Bobbi Satterfield, Carol Stamile, Karen Walsh, Robert Wolf

Special thanks to C. Herbert Feltner for ensuring the technical accuracy of this book.

Contents at a Glance

Contents

Introduction

Okay, so you've read *The Complete Idiot's Guide to Windows*, you've been ringing a few Windows bells and blowing a few Windows whistles, and you know, Windows isn't all *that* bad. Sure, it's not as intuitive as some Windows junkies would have you believe, and some of its quirks are enough to drive any sane person off the deep end, but it sure ain't brain surgery.

So why *another* Windows book? Surely you learned everything you need to know in *The Complete Idiot's Guide to Windows*. Why bother with the "Next Step" when the first step took you so far? Well, here are a few good reasons:

- If you use Windows every day, this book will show you how to make much of your day-to-day drudgery faster and easier. The result: you save enough time during the course of a day that you can have that third martini at lunch.
- Windows is bursting at the seams with wild and way-out features. Much of this stuff should be labeled "For Eggheads Only," but there are plenty of techniques that'll help you get ahead if you're using Windows at the office, or that can help you get the most out of your investment if you use Windows at home. For example, object linking and embedding, multimedia, and macros are powerful features, and when they're taught in this book's gentle, just-the-facts manner, they're quite easy to learn, too.
- This book places a special emphasis on learning by example. I've consistently found over the years that you can spew theory at people until you're blue in the face, and they'll just look at you like you're from Mars. Give them an example, however, and a whole new world opens for them. (Sometimes I swear I can see a little light bulb appear over their heads.) If you're looking for new Windows worlds to conquer, this book has plenty of examples.
- Troubleshooting Windows has become something of a cottage industry. Things always seem to be going wrong, whether you're running low on memory or suffering through an application that's traded its running shoes for lead boots. In recognition of this sad fact, this book has an extensive troubleshooting section (Part III) that diagnoses and shows you how to cure the most common Windowsmaladies.

- This book comes with a disk of free games, utilities, and just plain silly programs. (Elvis is on the disk, as well as a program that lets you delete files by flushing them down a toilet! Who said computers were no fun?)

What's that? You've forgotten most of what you learned in *The Complete Idiot's Guide to Windows*? Good for you; I always encourage people not to memorize anything related to computers. (I think you just end up frying circuits that could be used for more important things.) To get yourself back up to speed, all you have to do is read Chapter 1, "In Our Last Episode: What You Should Know About Windows." This chapter presents a quick tour of Windows' basics that should be enough to get you through.

The Lay of the Land: What's in the Book

The Complete Idiot's Next Step with Windows is designed more as a reference book than as a "how-to" that you're supposed to read cover-to-cover. Most of the chapters are self-contained, so you can leap around and just read whatever catches your fancy. If a topic requires knowledge of some tidbit discussed earlier, I'll point out the relevant chapter so you can get the info you need. Here's a summary of how the book is laid out:

Part I: A Potpourri of Cool Windows Stuff

The first part of the book presents a hodgepodge of sometimes fun, sometimes interesting, but always useful, Windows techniques. You'll learn how to customize Windows, how to make use of the Setup program after Windows has been installed, how to use the convenient Help system, and how to make DOS and Windows live together in harmony. Other topics include printing, fonts, object linking and embedding, INI files, and the omni-present multimedia.

Part II: Neat Things You Can Do with Windows Applications

The chapters in Part II, with one exception, cover specific Windows applications (Program Manager, File Manager, Write, Paintbrush, Terminal, and Recorder). I give you lots of tips and tricks for using these programs to your best advantage. The last chapter (Chapter 19) teaches you the very useful skill of uninstalling a Windows application you no longer need.

Part III: When Windows Won't Work: A Troubleshooting Guide

This section tells you what to do when Windows goes wonky. The chapters cover various problems that occur during installation and when you start Windows, as well as troubles related to memory, speed (or lack thereof), applications, and hardware. There's also a chapter that tells you how to avoid trouble by performing a few simple preventive maintenance chores.

The Complete Idiot's Next Step with Windows also includes the following, not-to-be-missed features:

- Sections titled "Exercises for the Anxious, Eager, and Adventurous." These sections take you through three practical examples of whatever subject we happen to be talking about. The exercises for the "anxious" are designed so you can get through them no matter what your level of computer expertise. The "eager" exercises are aimed at more of an intermediate audience: people who are relatively comfortable with Windows' basics, and would like to know more. The exercises for the "adventurous" explore more advanced features for the thrill-seekers in the crowd. You still won't need a degree in rocket science, though; just a willingness to venture into new territory.
- Several "(Not So) Real Life Example" sections that demonstrate Windows features using wacky and sometimes just plain weird examples. You'll need your tongue planted firmly in your cheek before reading these sections.
- "Do-It-Yourself" sections that provide hands-on experience working with Windows. These are usually step-by-step projects that take you through a real-world, practical Windows task.
- A glossary of computer and Windows terminology.
- A handy tear-out reference card that gives you easy access to some common Windows techniques and shortcuts.
- A "Freebies" disk jam-packed with programs that are useful, fun, stupid, and—best of all—free! Check out the "What's on the Freebies Disk" chapter at the end of the book to get the full scoop on this collection.

To make the instructions easier to read, *The Complete Idiot's Next Step with Windows* uses the following conventions:

- Text you're supposed to type appears in **bold**.
- Text that appears on your screen and text you select also appears in **bold**.
- The selection letter for commands that you select will appear in bold, such as **F**ile.
- If I tell you to "highlight" something, it means you should use your keyboard or mouse to move the cursor or highlight bar over the object. If I tell you to "select" something, on the other hand, it means that you should set whatever it is in motion. For a program icon, for example, it means start the program; for a menu command, it means run the command; for a command button, it means push the button.

Also, look for the following features that point out important information:

TECHNO NERD TEACHES...

This "Techno Nerd Teaches" icon gives technical information and potentially interesting asides you can use to impress your friends (and then forget five minutes later).

E-Z

Rearrange the letters in "complete idiot" and you get "de cool tip time." That's what this "E-Z" icon is all about: tips that show you easier ways to get things done.

OOPS!

There are always dangerous ways to do things on a computer, and this "OOPS!" icon will tell you how to avoid them.

SPEAK LIKE A GEEK

This "Speak Like a Geek" icon defines geeky computer terms in plain English.

Acknowledgments

Yikes, *another* book! This is, I think, my 14th solo effort, and I continue to be thoroughly amazed not only by how professional and downright competent everyone at Alpha Books continues to be, but also by how darn *nice* they all are. (I'm sure it has something to do with that fine Indiana air.) So, as usual, there are lots of people to thank. For openers, I'd like to thank Alpha Books Publisher Marie-Butler Knight for giving me my start in show-biz. Thanks are also a must for Acquisitions Editor Barry Pruett (for dialing my number yet again) and to Product Development Manager Faithe Wempen (for her sage advice and unflappable good humor). The book itself is a product of many fine hands, but I'd mostly like to thank Development Editors Heather Stith and Seta Frantz, Copy Editor Audra Gable, and Production Editor Mark Enochs.

Trademarks

Part I
A Potpourri of Cool Windows Stuff

Your "next step" tour begins with a look at some miscellaneous topics designed to round out your general Windows education. After beginning with a review of the basic Windows know-how you need to be familiar with, the rest of the chapters here in Part I check out a medley of semi-interesting things. Some of the stuff I cover extends what you've already learned in The Complete Idiot's Guide to Windows*: customizing, getting help, DOS, printing, and fonts. The rest of the chapters take you to new heights of Windows competence by tackling such topics as object linking and embedding (OLE), INI files, multimedia, and more.*

Chapter 1

In Our Last Episode: What You Should Know About Windows

In This Chapter

- Cranking Windows up to speed
- Getting comfy with the mouse and keyboard
- Playing with pull-down menus, dialog boxes, and windows
- Starting applications from Program Manager
- A no-muss, no-fuss primer designed to get you up and running with Windows in no time flat

In *The Complete Idiot's Guide to Windows,* I covered the basics of Windows for beginners and non-nerds alike. If you didn't read that book, this chapter culls out some of the basic know-how and condenses it into one easily digestible chunk. (If you did read the book, hey, thanks! I hope you enjoyed it. Use this chapter as a memory refresher.)

The topics covered here (using the mouse, pull-down menus, dialog boxes, and so on) are all things I'll assume you're familiar with throughout the rest of this book. To get the most out of your investment, I recommend that you read this material carefully.

First Things First: Starting Windows

One of the reasons Windows is so popular these days is that more and more computers are arriving at our doorsteps with Windows already set up and ready to go. Many of these machines also boast the added convenience of starting Windows automatically whenever you turn on or reboot the cranky beast.

The rest of us, however, still have to load Windows ourselves. To do so, follow these simple steps:

1. Exit any programs that are currently running. You should see the DOS prompt (the **C:\>** or **C>** thing) on your screen.
2. If you're not there already, switch to the drive where Windows is installed by typing the drive letter and a colon (:), and then pressing **Enter**. For example, to change to drive C, type **C:** and press **Enter**.
3. Type **win** and press **Enter**.

TECHNO NERD TEACHES...

Many people have this deep aversion to the Windows logo that appears each time you crank Windows up to speed. Their reasons seem to fall into two camps: the paranoids feel they're being brainwashed by Microsoft marketing hype, and the Type A's just want Windows to load faster.

If, for whatever reason, you want to avoid the Windows logo at startup, you can do it by typing **win** and a space, and then pressing **F7**. Your screen should now look something like this:

C:\>win ^@

Press **Enter** and Windows loads sans logo. (If you press **F7** and all you get is a list of DOS commands, it means you have something called *Doskey* loaded on your system. Doskey uses F7 to display a list of your most recent DOS commands, so you won't be able to use it to load Windows without the logo. Bummer.)

Becoming a Mouse Potato

The world's computer wags call anyone who spends a lot of time in front of the computer screen a *mouse potato* (which is, of course, the computer equivalent of the more familiar *couch potato*). This phrase, besides proving that at least some members of the digital set have a sense of humor, gives you an indication of how ubiquitous our little rodent friends have become. This is especially true in the world of Windows, because the program was designed from day one to be used with a mouse.

What do you use a mouse for? Well, when you move the mouse on its pad, a small arrow on-screen (called the *mouse pointer*) moves correspondingly across your monitor. The idea is that Windows (and Windows applications) will present you with various objects (such as dialog boxes, windows, and toolbars of one kind or another). Each of these objects has one or more features you can use to trigger certain actions, select from a list of choices, or whatever. The mouse makes it easy to use these features because you can usually access them directly instead of pressing a bunch of keys.

The mouse can do much more than move a little pointer around on-screen. The following list describes some of the amazing things you can do with a mouse:

Point To position the mouse pointer over a specific screen location. For example, if you position the pointer over one of the borders of the Program Manager window, the pointer changes to a two-headed arrow.

Click To quickly press and release the *left* mouse button. You normally point the mouse at a specific object first and then click. For example, point the mouse at the downward-pointing arrow in the upper right corner of Program Manager, and then click. This reduces the window to an icon (this is called *minimizing* a window; I'll tell you more about it later in this chapter).

Double-click To quickly press and release the left mouse button twice in succession. For example, if you minimized Program Manager above, double-click on the Program Manager icon to restore it.

Right-click To quickly press and release the *right* mouse button. Although Windows itself doesn't yet make use of the right mouse button, many of today's Windows applications use it as a shortcut to the program's features.

Drag To press and hold down the left mouse button, move the mouse, and then release the mouse button. For example, point the mouse at one of Program Manager's borders (to get the two-headed arrow), and then drag the mouse. When you release the button, Windows resizes the window (again, I discuss this in more detail later on).

Keyboarding for Curmudgeons

Just because Windows was designed for the mouse, don't think your keyboard is useless. You still have to type stuff, of course, and many Windows commands have keyboard shortcuts that can save you all kinds of time. And besides, your mouse may one day decide to go kaput, and then where will you be? (I once saw an otherwise-competent professional panic badly when, minutes before a crucial presentation, he realized he'd forgotten his mouse and had no idea how to work Windows from the keyboard. Don't let this happen to you!)

Happily, you don't have to become some kind of touch-typing tornado to get comfortable with your Windows keyboarding duties. It's really just a matter of learning the lay of the keyboard land and understanding a few basics. To get you started, the following diagram shows a typical PC keyboard layout.

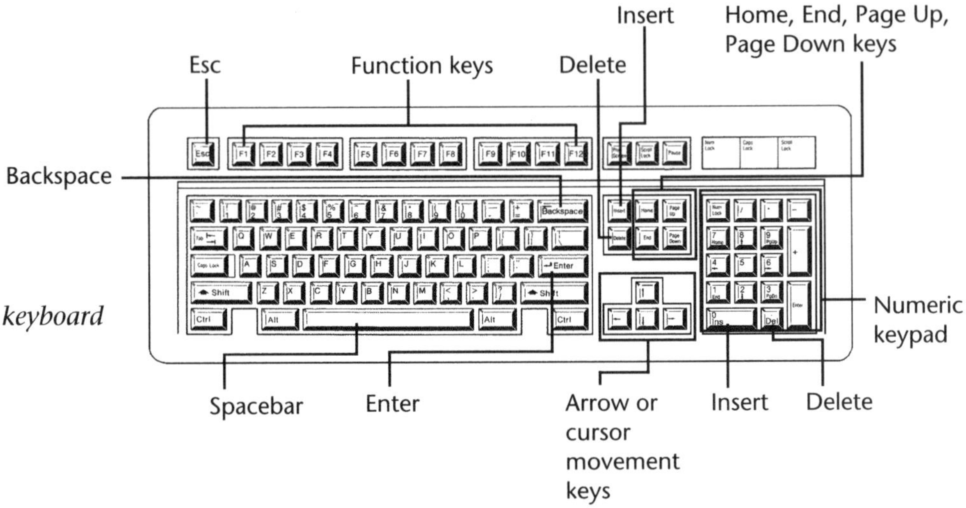

A typical keyboard layout.

Most of what you see is straightforward, but there are a few tricks you need to know. Here are some things to keep in mind.

- All keyboards have Ctrl (pronounced *control*) and Alt keys. You use these keys (and sometimes the Shift key) as part of *key combinations*—where you hold down one key and press another. For example, hold down the **Ctrl** key, press the **Esc** key, and then release **Ctrl**. (Throughout the rest of this book, I make instructions like this much simpler by saying "press **Ctrl+Esc**.") The Windows Task List appears on your screen. To remove the Task List, press **Esc** by itself.
- As its name implies, Esc (your keyboard may call it Escape) is Windows' all-purpose "bail out" key. If you find yourself in some strange neck of the Windows woods, you can usually extricate yourself by pressing Esc. (However, depending on how deep into the woods you are, you may have to press Esc two or more times to get back to some familiar territory.)
- Most keyboards have a separate numeric keypad that serves two functions. If the Num Lock key is on, the numeric keypad's numbers are active. If Num Lock is off, the keypad's navigation keys—the arrow keys, Home, End, Page Up, and Page Down—are enabled, and you can use them to navigate a document. Most newer keyboards (called *extended* keyboards) have a separate arrow keypad so you can keep Num Lock on all the time.
- As I've said, you can use the keypad's navigation keys to move around in an application. In a spreadsheet, for example, you might need to move to the left or right one or more cells. Each application has its own specific techniques, but you can almost always use the navigation keys for short trips. Here's a summary:

Press	To move
←	To the left
→	To the right
↑	Up one line
↓	Down one line
Home	To the beginning of the line
End	To the end of the line
Page Up	Up one screenful
Page Down	Down one screenful

Making Things Happen with Pull-Down Menus

One of the problems most mere mortals have with Windows is figuring out how to get it to do anything! In many cases, you can slam the keyboard or click the mouse until your fingers are sore, and Windows will just sit there, mocking your efforts. The reason for this is that almost everything that makes Windows go is hidden away in special *pull-down menus*. These menus contain lists of the commands that force Windows (or just about any other application, for that matter) to do your bidding.

Where are these menus hidden? Well, most applications have a *menu bar* on the second line of their window. In Program Manager, for example, the menu bar is the line with the words **F**ile, **O**ptions, **W**indow, and **H**elp. Each of these words is the name of a menu of related commands. For example, the **W**indow menu contains commands that let you work with Program Manager's windows (the program groups).

The following steps show you the basic technique for using pull-down menus:

1. With your mouse, point at one of the menu names in the menu bar, and then click.

   With your keyboard, first find the underlined letter in the menu name you want (this is called the menu's *hot key*). Now hold down the **Alt** key, press the underlined letter on your keyboard, and then release **Alt**. For example, if you want to work with the **F**ile menu, press **Alt+F**.

   In either case, Windows displays the menu of commands attached to the menu name, as shown in the following figure. (This is called *pulling down* the menu.)

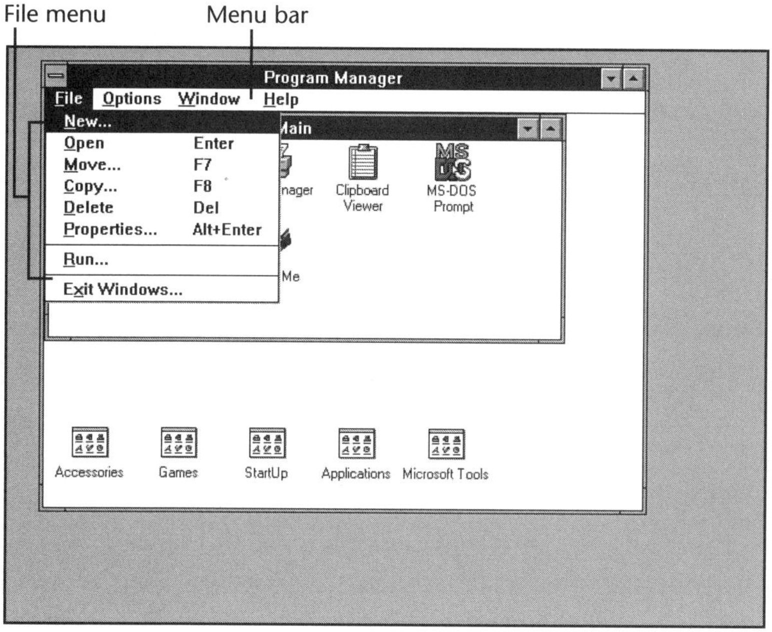

Program Manager's File menu.

2. Select the command you want either by clicking on it or by using the keyboard's up and down arrow keys to highlight the command and then pressing **Enter**. (Alternatively, look for the underlined letter in the command name, and press that letter on your keyboard.)

Depending on the command you select, one of three things can happen:

- Windows executes the command.
- Another menu appears (this is called a *cascade menu*). In this case, select the command you want to execute from the new menu.
- A dialog box appears to ask you for more information. See the section, "Using Dialog Boxes to Communicate with Windows" for the dialog box details.

OOPS!

If you decide you don't want to select a command after all, you can remove the menu from view by clicking on an empty part of the screen or by pressing **Alt** by itself.

On the Launch Pad: Starting Applications

Program Manager exists on this Earth for one reason and one reason only: to start applications. (Well, okay, you can also use it to exit Windows, but that doesn't count.) So, without further ado, here are the steps to follow to start an application from Program Manager:

E-Z

To navigate a program group quickly with your keyboard, press the first letter of the icon name you want. Windows will highlight the first icon that begins with that letter. If that's not the one you want, keep pressing the letter until you get the correct icon.

1. Open the program group that contains the icon of the application you want to load. (If the program group you want appears as an icon, you can open it either by double-clicking on the icon, or by pulling down the **W**indow menu and selecting the group.)
2. Either double-click on the icon, or use the arrow keys to highlight the icon and press **Enter**.

Windows actually has more methods for starting applications than you can shake a stick at. Many of these methods are actually quite handy, so I've compiled a list of them and stuffed everything into Chapter 12, "Let's Do Launch: Interesting Ways to Start Applications."

Using Dialog Boxes to Communicate with Windows

Computers, being the fastidious beasts they are, don't tolerate vague commands. If you say, for example, that you want to print something (by selecting some sort of Print command, presumably), it's likely the application will also want to know how much of the document to print, how many copies you want, which printer to use, and who knows what else.

In the dark days before Windows came along, filling in these blanks was often an exercise in frustration. You might have to type in the info by hand, answer all kinds of incessant prompts, or jump through any number of absurd hoops.

However, Windows changes all that. When it needs some feedback from you, it displays a *dialog box*—a small window that lays out all your choices in front of you. You make whatever selections are appropriate, and then get on with your life.

> **TECHNO NERD TEACHES...**
>
> In most cases, you can tell in advance when a dialog box will appear. When you pull down a menu, check the command to see whether it's followed by three dots (...). These three dots (they're called an *ellipsis*) tell you that some kind of dialog box will appear if you select the command.

Here are a few notes to mull over when dealing with dialog boxes:

- As you can see in the picture below, dialog boxes contain various objects you use to make your selections. They're called *controls* because you use them to control the way the dialog box works. (I explain how you work each type of control in a sec.)

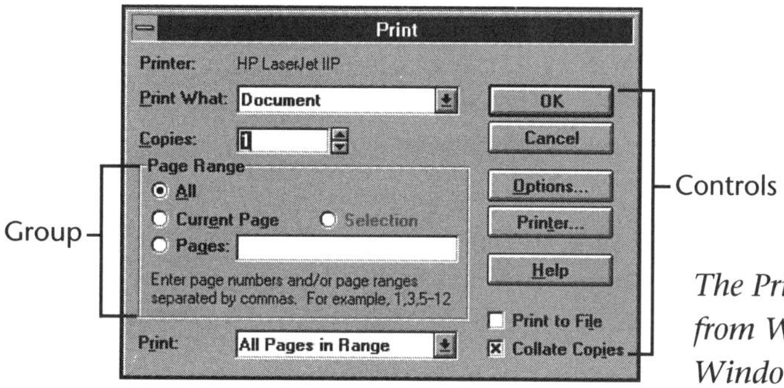

The Print dialog box from Word for Windows.

- If you're using a mouse, you can navigate the controls simply by clicking on them. For keyboardists, press the **Tab** key to move forward through the controls ("forward" means you move either left-to-right or top-to-bottom, depending on how the dialog box is laid out). You can also press **Shift+Tab** to move backward.
- Several similar controls surrounded by a box indicate that the controls form a *group*. In the Print dialog box shown earlier, the box labeled "Page Range" groups together the All, Current Page, and Pages controls. You first use the Tab key to get into the group, and then use the arrow keys to move within the group itself.

- Most dialog boxes like to monopolize your attention. While they're on-screen, you can't do anything else (such as select a pull-down menu command). If you try, your computer beeps at you to let you know you're doing something silly.

Dialog boxes display all different kinds of flora and fauna. Here's a field guide to the various types of controls you'll encounter in your Windows travels:

Control	Example	What it does
Check box		Toggles a setting on or off. The setting is "on" when an X appearsinside the box; it's "off" when no X appears. You toggle the X by clicking on the check box, or by highlighting it and pressing the **Spacebar**.
Option button		The equivalent of a multiple-choice question. You're given two or more option buttons in a group, and you can only pick one.
Text box	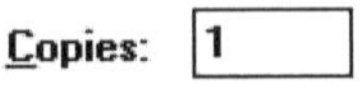	Accepts text information, such as a description or the name of a file or numbers.
List box	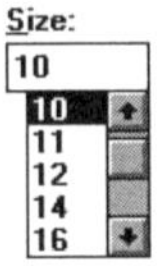	Presents a list of choices. You can either type in your choice or select it from the list.
Drop-down list box	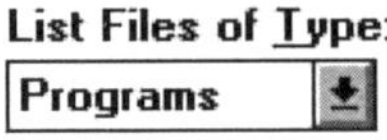	Also presents a list of choices, but normally only displays the current selection. To see the list, click on the downward-pointing arrow or press the down arrow key.

Control	Example	What it does
Command button		Executes the command written on the face of the button. Most dialog boxes have an OK button that you select to exit the dialog box and put your settings into effect. You also usually see a Cancel button that lets you abandon the dialog box without doing anything.
Spinner	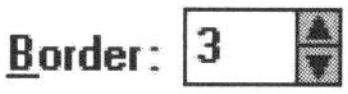	Accepts numerical values. Click the upward-pointing arrow to increase the value; click the downward-pointing arrow to decrease the value.
Scroll bar		Accepts numerical values. (The current "value" is given by the position of the box.) Click the left-pointing arrow to decrease the value; click the right-pointing arrow to increase the value.

Working with Windows' Windows

Working in Windows means, literally, working in windows—those rectangular objects that house your applications and their documents. So it should come as no surprise that learning how to work with windows is part of the core curriculum in your Windows education. This section takes you through the basics.

TECHNO NERD TEACHES...

Just for the sake of complicating an otherwise simple issue, Windows wonks differentiate between two types of windows: *application windows* and *document windows*. An application window holds an entire application (the Program Manager window is an example). A document window, on the other

continues

continued

hand, holds data created *within* the application (such as the program groups—Main, Accessories, and so on—you see inside Program Manager). In this case, "document" is a generic term that covers not only word processing documents, but spreadsheets, database tables, graphics, and anything else you've managed to coax out of an application.

The picture below points out the various parts that are common to all windows.

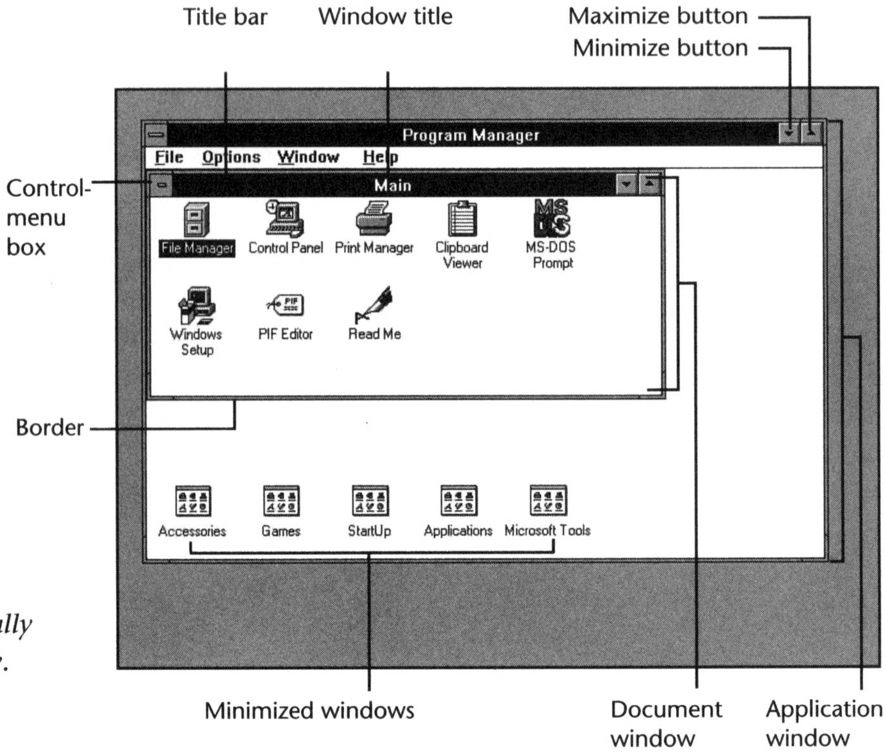

The anatomically correct window.

The following list discusses various window actions you can perform, discusses the window parts in more detail, and shows you how to use them to play around with your windows:

The active window The first concept you need to be comfortable with is the idea of the *active* window. Windows lets you open all kinds of windows at the same time, but to keep things simple, it only lets you work in one window at a time. The window you can work in is called the active window. How can you tell which window is active? Easy: just look at the title bar. If it shows white letters on a dark background, it's the active window; if it shows black letters on a white background, it's an inactive window.

Opening a window How do you display windows on-screen? Well, Program Manager's windows are always on display, so it's a bad example. The vast majority of Windows applications require you to pull down their **F**ile menu, and select the **O**pen command. The Open dialog box that appears allows you to choose the file you want to work with. When you select **OK**, the application opens the file in its own window.

Activating a window To make an inactive window active, just click on it with your mouse. However, because Windows are allowed to overlap each other, you may not be able to see the one you want. In this case, the application will usually have a **W**indow menu that can get the job done. Pull down the **W**indow menu, and a list of all the open windows appears at the bottom. (If you pull down Program Manager's **W**indow menu, for example, you see a list of all your program groups.) You can then activate the window you want by selecting it from this menu.

Using the Control menu Every window has a Control-menu box in its upper left corner. This box contains a menu—called the Control menu—that allows keyboard users to manipulate the window. To display this menu, press either **Alt+Spacebar** (for an application window) or **Alt+– (hyphen)** for a document window. (You can also click on the **Control-menu box**.)

Moving a window If you have multiple windows open, you may need to rearrange them to get a better view. To move a window with your mouse, use either of the following techniques:

- With your mouse, point at the window's title bar, hold down the left mouse button, and then drag the title bar. As you're dragging, Windows displays a gray outline of the window's borders. When the outline seems like it's in the right position, release the mouse button. Windows moves the window.
- With your keyboard, display the Control menu, select **M**ove, use the arrow keys to move the window outline, and then press **Enter**.

> **E-Z**
>
> Instead of moving and sizing windows yourself, you can usually make Windows do much of the work for you. Most applications have Cascade and Tile commands on the Window menu. The Cascade command arranges your windows in an overlapping pattern that places the active window on top and shows you only the title bars of the other windows. The Tile command parcels out an equal amount of screen real estate to each window.

Sizing a window You can also rearrange your windows by changing their sizes. Here are the mouse and keyboard instructions:

- To size a window with your mouse, position the pointer over a window border (the pointer changes to a two-headed arrow), hold down the left mouse button, and then drag the border. Again, a gray outline shows the new border position. When things look about right, release the mouse button.
- Keyboard types need to display the Control menu, select Size, use the arrow keys to move the borders, and then press **Enter**.

Minimizing a window If you don't need a window for a while, you can minimize it down to a small, out of the way icon. Here's how it's done:

- With a mouse, click on the **Minimize** button (the downward-pointing button in the upper right corner of the window).
- With the keyboard, select the Control menu's Minimize command.

Maximizing a window If you want the largest possible work area, you need to maximize a window:

- Mouse users click on the **Maximize** button (the upward-pointing button in the upper right corner of the window).
- Keyboardists select the Control menu's Maximize command.

Restoring a window After you've maximized or minimized a window, you may need to return it to its previous size and position. This is called *restoring* the window, and it's done like this:

- If you minimized the window, double-click on its icon. If you maximized the window, the Maximize button appears now with double arrows (one pointing up, the other pointing down); just click on this button to restore the window.

- If you minimized the window with your keyboard, pull down the **W**indow menu and select the window you want to restore. If you maximized the window, display the Control menu and select **R**estore.

Closing a window When you're done with a window, you can close it by using any of the following techniques:

- Pull down the application's **F**ile menu, and select the **C**lose command.
- Double-click on the window's Control-menu box.
- Press **Ctrl+F4**.
- Select the Control menu's **C**lose command.

Bailing Out of Windows

When you've finished working with Windows, you need to exit the program. Here are the steps to follow:

1. Pull down Program Manager's **F**ile menu and select the E**x**it Windows command, or press **Alt+F4**. Windows displays a dialog box that tells you what you already know: that you're about to end your Windows session (see below).

> **OOPS!**
>
> Never, I repeat never, shut down your computer while Windows is still running. Doing so could result in lost data, damage to Program Manager and other files, and premature graying.

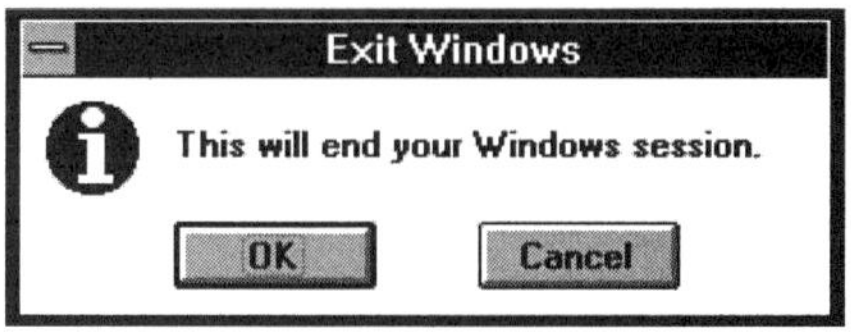

When you select Program Manager's Exit Windows command, Windows gives you a second chance to change your mind.

2. Select the **OK** button or press **Enter**. Windows shuts down and returns you to the DOS prompt. (If you change your mind and decide to continue messing about with Windows, select the **Cancel** button instead.)

The Least You Need to Know

This chapter took a quick look at a few Windows fundamentals that will hold you in good stead throughout the rest of this book. Here's a recap of the recap:

- Type **win** and press **Enter** to start Windows.
- To pull down a menu with the mouse, click on the menu name in the menu bar. To pull down a menu with the keyboard, look for the menu's hot key, press and hold **Alt**, and press the key on your keyboard.
- To display a document window's Control menu, press **Alt+–** (**hyphen**) or click on the **Control-menu box**.
- To move a window, drag its title bar, or select **M**ove from its Control menu and use the arrow keys. To size a window, drag its borders, or select **S**ize from its Control menu and make your adjustments with the arrow keys.
- To minimize a window, click on the **Minimize** button or select the Mi**n**imize command from the window's Control menu. To maximize, click on the **Maximize** button or select the Control menu's Ma**x**imize command.
- To exit Windows, pull down Program Manager's **F**ile menu, select the E**x**it Windows command, and then select **OK** in the dialog box that appears.

Chapter 2
Dressing Windows for Success: Customization Fun

In This Chapter

- Customizing Microsoft's new mouse
- Sprucing up the desktop with wallpaper
- Doing Windows' colors
- Trying out Control Panel's International settings
- How to turn yourself into a veritable Windows fashion plate

When you install Windows right out of the box, it comes in a basic, one-size-fits-all outfit. This off-the-rack approach is fine for some people, but the rest of us prefer a little more individuality in our Windows wear. We want our version of Windows to reflect our impeccable tastes, our inimitable personality, and our charming quirks.

Windows, thankfully, is only too happy to oblige such rugged individualism. The program comes with a fistful of features that allow you to customize to your heart's content. This chapter looks at many of these features, including customizing the new Microsoft mouse, working with wallpaper and colors, and more. To max out your customization good times, you need to know how to whip Windows' INI (initialization) files into shape. See Chapter 9, "Learning to Love Those Strange INI Files," to learn the ins and outs of INI files.

Checking Out Microsoft's New Mouse

In 1993, Microsoft released a new version of its venerable mouse. This updated version is a little more aerodynamic than its predecessor and it comes with an entirely new set of customization options. If you use this new mouse, follow these steps to customize the little critter to your liking:

1. Start the Control Panel by selecting the **Control Panel** icon in the Main program group.
2. Double-click the **Mouse** icon, or pull down the **S**ettings menu and select **M**ouse. Windows displays the Mouse Manager dialog box, as shown below.

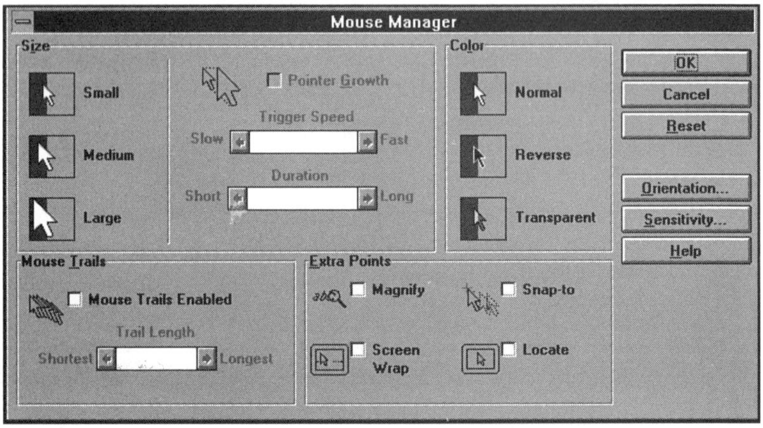

The Mouse Manager dialog box for the new Microsoft Mouse.

3. Make your changes to the Mouse Manager controls (as explained in the next few sections), and then select **OK**. (If you've made changes, but you'd like to start over, select the **R**eset button.)
4. Pull down Control Panel's **S**ettings menu and select Exit (or press **Alt+F4**). Windows returns you to Program Manager.

If you see the Mouse dialog box instead of the Mouse Manager, it means you're using either an older version of the Microsoft mouse, or some other species of mouse. I covered the options in the Mouse dialog box in *The Complete Idiot's Guide to Windows*. Many of the controls in this dialog box are carryovers from the old Mouse dialog box. The next few sections give you a summary of the new features.

A Pointer Size for All Seasons

The Mouse Manager's Size options control the size of the mouse pointer. Small is the normal size, but you can select either Medium or Large if you're having trouble seeing the pointer. If you select Medium or Large, you can also activate the Pointer Growth check box. In this case, the pointer only grows to the new size you selected while you move the mouse. This ensures that you maintain fine control over the pointer when you point at smallish targets such as option buttons and window borders. The growth is controlled by two scroll bars:

Trigger Speed tells Windows when to trigger the pointer growth. Slow means the pointer grows even when you're just toddling along; Fast means you have to really fly to initiate the growth.

Duration controls how long it takes for the pointer to shrink back to its normal size.

Controlling the Appearance of the Pointer

The Color options affect the color of the pointer. Normal gives you a white pointer, Reverse gives you a black pointer, and Transparent gives you an interesting see-through effect.

If you're using the large pointer and you're still having trouble seeing the mouse (especially if you're using a notebook computer with one of those hard-to-read liquid crystal displays), try activating the **Mouse Trails Enabled** check box. With this feature turned on, the mouse leaves a cool trail of pointers as you move it around the screen. You can also use the Trail Length scroll bar to adjust the length of the trail. By sliding the scroll box to the left or right, you can generate shorter or longer trails.

Making the Mouse Sensitive to Your Needs

Whether you're a beginner who has trouble making the pointer behave itself or a virtuoso who has achieved pinpoint control through incessant hours of pointing, clicking, and dragging, you can adjust the *sensitivity* of the mouse so it responds properly to your movements. (Some of my female friends would love to just click a button or two to make the males in their life more sensitive.)

Select the **Sensitivity** button to display the Sensitivity dialog box. Use the Overall Pointer Speed scroll bars to adjust how fast the pointer moves when you move the mouse. (You can set both the Vertical and Horizontal speed.) You can also select an acceleration value to make the mouse accelerate as you move it. I'd suggest starting out at the Low setting until you get used to this feature. Medium and High are really hard to control.

The **Double-Click Speed** scroll bar controls the threshold by which Windows differentiates between a double-click and two single-clicks. If Windows doesn't always recognize your double-clicks, set up a slower double-click speed by moving the scroll box to the left. If Windows sometimes interprets two single-clicks as a double-click, set up a faster double-click speed by moving the scroll box to the right. (To test the new speed, double-click on the **Test** area. The clapper board moves up and down if Windows recognizes your double-clicks.)

Some Mouse Extras

The **Extra Points** section gives you the following options:

The **Magnify** check box lets you blow up a small chunk of the screen to get a good look at hard-to-read text or graphics. When you select Magnify, a list appears from which you can select the keyboard/mouse combination that activates the magnification (you need to double-click on the selection). For example, selecting **Alt+Secondary** means the magnification kicks in when you hold down Alt and right-click. (Microsoft uses the terms "Primary" and "Secondary" just in case you've reversed your left and right mouse buttons, as described in the following sidebar.)

Snap-to is a handy feature that can make it easier to navigate dialog boxes. Most dialog boxes have a default command button (usually, but not always, the **OK** button) that you can select by pressing **Enter**. When you activate the **Snap-to** check box, Windows automatically places the mouse pointer over the default button. So, to select this button, you just have to click.

Screen Wrap is one of my favorite features of the new mouse. If you activate this button and then, say, move the mouse pointer off the left edge of the screen, it comes back in on the right side! It's not for everyone, and it does take some getting used to, but it can make mousing around remarkably easier.

If you've ever lost your pointer in the midst of a crowded screen (especially you notebook users), the **Locate** option is for you. When you activate this check box, you're presented with the same list of keyboard/mouse combinations you saw for the Magnify option. Double-click on the one you want, and then try it out. Like magic, the pointer appears instantly right smack in the middle of the screen.

TECHNO NERD TEACHES...

If you're left-handed, you can reverse the functions of the left and right mouse buttons for a more comfortable fit. Select the **O**rientation button to display the Orientation dialog box. Select Set **B**uttons, click the right mouse button, and then click on **OK** (using the right button this time). From now on, Windows assumes you're doing the clicking thing with the right mouse button.

A Desktop with a View

The background on which your windows, icons, and dialog boxes appear is called the *desktop*. In its default incarnation, the desktop is a drab, lifeless gray: a real yawning festival. If you prefer something with a little more character, the Control Panel has umpteen ways to remake the desktop in your own image. For starters, load the Control Panel (by double-clicking the **Control Panel** icon in Program Manager's Main group), and then either double-click the **Desktop** icon or select the **S**ettings menu's **D**esktop command. Windows displays the Desktop dialog box, shown in the following figure.

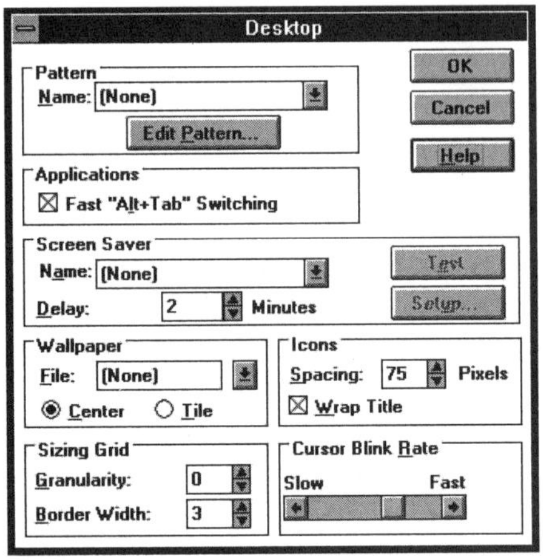

Use the Desktop dialog box to customize the look and feel of the Windows desktop.

Sprucing Up the Desktop with Wallpaper

The easiest way for you would-be Windows interior decorators to get a new look is to wallpaper the desktop. In Windows, a *wallpaper* is just a pattern or image that covers some or all of the desktop. To check it out, find the Wallpaper group in the Desktop dialog box, drop down the **File** list (by clicking on the downward-pointing arrow or by pressing **Alt+F** and then **Alt+down arrow**), and then select one of the file names (ARCHES.BMP and MARBLE.BMP are pretty cool). Most of these images are just small rectangles, so to get the full effect you also need to activate the **Tile** option. Select **OK**, and Windows displays the wallpaper. (To get a good look at it, you should probably minimize any running applications.)

If you'd like a different wallpaper to appear automatically every time you start Windows, pay a visit to Chapter 18, "Windows Robotics: Recording Recorder Macros," to find out how that's done.

Do-It-Yourself: Creating Your Own Wallpaper

The wallpapers provided by Windows are pretty good, but you might prefer to see something a little more personal. For example, you might want to display your company logo, a photo of a loved one, or a picture done by the kids. Here's the secret: each of the wallpapers in the **File** list are actually files residing in your Windows directory. (They're called *bitmap* files, which is why they all end with .BMP—BitMaP, get it?) So all you have to do is create your own bitmap images and store them in the WINDOWS directory.

The tricky part, of course, is creating your own bitmap files. Here are a few ideas:

- If you have access to a scanner, you can save the images to a .BMP file in the WINDOWS directory. (A *scanner* is a machine something like a photocopier; it copies images, but instead of creating a hard copy, it stores the image as a file on your computer.)
- Many CD-ROMs come packed with interesting photos and graphics. If these are already in .BMP format (i.e., if the file name ends with .BMP), use File Manager to copy the files you want to the WINDOWS directory. If they're not in .BMP format, you can often use Paintbrush to convert them. See Chapter 15, "A Master Class in Paintbrush," for details.
- You can use Paintbrush to create your own bitmap images. When you save the image, select one of the .BMP formats from the Save File as Type list (Paintbrush always defaults to a .BMP format, so you probably don't have to worry about this). Also, make sure you save the image in the WINDOWS directory (again, this is the default location for Paintbrush files).

Whichever method you use, Control Panel automatically picks out any .BMP files in the WINDOWS directory and displays them in the wallpaper list. The picture below shows the company logo I created in Paintbrush proudly displayed as wallpaper.

My company logo as wallpaper.

A (Not So) Real-Life Example

If your computer sits where other people can see it, why not put it to good use when you're not working with it? Specifically, I'm talking about having your computer display some kind of promotional material for an upcoming event you're involved with. All you have to do is create a snappy ad in Paintbrush, save it as a .BMP file in your WINDOWS directory, and then display it as wallpaper. (For best results, make sure you minimize all your running applications.) The picture below shows an example.

You can use wallpaper to turn your computer into a mini-billboard.

Screen Saver Silliness

In olden times (say, five or six years ago), monitors weren't as good as they are today, and most of us struggled along using ugly DOS screens. One of the problems people faced was leaving their monitors on too long and ending up with some DOS hieroglyphics burned permanently into the screen. To prevent this from happening, some genius came up with the idea of a *screen saver*: a program that would automatically kick in after the computer was idle for a few minutes. The screen saver would display some kind of moving pattern that would help prevent burn-in. A simple touch of a key or jiggle of a mouse, and the normal screen would return unharmed and none the worse for wear.

Nowadays, it's pretty tough to burn an image into your screen. Improvements in monitor quality and the graphical nature of Windows have made such a fate virtually impossible. Curiously, though, screen savers are still around and are, in fact, flourishing. The reason: most of them are just plain cool. Who cares about preventing burn-in when we can watch wild, psychedelic patterns every few minutes?

There are scads of commercial screen savers on the market (forge ahead to Chapter 10, "A Few of My Favorite Windows Things," to get the lowdown on some of the more interesting ones), but Windows comes equipped with some of its own. To try them out, find the Screen Saver group in the Desktop dialog box, drop down the Name list, and select a screen saver. You can also choose the following options:

Delay This spinner controls the amount of time your computer must be inactive before the screen saver goes to work. You can enter a number between 1 and 99 minutes.

Test Select this button to give the screen saver a trial run. To return to the Desktop dialog box, move your mouse or press any key (I suggest pressing a harmless key such as Shift or Ctrl).

Setup Select this button to set various options for the screen saver. The Setup dialog box that appears depends on which screen saver you chose. You usually see some options that control the speed of the screen saver, and the number and type of the patterns available. You can also assign a password to a screen saver. See Chapter 20, "An Ounce of Prevention: Avoiding Trouble," to get the full password poop. Make your selections, and then select **OK** to return to the Desktop dialog box.

Even More Desktop Customization Tomfoolery

The Desktop dialog box is jam-packed with all kinds of customization fun. I won't go through everything, but here's a quick lowdown on a few of the other features you might want to give a whirl.

The **Icons** section controls two properties of the Windows icons:

- The Spacing spinner (sounds like an amusement park ride, doesn't it?) controls the amount of horizontal space Windows allows between icons. If you find some of your icon titles are bumping into each other and causing fights, increase this number to 100 or so (you can, if you like, go as high as 512). Conversely, if you'd like to cram more icons into a limited space, reduce the value (the minimum allowed is 32).

- Activating the **W**rap Title check box tells Windows to display really long icon titles on multiple lines (up to a maximum of four lines).

The Sizing Grid options can make it easier to size windows (as described in the last chapter):

- The Windows desktop has an invisible grid that determines how window borders are sized and moved. The **G**ranularity (who comes up with these words?) is just a fancy name for the size of the grid. The larger the number (the max is 49), the faster your windows leap across the screen as you move and size them. The downside is that larger numbers give you much less control over the placement of a moved or sized window. Entering 0 in this spinner turns the grid off.
- The **B**order Width spinner controls the size of the borders that surround each window. If you're having trouble grabbing a border when you try to size a window, increase this number (you can go up to 50, but you shouldn't need anything larger than 10 or so).

The Cursor Blink **R**ate scroll bar controls the speed at which the insertion point cursor winks on and off. A faster speed may help you see the cursor better, but it just gets annoying if it's too fast.

Color Your Windows World

Most of us have seen (or lived in) neighborhoods where all the houses seem to be formed from the same mold (the old cookie-cutter approach to house building). What redeems these areas for me is that most owners are determined to make their homes stick out from the herd by adding a splash of color to a garage door or a gutter.

If you'd like to stand out from the Windows crowd, one of the best ways to do it is to customize Windows' colors. You can change the color of not only the desktop but also the title bars, menu bars, buttons, and more. To do Windows' colors, start Control Panel and then either double-click on the **Color** icon or pull down the **S**ettings menu and select the Color command. The Color dialog box appears, as shown below.

Watch these fake windows to see what effect your colors will have.

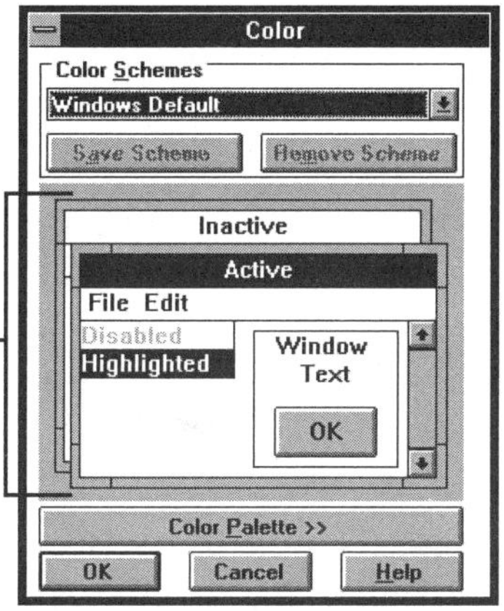

Use the Color dialog box to put some color in Windows' cheeks.

Picking Out a Color Scheme

The Windows creators thoughtfully included a number of built-in color schemes that range from the staid and conservative to the wild and wacky. To select one of these schemes, drop-down the Color **S**chemes list and choose a scheme that sounds interesting. Keep your eyes peeled on the faux windows below the Color **S**chemes list to see what each scheme looks like. When you've picked out a scheme that suits your fancy, select **OK** to put it into effect.

E-Z

If you're using Windows on a notebook computer, be sure to check out any of the "LCD" color schemes (such as **LCD Default Screen Settings**). They're designed to make Windows easier to view on those unattractive notebook screens.

Do It Yourself: Creating Your Own Personal Color Scheme

Some of the prefab color schemes are bizarre to say the least. (I suggest wearing sunglasses if you plan to view the Hot Dog Stand scheme for more than a few seconds.) If you can't find a color scheme you can live with day in and day out, don't sweat it because it's easy to create your own. Here's how:

1. In the Color dialog box, select the Color **P**alette button. Windows expands the dialog box to display more options.
2. Use the Screen **E**lement drop-down list box to select which component of the Windows screen you want to change. (Or you can click on the appropriate element in the fake windows on the left side of the dialog box.)
3. Use the color boxes in the **B**asic Colors collection to specify a color for the selected element. You can either click on the color box you want, or you can press **Alt+B**, use the arrow keys to highlight a color, and then press the **Spacebar**. The fake windows on the left side of the dialog box show you what the new color will look like in the heat of battle.

TECHNO NERD TEACHES...

> If none of the 48 available colors do anything for you, create your own. Select one of the boxes in the **C**ustom Colors area, and then select the **D**efine Custom Colors button. In the Custom Color Selector dialog box that appears, click on the color you want, select **A**dd Color, and then select **C**lose.

4. Repeat steps 2 and 3 to establish colors for the other screen elements you want to change.
5. When you're done, select the S**a**ve Scheme button. Windows displays the Save Scheme dialog box.
6. Enter a name for the scheme in the text box provided, and then select **OK** to return to the Color dialog box.
7. Select **OK** to return to the Control Panel and put your shiny new color scheme into effect.

A (Not So) Real-Life Example

If you want to be truly "cool" these days, black is *the* choice for your fashion color. It's not all that unusual to see people dressed entirely in black—right down to their lipstick and nail polish. (These monochrome bohemians are called PIBs—Persons in Black.) If this style appeals to you, why not set Windows up the same way? The picture below shows you what Windows looks like if you select black for *everything* in the Screen Element list. Way cool.

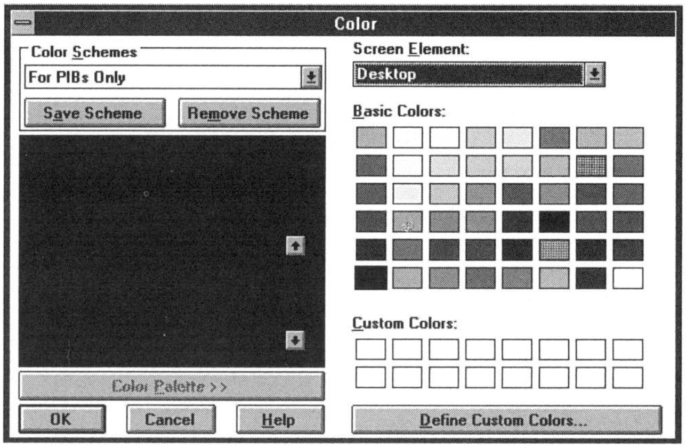

A Windows color scheme for the cool.

Going Global with Control Panel's International Settings

It is, as the song says, a small world after all, and you may need to add an international flavor to your Windows work. Control Panel's International settings do two things that are of interest to us: they provide many Windows applications with default values for things like date, time, currency, and number formats, and they specify a default keyboard layout so you can easily type foreign characters in your documents. Consider the following uses for the International settings:

- You might need to format your dates to conform to the standard of another country. For instance, in Britain, the date 5/7/94 means July 5, 1994; the same thing in the U.S. means May 7, 1994.
- You might want currency values in a spreadsheet or database to always appear with, say, a pound sign (£).
- You might need to use foreign characters (such as á, ç, or ö) in your documents. If you only need the occasional foreign character, Windows' Character Map application can do the job. (I covered the Character Map in *The Complete Idiot's Guide to*

Windows.) However, that becomes a pain if you need these characters regularly.

To modify the International settings, follow these steps:

1. In Control Panel, double-click on the **International** icon or select International from the Settings menu. The International dialog box appears, as shown below.

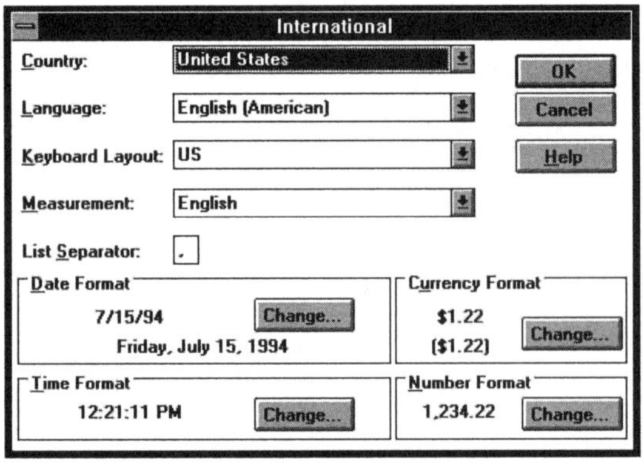

Use the International dialog box to broaden Windows' horizons.

2. Use the Country drop-down list to select a country. Windows alters the formats at the bottom of the dialog box to conform to the standards of the country you select.
3. In the Keyboard Layout drop-down list, select **US-International**.
4. Select **OK**. If this is the first time you've used the US-International keyboard, Windows displays the Install Driver dialog box that asks you to insert one of the Windows installation disks.
5. Insert the appropriate disk and select **OK**. Windows copies a special file from the disk and returns you to the Control Panel.

Your keyboard is now set up to type accented foreign characters in your documents. To try this out, load Write or your favorite word processor. Now type a back quote (') and the letter **a**. Voilà! Windows produces an à. In the new keyboard layout, the back quote is a special character that adds accents to letters. The following table shows you the characters you can use and the accents they produce:

Press	To get the following accent
Back quote (‘)	Grave (à, è, ì, ò, ù)
Tilde (~)	Tilde (ñ)
Caret (^)	Circumflex (â, ê, î, ô, û)
Apostrophe (’)	Acute (á, é, í, ó, ú) or cedilla (ç)
Quotation mark (“)	Dieresis (ä, ë, ï, ö, ü, ÿ)

In each case, you first press the special character (‘, ~, ^, ’, or “) and then the letter. If you want to use a special character by itself, type a space after it.

You can also use the *right* Alt key to generate other useful characters. (The left Alt key's behavior remains unchanged.) The following table lists a few interesting possibilities:

Press	To get
Right Alt+C	©
Right Alt+Shift+C	¢
Right Alt+R	®
Right Alt+6	¼
Right Alt+7	½
Right Alt+8	¾
Right Alt+$	£

The Least You Need to Know

This chapter showed you how to dress up Windows so you can take it anywhere. Here's a review of this chapter's fashion highlights:

- If you use Microsoft's slick new mouse, you can customize it by selecting the Control Panel's **Mouse** icon. Use the Mouse Manager dialog box that appears to rearrange your rodent.
- To liven up your desktop with some wallpaper, select Control Panel's **Desktop** icon, and then use the Wallpaper group's **F**ile list to select a wallpaper.
- To activate the Windows screen saver, select Control Panel's **Desktop** icon, and then choose a screen saver from the N**a**me list.
- You can show your Windows colors by selecting the **Color** icon in Control Panel, and then selecting a color scheme from the Color **S**chemes list. If you'd like to try your hand at creating your own color scheme, select the Color **P**alette button and then assign a color to the various items in the Screen **E**lements list.
- The International settings control the default date, time, currency, and number formats used by some Windows applications, and they let you easily type accented characters. To change these settings, choose the **International** icon in the Control Panel.

Chapter 3
Tweaking Windows with Setup

In This Chapter

- Changing the settings for your display, mouse, and keyboard
- Telling Windows about applications that are already on your hard disk
- Adding and removing Windows components
- Using the DOS Version of Setup
- Using Setup to alter the cut of Windows' jib

The Windows installation is handled by a program called Setup that does two things: it configures Windows so it will get along with your system's hardware, and it copies and sets up the files necessary to operate Windows. In most cases, Windows runs fine right out of the box, and you never have to worry about adjusting its configuration again. But what if you get a new monitor or a new mouse? Or what if you're running out of disk space and you'd like to blow away one or two of the Windows applets?

For this sort of periodic maintenance, you need to return to the Setup program and use it to keep you and Windows on the same page. With Setup you can tell Windows about new hardware (video, mouse, or keyboard), add and remove Windows components, and even set up your existing DOS applications so you can launch them from within Windows. This chapter shows you how to do all these things.

Messing Around with Your Hardware Settings

In order for your software to work properly, it must be able to coexist relatively peacefully with your hardware. The problem is, software and hardware speak completely different languages. Put them in the same room together, and they end up just staring at each other with perplexed looks on their digital faces.

To bridge the gap, the world's programming eggheads came up with tiny little programs called *device drivers*. These drivers are highly specialized creatures that exist only to translate signals back and forth between a hardware device and your software. For example, whenever you click your mouse, the mouse's device driver gets a signal that says something like, "tell whatever software is running that the left mouse button has just been clicked." The driver translates this signal into softwarese, and passes the message on to Windows.

During installation, the Setup program noses around in your system to check out what kind of hardware you've got hooked up. It looks at, among other things, your video display card (this is an internal component that generates the stuff you see on your monitor), your keyboard, and your mouse. Setup then copies the appropriate device drivers to your hard disk so Windows can use them. Each time you start Windows, these device drivers are loaded into memory, where they patiently await the signals that give meaning to their lives.

But what happens if you change your mouse or keyboard? Or what if you have a video card that can handle different resolutions? (I explain what *resolutions* are shortly.) Because most device drivers are designed to work only with specific devices, you need to tell Windows to switch to a different driver that works with the new device. Fortunately, this is quite easy because all you do is invoke Setup again and tell it to make the switch.

A Thing or Two About Video Resolutions

Before we get down to the nitty-gritty of specifying new device drivers, let's have a brief chat about *video resolutions*. The resolution of your video system is a measure of how much detail it can display. (The resolution is also known as the *display mode*.) Everything you see on your monitor is displayed using tiny pinpoints of light called *pixels* (which is short for *picture elements*). A typical VGA (Video Graphics Array) system might have 640 columns of pixels arranged in 480 rows, and so it's said to have a 640-by-480 resolution. This provides over 300,000 total pixels for displaying all your windows, dialog boxes, and graphics. That's a lot of pixels, but many of today's new Super VGA systems can handle resolutions of 800-by-600 (480,000 pixels) and even 1,024-by-768 (a mind-blowing 786,432 pixels!).

What do these different resolutions mean in the real world? Well, for one thing, more pixels mean you can display things like graphics in greater detail. The big advantage you get with higher resolutions, though, is more screen space. For example, the picture below was shot in the standard 640-by-480 resolution.

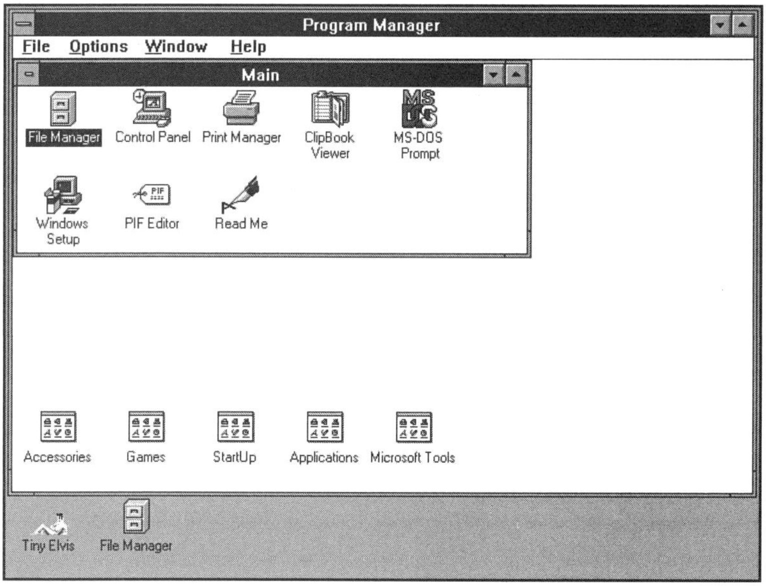

Windows in yer basic 640-by-480 video mode.

Now take a look at the following figure. This baby was shot in 1,024-by-768 resolution. As you can see, this display has *way* more room to display windows, which comes in handy if you work with multiple applications. The disadvantage is that the letters of the icon labels and menu bar names also become smaller and can be hard to read. (Some video cards have drivers that can display fonts in a larger type size at higher resolutions.) Most people find that the 800-by-600 resolution provides just the right balance between extra screen real estate and legibility.

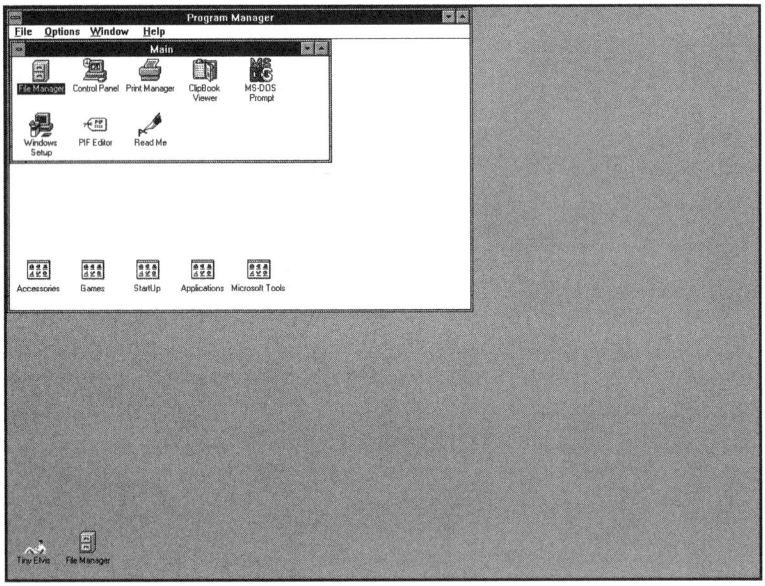

The same screen in the fancy-shmancy 1,024-by-768 mode.

TECHNO NERD TEACHES...

Why do things shrink in the higher resolutions? The reason is that most Windows features are of a fixed size. For example, consider a dialog box that is 160 pixels wide. In 640-by-480 mode, the dialog box is 1/4 as wide as the screen; in 1,024-by-768, however, the same 160 pixels take up only about 1/7th of the screen width.

The interesting thing is that many of today's video cards and monitors can handle multiple resolutions. A high-end Super VGA card is just as happy to display Windows in 640-by-480 mode as it is in 1,024-by-768 territory. So if you need more room to display multiple windows, you can run Windows in a higher resolution; if you want something a little easier on the eyes, you might move down to a lower resolution. In either case, you have to use Setup to load the appropriate device driver for that resolution.

Specifying a New Device Driver

Okay, enough of the long-winded explanations. Without further ado, here are the steps to follow to specify a different device driver:

1. In Program Manager, open the **Main** group and select the **Windows Setup** icon. The Windows Setup window appears.
2. Pull down the Options menu and select Change System Settings. Setup displays the Change System Settings dialog box, as shown below.

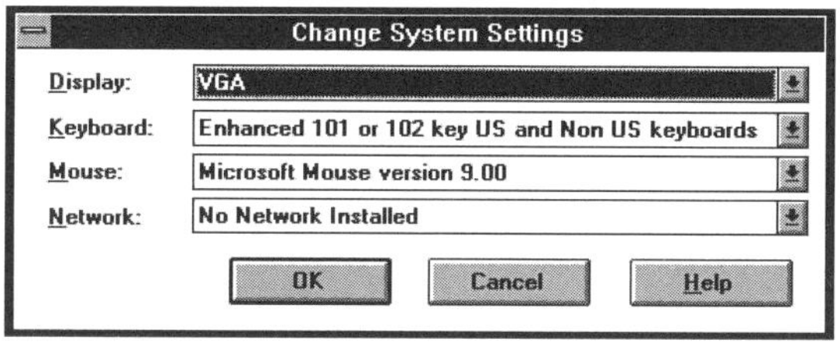

Use the Change System Settings dialog box to select a device driver.

3. Use the appropriate drop-down list (Display, Keyboard, Mouse, or Network) to select the driver you want to use. If you don't see the driver you want, you need to load it from the disk of drivers that came with the hardware. In this case, move to the bottom of the list and select **Other**. (In the Display list, for example, select **Other display**.)
4. Select **OK**.

5. Depending on the driver you selected, one of the following happens:
   - If the driver already exists on your system, Setup lets you know and asks whether you want to use the current driver or a new one. To use the current driver, select Current and skip to step 7; to load the new driver, select New. In the latter case, Setup prompts you to enter one of your Windows installation disks.
   - If Setup can't find the driver, it prompts you to enter one of your Windows installation disks.
   - If you select **Other** from the list, Setup prompts you to enter the disk of drivers that came with the device.
6. If Setup asked you for a disk, insert the disk and select **OK**. If you're installing drivers for a new device (i.e., if you chose **Other** in the driver list), Setup displays a list of drivers. Choose the one you want and select **OK**.
7. In the dialog box that appears, select Restart Windows to restart Windows and load the new device driver into memory.

Setting Up DOS Applications with Setup

If you used your machine before discovering the wonderful world of Windows, you've probably worked with a few DOS programs in your day. Windows, of course, is only too happy to run DOS applications from Program Manager, so it makes sense to create icons for your DOS software. This isn't any big whoop if you just have a program or two, but if you have a fistful to set up, you might consider letting Setup handle this chore for you. (Not sure how to create an icon in Program Manager? Don't sweat it: just leap ahead to Chapter 12, "Let's Do Launch: Interesting Ways to Start Applications," to find out how it's done.)

Setup's brain is stuffed with the pertinent details of many major DOS applications. The idea is that Setup scours your hard drive looking for DOS programs. (Setup actually picks out both DOS and Windows applications. I'm assuming, however, that your Windows applications are already set up in Program Manager, so I'm just concentrating on DOS stuff here.) The ones it recognizes are then displayed in a list that you use to select which ones to add to Program Manager. It's quite painless, really; the following steps give you the details:

1. Open Program Manager's **Main** group and select the **Windows Setup** icon to display the Windows Setup window.
2. Pull down the Options menu and select the Set Up Applications command. The Setup Applications dialog box appears.
3. Make sure the **Search for applications** option button is active and select **OK**. Setup now asks where you want it to search for the applications.
4. Unless you want to restrict the search, you should select each item in the Setup will search list either by clicking on it, or by highlighting it and pressing the **Spacebar**. When you're done, select the Search Now button. Setup trudges through your hard disk looking for applications.
5. If Setup can't figure out an application, you may see a dialog box that shows you the name of the file that starts the program and a list of possible suspects. Highlight the appropriate application (or select **None of the above**, if you're not sure), and then select **OK**.
6. When Setup is done, it displays the Setup Applications dialog box shown below. The Applications found on hard disk(s) list shows you the programs Setup found. Highlight each one you want to create an icon for and select Add. If you add the wrong application by accident, highlight it in the Set up for use with Windows list and select Remove.

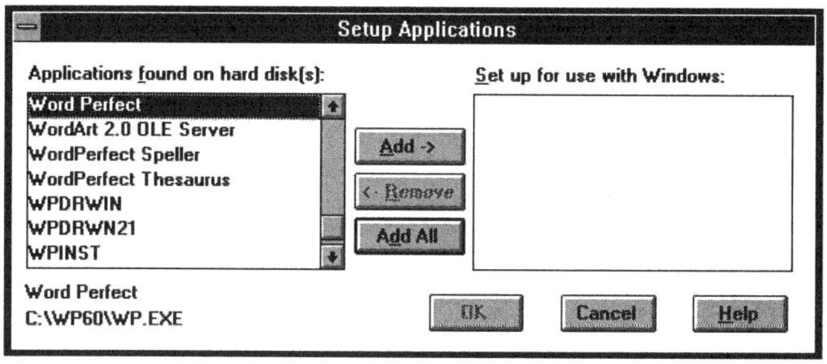

Use the Setup Applications dialog box to specify which applications you want to create icons for.

7. When you're done, select **OK**. Setup creates a new group named Applications (if you don't have one already), and then adds an icon for each application you selected. When it's done, you're returned to the Windows Setup window.

8. Exit Setup by pulling down the Options menu and selecting Exit.

Adding and Removing Chunks of Windows

Windows isn't just one big mega-program. It actually comes in relatively small, bite-sized chunks such as the accessories (for example, Write), the games (for example, Solitaire), and things like the wallpaper files we looked at in the last chapter. The great thing about this approach is that it makes it a breeze to create your own custom version of Windows that includes only those components you use. And it can be a real lifesaver in the cramped confines of an overburdened, bursting-at-the-seams hard disk.

This section explains how to use Setup to add and remove Windows components. Keep in mind that Setup only deals with certain trees in the Windows forest. If your hard disk is desperately low on space (which most notebook users can probably relate to), there are other files you can kevork. ("Kevork" is Internet jargon for "delete.") Turn to Chapter 13, "Fiddling Around with File Manager," to find out more. You might also want to check out Chapter 19, "How to Uninstall a Windows Application," to learn how to rid your machine of programs that have worn out their welcome.

The following steps show you how to use Setup to add and remove Windows components:

1. Start Setup by opening the **Main** group in Program Manager and selecting the **Windows Setup** icon.

2. Pull down the Options menu and select Add/Remove Windows Components. The Windows Setup dialog box appears, as shown below.

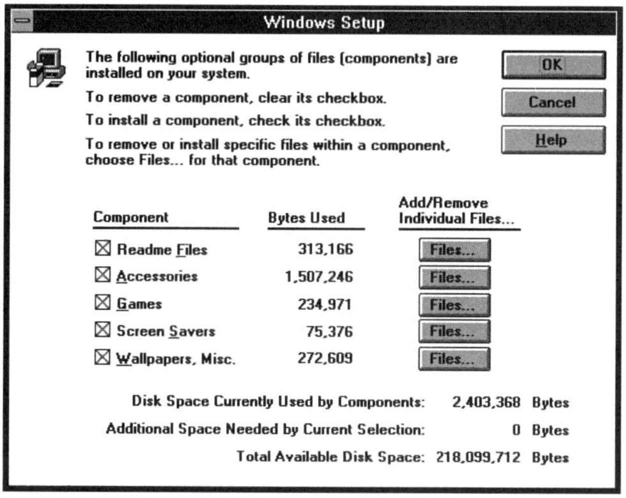

Use the Windows Setup dialog box to add or remove Windows components.

3. The check boxes under the Component column represent various chunks of the Windows system. You have three options at this stage:

   - You can remove a component by deactivating its check box.
   - You can add a previously removed component by activating its check box.
   - Because each component is actually composed of several files, you can add or remove only specific files. To do this, first select the **Files** button for the component you want to work with. In the dialog box that appears, you can remove a file by highlighting it in the **Install these files on the hard disk** list and then selecting Remove. If you're adding a file, highlight it in the **Do not install these files** list and select Add. When you're done, select **OK**.

TECHNO NERD TEACHES...

If a component has some files added and some removed, its check box is a solid gray to let you know.

4. Select **OK**. One of two things happens:

   - If you're deleting files, Setup asks you to confirm the deletion. You can either select Yes for each file, or you can select Yes to All to avoid being prompted for every file.
   - If you're adding files, Setup may prompt you to insert the appropriate installation disk. Place the disk in the drive and select **OK**.

5. When you're back in the Windows Setup window, pull down the Options menu and select Exit to return to Program Manager.

A Note About the DOS Version of Setup

You may sometimes find that you can't access the Setup application from within Windows. For example, you may be using a video driver that suddenly goes haywire, and you can't make heads or tails out of what you see on-screen. Fortunately, Windows also has a DOS version of Setup that you can use to (hopefully) get yourself up and running again. Here's how it works:

1. Close all your running applications and exit Windows. (If you can't exit Windows because your video is all messed up, just keep pressing **Alt+F4** and **Enter** until you get to the DOS prompt.)
2. If the DOS prompt says C:\WINDOWS, skip to step 3. Otherwise, type **CD\WINDOWS** and press **Enter** to change to your Windows directory.
3. Type **SETUP** and press **Enter**. The Windows Setup screen appears, as shown below.

OOPS!

Don't try to run the DOS version of Setup from a Windows DOS session. If you do, Windows gets all huffy and displays an error message.

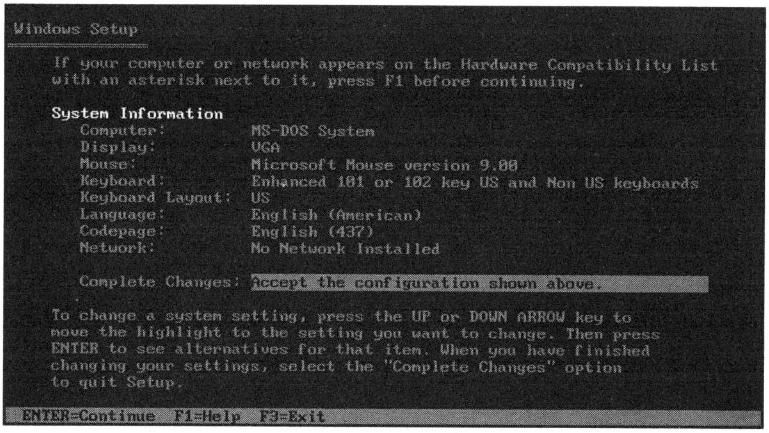

The main screen of the DOS version of Setup.

4. Use the up and down arrow keys to highlight the setting you want to work with, and then press **Enter**. Setup displays a list of options for the setting. For example, the Display setting displays a list of video drivers.
5. Highlight the item you want and press **Enter**. Depending on the item you choose, Setup may ask you whether you want to use the current driver, or it may ask you to insert a disk.
6. Follow the instructions on-screen until you return to the Windows Setup screen.
7. Press **Enter** to return to the DOS prompt.
8. Type **win** and press **Enter** to restart Windows.

The Least You Need to Know

This chapter showed you how to use Setup to tweak various aspects of Windows. Here's a summary of what you need to know:

- Device drivers are mini-programs that translate signals between a hardware device and your software.

continues

continued

- Video resolution is a measure of how much detail your monitor can display. The resolution is measured in pixels arranged in columns and rows.
- To specify a new device driver, start Setup, pull down the **O**ptions menu, and select **C**hange System Settings.
- To have Setup automatically set up DOS applications, pull down Setup's **O**ptions menu and select the **S**et Up Applications command.
- To add or remove Windows components, pull down Setup's **O**ptions menu and select the **A**dd/Remove Windows Components command.
- If you can't access Setup from Windows, you can run the DOS version by exiting Windows, changing to the WINDOWS directory, typing **SETUP**, and pressing **Enter**.

Chapter 4
Secrets of the Windows Help System

In This Chapter

- A review of the Help system basics
- Navigating the Help jungle
- Searching for a long lost Help topic
- Using bookmarks to mark regular stops on your Help tours
- Lots of little-known factoids that give you the Help help you need

With both *The Complete Idiot's Guide to Windows* and *The Complete Idiot's Next Step with Windows* in your computer library, you don't have to go far to find what you need to know about most Windows features. However, my purpose in these books is not to cover absolutely every little Windows component. There are still plenty of Windows stones I've left unturned. If you decide to take a look under some of these rocks, you may be perplexed at some of the flora and fauna you see, but where do you go for help? You could try plowing through the manual, but that can be, at best, time-consuming, and, at worst, downright frustrating (we're talking major geekspeak).

The solution is to take advantage of Windows' online Help system, which can give you assistance on any aspect of Windows with a few simple mouse clicks or keystrokes. This chapter delves into the inner recesses of Help to show you how to get the most out of this valuable resource.

Getting Help: The Basics

If you run into a problem with Windows, or if you simply find yourself in a strange part of town, you want to get help fast before panic sets in. Thoughtfully, the Windows programmers have provided you with no less than three ways to access the Help system:

- Press **F1** to get help that is *context-sensitive*. This means the help screen that appears is related to the Windows area you were in when you pressed F1. For example, when you're in Program Manager, pressing F1 displays the Program Manager Help window (see the picture below).

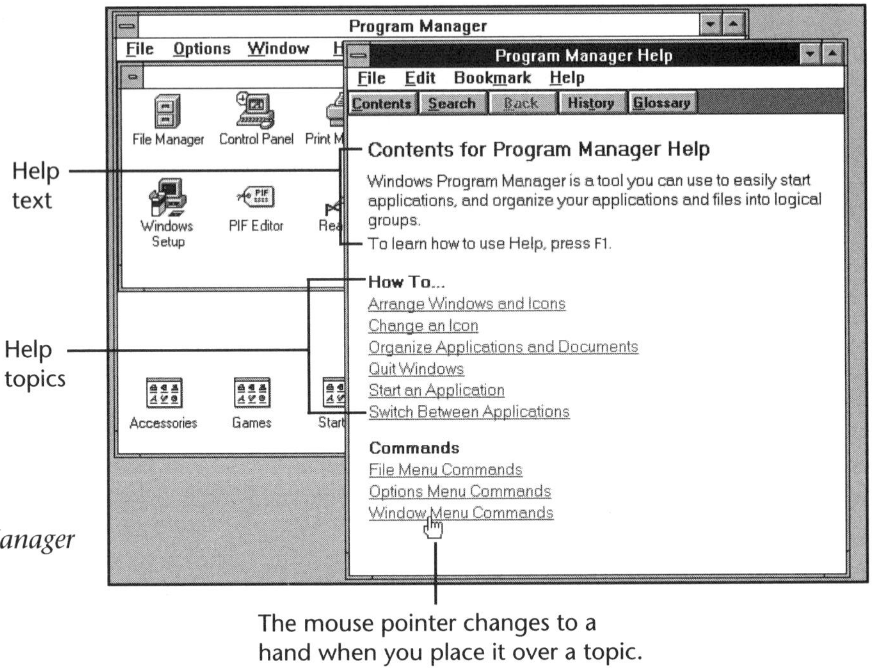

The Program Manager Help window.

- Click on a **H**elp button in a dialog box. The help window that appears is related to the dialog box.
- Select a **H**elp menu command. Most Windows applications have a **H**elp menu that contains various commands for accessing the Help systems. For example, Program Manager's **H**elp menu sports the following commands:

  Contents displays a list of the Program Manager Help contents (see the picture shown earlier).

  Search for Help on displays the Search dialog box, from which you can search for help by entering a keyword or phrase. (See the section titled "Seek and Ye Shall Find Help," later in this chapter.)

  How to Use Help gives you help on using the Help system.

  Windows Tutorial runs a tutorial designed for new Windows users. The Mouse lesson is especially useful if you're a first-time mouse user.

  About Program Manager displays information about Program Manager. What does it have to do with the Help system? Beats me.

> **E-Z**
>
> In some Windows applications (such as Word and Excel), pressing **Shift+F1** adds a question mark to the mouse pointer. You can then click on one of the application's features (such as a toolbar button) to get context-sensitive help on that feature.

Help is actually a Windows application, so the information you see is displayed in an application window complete with its own menu bar and button bar. The rest of this chapter shows you how to wield these tools to make Help do your bidding.

Getting Around in the Help System

The hardest part about working with Help is getting used to the way things are organized. It's remarkably easy to get lost as you leap around from topic to topic. So our first order of business will be to knock some sense into the structure of a typical Help file.

Making the Jump to Hyperspace: Displaying Related Topics

When you invoke the Help system, the window that appears gives you help in the form of a brief description or set of instructions. If this answers your questions, fine. More often than not, however, you need more specific help. To accommodate this, most Help screens provide a list of related topics that, when selected, take you to a different Help screen. These topics appear in underlined green text (if you don't have a color monitor, the keywords appear in a lighter, underlined text). For example, the Contents for Program Manager Help screen has a Quit Windows topic. Selecting this topic displays another screen that shows you how to quit Windows.

How do you select these topics? You can use any of the following methods:

SPEAK LIKE A GEEK

The phrases that are shown in green with the solid underline are called either **jumps** or **hyperlinks.**

- With your mouse, position the pointer over the topic (the pointer changes to a hand, as shown in the picture you saw earlier) and then click.
- From the keyboard, press **Tab** to move the highlight down through the topics (use **Shift+Tab** to move back up) and when you get to the topic you want, press **Enter**.
- A keyword or phrase with a dotted underline has a definition associated with it. When you select one of these topics, Help displays the definition. (To remove the definition, click the mouse or press **Esc**.)

TECHNO NERD TEACHES...

Do you find the green jump text hard to read? Many people do, but not too many of them know that it's possible to change the color of this text to something more legible. How does one perform this magic? Turn to Chapter 9, "Learning to Love Those Strange INI Files," to find out.

Point-and-Shoot Navigation with the Button Bar

As I've said, once you've jumped around to a topic or two, it's easy to get lost in most Help files. How do you get back to a topic you saw earlier? Is there any way to find a specific topic? What if I just want to get back to the Contents screen and start over? To resolve these problems, most Help windows contain a *button bar* just below the menu bar. These buttons provide several handy navigation aids—and they're just a simple mouse click away. (The buttons also have underlined hot keys so keyboard users can get into the act as well.) Here's a summary of the buttons:

Select	To
Contents	Return to the Contents screen.
Search	Search for a specific topic. See the section titled "Seek and Ye Shall Find Help," later in this chapter.
Back	Move back through topics you've selected. (This button is dimmed when you first start Help.)
History	Display the Windows Help History window (see the following figure). This box shows you a sequential list of all the Help topics you've selected. The current topic is at the top, and the first topic displayed appears at the bottom. To redisplay one of these topics, double-click on it, or use the up and down arrows to highlight it and then press **Enter**. To remove the window, double-click on the **Control-menu box** in the top left corner or press **Alt+F4**.
Glossary	Display a glossary of Windows terms. The window that appears contains, in alphabetical order, a list of words and phrases in the green, dotted-underlined text we looked at earlier. To close the glossary, double-click on the **Control-menu box** in the top left corner or press **Alt+F4**.
<<	View the previous topic from a sequence of related topics. (This button is only available in some applications.)

continues

Continued

Select	To
	View the next topic from a series of related topics. (Again, only some applications include this button in their Help.)

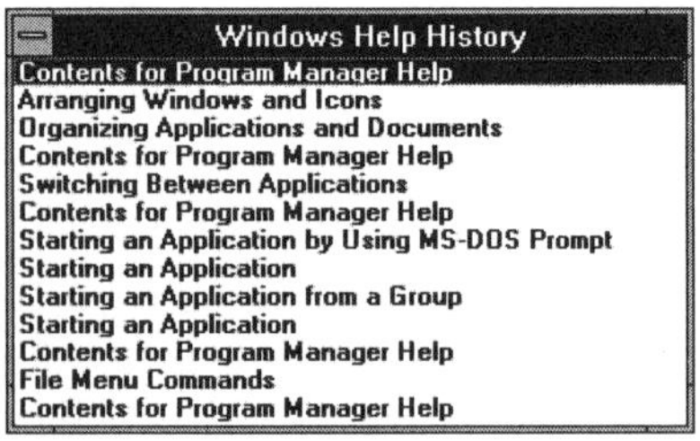

The Windows Help History windows shows you a list of the topics you've jumped to.

Seek and Ye Shall Find Help

As handy as the Help system is, it can quickly become frustrating as you leap madly from topic to topic without ever finding exactly the info you need. To avoid this maze, the Help system includes a Search feature that lets you seek out a particular Help topic by using an alphabetical list of topics or by typing a keyword or phrase. Here's what you do:

OOPS!

Windows wipes out the History list each time you exit the Help system. To keep the History intact, leave Help up and running while you use the application.

1. In an application, pull down the **H**elp window and select the **S**earch for Help on command, or if you're already in the Help system, select the **S**earch button. The Search dialog box appears.
2. Select the topic you want either by scrolling through the list or by typing the first few letters of the topic you want in the text box. For example, if you're working in Program Manager's Help system and you type **s**, Search moves to **starting applications**. If you then type **w**, Search moves to **switching between applications**, as shown in the following figure.

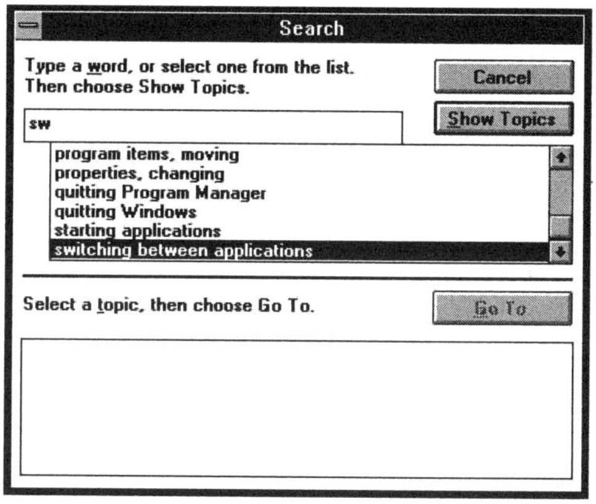

Peck out the first few letters of the topic you want in order to display that topic.

3. Select the Show Topics button or press **Enter** to display a list of topics associated with the highlighted phrase. This list appears in the box at the bottom of the Search dialog box.
4. If more than one topic is listed, highlight the one you want.
5. Select the Go To button to display the Help for that topic.

Making Your Mark in Help

If you find yourself referencing a particular topic regularly, it can be a pain to navigate a bunch of screens to get where you want to be. Instead, you can set up an electronic bookmark to help you access the topic quickly. Here are the steps you need to follow:

1. Display the Help topic you want to mark.
2. Select the Bookmark Define command. Help displays the Bookmark Define dialog box, as shown below.

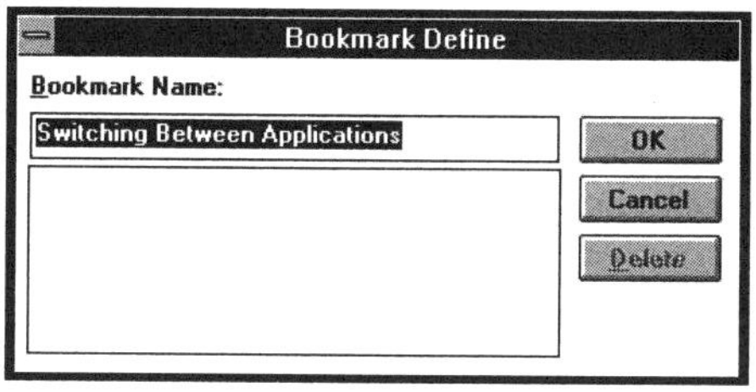

Use the Bookmark Define dialog box to define your bookmark.

3. If you don't like the default bookmark name that Help provides, type your own description in the **B**ookmark Name text box.
4. Select **OK**.

Once you've defined a bookmark, you can jump quickly to that topic by pulling down the Book**m**ark menu and selecting it from the list of bookmarks that appear.

> **TECHNO NERD TEACHES...**
>
> The Book**m**ark menu can hold up to nine different bookmarks. If you have ten or more bookmarks defined, a **M**ore command appears at the bottom of the menu. When you select this command, Help displays the Bookmark dialog box with a list of all your bookmarks. Highlight the one you want and select **OK**. If you'd like to keep your bookmark list manageable, you can delete bookmarks. Just select the Book**m**ark menu's **D**efine command to display the Bookmark Define dialog box, highlight the bookmark you want to delete, and then select the **D**elete button.

More Help System Options to Play Around With

Once you've found the topic you want, Help offers a number of options for working with the text, such as printing the topic or adding your own notes. The next few sections give you the nitty-gritty.

Getting a Help Topic Hard Copy

Some people like to make hard copies of Help topics to include as part of instruction manuals and such. (Keep in mind, though, that you can't just cobble together some Help topics and then start selling them on the street. Can you say *copyright infringement*? I knew you could.) If you want to print out a Help topic, you can do it by following these steps:

1. Make sure your printer is turned on and is online.

2. Display the topic you want to print.
3. Pull down the **File** menu and select the **Print** Topic command. Help prints the topic.

Copying a Help Topic

Why would anyone want to make a copy of a Help topic? Well, some folks prefer to create their own Help systems by copying selected topics from various Help files and combining them into a single document in another application (usually a word processor). Help's Copy feature makes this a breeze. The following steps show you how to copy a Help topic into another application:

1. Display the Help topic you want to copy.
2. Pull down the **Edit** menu and select the **Copy** command. Help displays the Copy dialog box, as shown below.

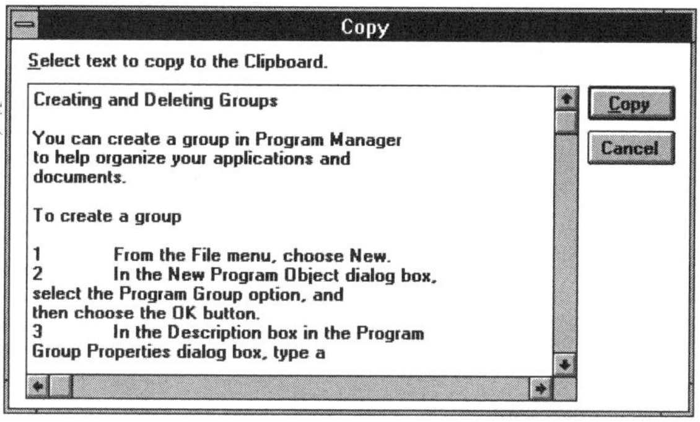

Use the Copy dialog box to select the Help text you want to copy.

3. If you only want to copy part of the topic, highlight the appropriate text. To do this with a mouse, simply drag the mouse over the text. From the keyboard, hold down the **Shift** key and use the arrow keys to highlight the text.
4. Select the **Copy** button.
5. Open the application you want to copy the Help info to, and position the cursor where you want the text to appear.
6. Pull down the application's **Edit** menu and select the **Paste** command. Windows pastes the copied text at the cursor position.

Adding Your Own Notes to a Topic

Although the Help system is extensive, it can't cover everything. You can add your own notes to the topics to record tidbits you've gleaned from other sources. Here's how to do it:

1. Display the topic to which you want to add a note.
2. Pull down the **Edit** menu and select the Annotate command. Help displays the Annotate dialog box.
3. Enter your note in the Annotation text box (see below).

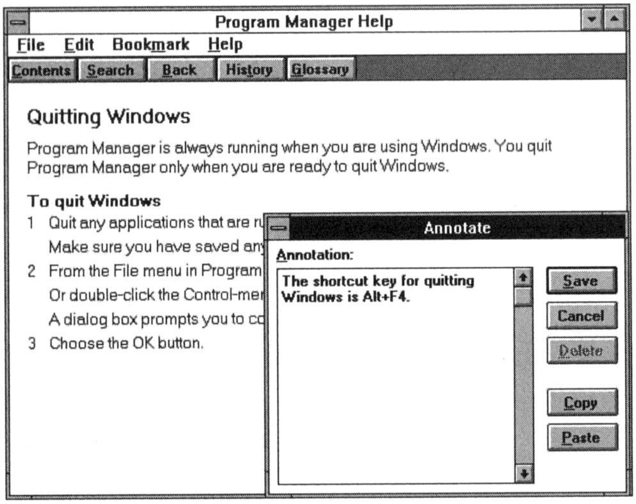

Use the Annotate dialog box to add your own notes to the Help system.

4. Select the **Save** button. Help displays a paper clip icon to the left of the topic title. This tells you that you have a note attached to this topic.

Once you've added a note to a topic, you can view it by clicking on the paper clip icon, or by pressing **Tab** until the paper clip is highlighted and then pressing **Enter**.

The Least You Need to Know

This chapter showed you how to get help by using Windows' online Help system. Here are a few pointers to take with you on your travels:

- To invoke the Help system, press **F1**, select a **H**elp button in a dialog box, or choose a command from an application's **H**elp menu.
- To display a related Help topic, click on a jump phrase, or press **Tab** to highlight the topic and press **Enter**.
- To avoid the Help maze, select the **S**earch button to search for a specific Help topic.
- For quick access to a topic you view regularly, set up a bookmark by pulling down the Book**m**ark menu and selecting the **D**efine command.
- The Help system menu bar contains other commands for working with Help topics: in the **F**ile menu, select **P**rint Topic to get a hard copy of the current topic; in the **E**dit menu, select **C**opy to make a copy of a topic to be pasted in another application; or in the **E**dit menu, select **A**nnotate to add your own notes to a topic.

Chapter 5
Taming the DOS Beast

In This Chapter

- Cranking up a DOS session
- Doling out DOS commands from Windows
- Using the mysterious PIF Editor
- Customizing the current DOS session
- Valuable tips and techniques that let you show DOS who's boss

If you've ever read the letters section of a computer magazine or spent any time online in the Internet or in a service such as CompuServe, you've probably come across a "holy war" or two. In computing circles, a holy war is a never-ending debate on the merits of one thing versus another, where people use the same arguments over and over, and nobody's opinion ever budges even the slightest one way or the other.

The mother of all holy wars is the DOS versus Windows debate. I shudder to think how much energy some people spend extolling the virtues of one system and the shortcomings of the other. In the end, it's all a complete waste of effort because both DOS and Windows do certain things well. The smart computer user recognizes this and maintains a foot in both camps.

If you have a strong relationship with Windows but would like the occasional fling with DOS, this chapter's for you. I show you how to get the most out of your DOS sessions, and how to avoid Windows and DOS running into each other on the street.

Dirty DOS Dancing: Starting DOS Sessions

From Windows' point of view, DOS is a program more or less like any other. You start it up, work in it, and then shut it down when you're done. You can even display your DOS session in a window and move it around on-screen or minimize it to an icon.

> **SPEAK LIKE A GEEK**
>
> A holy war is also known as a **FAWOMPT**: a Frequently Argued Waste of My Precious Time.

When you start a DOS session, you have two choices: you can load a DOS application, or you can run COMMAND.COM, the DOS *command interpreter*. To run a DOS program, just double-click its icon in Program Manager, and you're off to the races. (If you need to create icons for your DOS programs, Chapter 3 explains how.) A COMMAND.COM session is a little different, however. COMMAND.COM displays the DOS prompt so that you can enter DOS commands, then it translates these commands into a language DOS can understand. Lastly, it executes the commands.

To start a COMMAND.COM DOS session, you have two choices:

- In Program Manager, open the **Main** group and select the **MS-DOS Prompt** icon.
- In either Program Manager or File Manager, pull down the **F**ile menu and select **R**un. In the Run dialog box that appears, enter **COMMAND.COM** in the **C**ommand Line text box, and then select **OK**. The advantage to doing this in File Manager is that Windows begins the DOS session in the currently selected File Manager directory.

Once the DOS prompt appears, you're free to enter DOS commands, start DOS programs, or do whatever other DOS stuff suits your fancy. (I'm assuming here, of course, that you have at least a basic understanding of all this DOS voodoo. If you don't, may I suggest picking up a copy of *The Complete Idiot's Guide to DOS*, by the lovely and talented Jennifer Fulton.)

Remember, Windows treats each DOS session like another program. So, if you need to switch to another application, you can use the **Alt+Tab** "cool switch" (hold down **Alt** and press **Tab** until you get to the application you want). If you prefer your DOS session to appear in a window, press **Alt+Enter**. (You're not able to do this if you're running Windows on a 286 computer.) When you're done dealing with DOS, type **Exit** and press **Enter** to return to Windows.

If you want to run just a single *external command* in your DOS session, you may be able to avoid the hassle of opening the DOS session and then running the command. External commands are DOS commands that are actually separate, stand-alone programs in their own right. Examples include EDIT—the DOS text editor—and FORMAT—the DOS command that formats floppy disks. To run these commands, pull down Program Manager's (or File Manager's) **F**ile menu, select **R**un, and enter the following in the **C**ommand Line text box:

COMMAND.COM /C *command*

Here, *command* is the name of the DOS command you want to run. For example, to format a floppy disk in drive A without bothering with File Manager, you'd select the **R**un command and enter the following:

COMMAND.COM /C FORMAT A:

The /C thing (it's called a *switch*) tells DOS that you want to run a temporary COMMAND.COM session. This means that when the command finishes executing, the entire DOS session ends and you're plopped back in Windows.

The problem with this switch is that it isn't effective if you're running a command such as DIR or MEM that displays its findings on-screen. (DIR produces a listing of files in the current directory, and MEM tells you how your system's memory is being used.) If you try running these commands with COMMAND.COM /C, you just see a quick flash of info before you end up back in Windows. If you have at least DOS 6, you can use the new /K switch to tell DOS not to exit the session automatically. For example, to get a memory listing, you enter the following command in the Run dialog box:

COMMAND.COM /K MEM

If you have an older version of DOS, check out the "Exercises for the Anxious, Eager, and Adventurous," later in this chapter to learn other ways around the limitation of the /C switch.

Figuring Out the PIF Editor

You've probably noticed an icon named PIF Editor in Program Manager's Main group, and you've probably wondered just what the heck is a PIF, and why would anyone want to edit one? Allow me to explain. Windows has no trouble running a Windows application because it knows, more or less, what to expect. DOS applications, however, are a whole other kettle of digital fish. Windows doesn't know in advance what kind of mischief a DOS program might get into, so it likes to set up a few ground rules in advance. These ground rules are contained in something called a *program information file*, or PIF for short. The PIF Editor, then, is just a mechanism by which the likes of you and I can create our own PIFs and modify existing ones. Do you have to use a PIF to run a DOS program? Technically, no. But I'd recommend it because PIFs can help you avoid problems like running out of memory, and having a DOS program step on the toes of a Windows application.

Before getting into the rigamarole of editing PIFs, check to see whether you need to bother. The manufacturers of many of today's DOS applications recognize that a sizable chunk of their users will run the program under Windows; therefore, they have thoughtfully included ready-made PIFs. When you create icons for your DOS programs, look for a PIF (you'll find most PIFs either in the WINDOWS directory, or in the application's main directory) and enter its name in the Command Line text box of the Program Item Properties dialog box. (All PIFs end with the extension .PIF.) The picture below shows an example from WordPerfect for DOS 6.0 (which comes with a PIF named WP60.PIF).

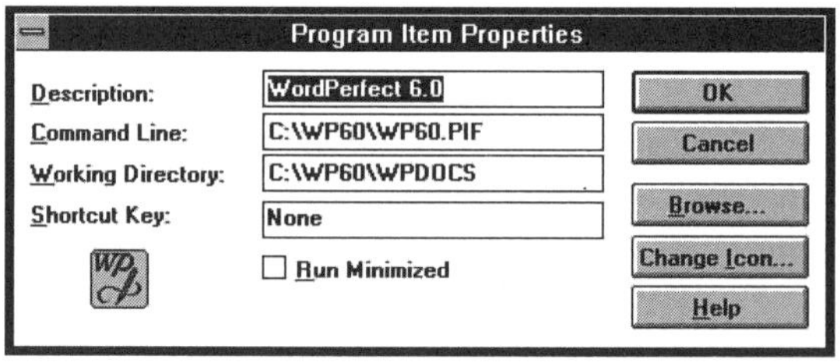

An example of a Program Item Properties dialog box that uses a PIF to start a DOS program.

PIF Editing

If you need to make changes to or create a PIF, here are the general steps to follow:

1. In Program Manager's **Main** group, select the **PIF Editor** icon. The PIF Editor window appears, as shown below.

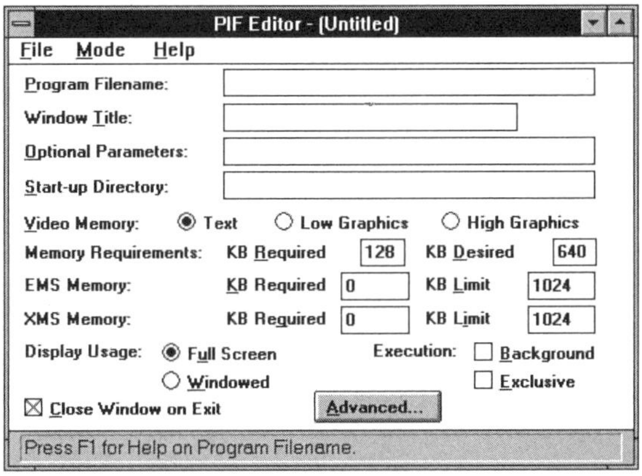

Use the PIF Editor window to create and modify your PIFs.

2. If you want to modify an existing PIF, pull down the File menu, select Open, and then choose the PIF you want from the Open dialog box that appears.

3. Fill in or edit the PIF settings. (See the next section, "Perusing the PIF Options," for the lowdown on the controls in the PIF window.)

4. Select the File menu's Save command, then enter a name for the file. You don't have to bother with an extension because the PIF Editor adds its .PIF extension for you automatically. Ideally, you should store all your PIFs in the WINDOWS directory.

5. Pull down the File menu and select Exit. Windows returns you to Program Manager.

6. If you've created a PIF for an existing icon, highlight the icon and press **Alt+Enter**, or hold down **Alt** and double-click on the icon. If you're creating a new icon, select the File menu's New command, and then select **OK** in the dialog box that appears. In either case, Windows displays the Program Item Properties dialog box.

7. In the Command Line text box, enter the name of the PIF, including the drive and directory if the PIF isn't in the WINDOWS directory.
8. Fill in the rest of the dialog box, if necessary, and then select **OK** to return to Program Manager.

Perusing the PIF Editor Options

The PIF Editor is bursting at the seams with intimidating and just plain scary-looking controls. Most of them appeal only to technogeeks, but there are some that the rest of us might find useful. The following summary brings these options into the realm of mere mortals.

Take note: the following summary doesn't cover any settings with the word "memory" in them. There just isn't any point in cramming this stuff in until you learn some memory fundamentals. You'll tackle that all-important subject in Chapter 23, "Maneuvering the Memory Maze."

Program Filename This is the name of the file that starts the DOS application (including its extension—usually either .EXE or .COM). Be sure to include the drive letter and directory where the file resides. For example, if you were setting up a PIF for Lotus 1-2-3, you might enter something like **C:\123\123.EXE**.

Window Title This is the text that appears in the title bar when you switch the DOS application to a window (by pressing **Alt+Enter**). Well, sort of. If you create an icon for the PIF in Program Manager and start the application using this icon, Windows uses the **D**escription line from the Program Item Properties dialog box as the window title. The only time this PIF text is actually used as the window title is if you run the PIF using the **R**un command in Program Manager or File Manager.

Optional Parameters This text box holds any extra stuff that you'd normally place after the startup file name (the file name you entered in the **P**rogram Filename box). In FoxPro for DOS, for example, you can add **-t** to prevent the FoxPro logo from appearing. More commonly, you can add the file name of a data file (such as a document for a word processor) in this space. This tells the application to load the data file automatically at startup.

Start-up Directory This is the directory that will be active when you start the program. Many people like to use the directory where they store their data files for the application. Again, however, if you start the PIF from a Program Manager icon, the **W**orking Directory entry in the Program Item Properties dialog box takes precedence.

Display Usage As I've mentioned, you can toggle your DOS programs between the full-screen view and a window by pressing **Alt+Enter** (as long as you have a 386 computer or better). These option buttons determine the default view you get when you first start the program: F**u**ll Screen or **W**indowed.

Execution This has nothing to do with firing squads (although I've met a few DOS applications in my day for which a firing squad would be too good a fate). Instead, these two check boxes control how Windows runs the DOS program. If you activate the **B**ackground check box, the DOS program keeps running even if you switch to another application. This is crucial if you plan to, say, start a large print job in the program and then switch to something else. Similarly, if you use a DOS communications program, activating **B**ackground allows you to perform file transfers while working in another application. The **E**xclusive check box gives you the opposite effect: it tells Windows that you'll use the DOS program and only the DOS program. This forces Windows to give its full attention to the DOS session, which can result in a much snappier performance. (See Chapter 22, "From Slowpoke to Speed Demon: Making Windows Fly," to learn more speedup tricks.)

> **SPEAK LIKE A GEEK**
>
> Windows' deft ability to do two things at once is called **multitasking**.

Exercises for the Anxious, Eager, and Adventurous

So far in this chapter I've discussed various ways to get a DOS session up and running. To make sure you're comfortable with some of the ideas I've foisted upon you, the next few sections take you through some related exercises of increasing complexity.

For the Anxious: Creating an Icon for a DOS Command

If you have a favorite DOS command you run regularly, it can be a pain to always open a COMMAND.COM session, or even to use the **R**un command. Instead, why not create an icon in Program Manager so you can execute the command with a simple double-click? As an example, create an icon that copies all the files in a directory to a floppy disk. (Ideally, you'd use this command as a makeshift backup utility that copies all your work files to a floppy disk.) Here's what you do:

1. In Program Manager, open the group you want to use for the icon.
2. Select the **F**ile menu's **N**ew command, and then select **OK** in the dialog box that appears. Windows displays the Program Item Properties dialog box. (You can also get to the Program Item Properties dialog box by holding down **Alt** and double-clicking an empty area inside the group.)
3. Use the **D**escription text box to enter a description of the command (for example, **Back Up Documents to Drive A**).
4. In the **C**ommand Line text box, enter **COMMAND /C**, a space, and the command you want to run. For example, to copy all the files in the directory C:\DOCS to drive A, you'd enter the following:

   COMMAND /C XCOPY C:\DOCS A:

5. Select **OK**. Windows adds the icon to Program Manager.

TECHNO NERD TEACHES...

Windows assigns the same boring icon to each of your DOS commands. To use something with a little more pizzazz, select the Change **I**con button, then select **OK** in the dialog box that appears. In the Change Icon dialog box, type **MORICONS.DLL** and press **Enter**. Select the icon you want from the **C**urrent Icon list and select **OK**.

For the Eager: Prompting for PIF Parameters

As you saw earlier, you can use the PIF Editor's **O**ptional Parameters text box to include parameters such as the name of a data file. This means you can create separate PIFs for files you use regularly. But what if you don't know in advance which file you want to open? To get around this problem, you can make Windows prompt you for a parameter before it loads the program. How? Easy: just add a question mark (?) in the **O**ptional Parameters text box.

To see how this works, let's try out an example in which you create an icon that runs the DOS 6 Help application and prompts you to enter the Help topic you want to view:

1. Open the PIF Editor and enter **C:\DOS\HELP.COM** in the **P**rogram Filename text box.
2. In the **O**ptional Parameters text box, enter a question mark (**?**).
3. Enter any other PIF options you want, save the PIF, and then exit the PIF Editor.
4. In Program Manager, create an icon for the PIF you just created. (See the preceding exercise for more specific insructions on how to do this.) Make sure you enter the name of the PIF in the Command Line text box.

When you double-click the icon, a dialog box appears so that you can enter the name of the topic you want (see the example shown below). When you select **OK**, Windows runs Help and displays the topic you entered.

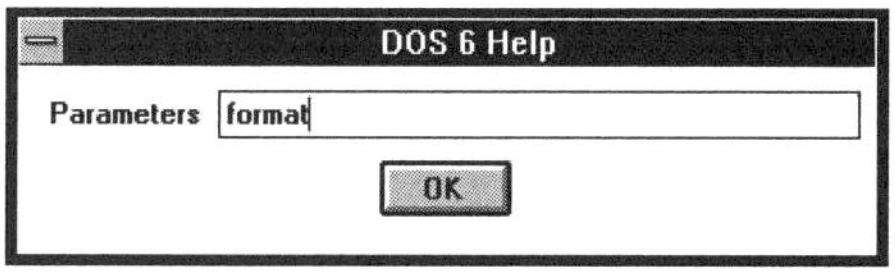

Windows displays a dialog box like this when prompting you for parameters.

For the Adventurous: Running Multiple DOS Commands

Sometimes a single DOS command just won't cut the mustard. For example, in our simple backup utility we looked at earlier, you might need to copy files from several directories to a floppy disk. The most obvious solution, of course, is to create separate icons for each command and then run them individually. Sounds like *way* too much work to me, though.

Instead, you can create special files—called *batch files*—that can contain any number of DOS commands. You just run the batch file, and DOS executes every command.

To see how batch files work, let's create one that copies files from two different directories (C:\DOCS and C:\DATA) to drive A and then displays a directory listing (using the DIR command) so you can see how much space is left on the floppy disk:

1. Open Program Manager's **Accessories** group and select the **Notepad** icon.
2. Enter the following five lines in Notepad. (Substitute your own data directories for C:\DOCS and C:\DATA.) The picture below shows you what your screen should look like.

```
@ECHO OFF
XCOPY C:\DOCS A:
XCOPY C:\DATA A:
DIR A:\
PAUSE
```

TECHNO NERD TEACHES...

Most batch files start with the special **@ECHO OFF** command. This just keeps things tidy by telling DOS not to display the commands as they're executed. The **PAUSE** command tells DOS to stop executing until you press a key. This enables you to see the results of the DIR listing.

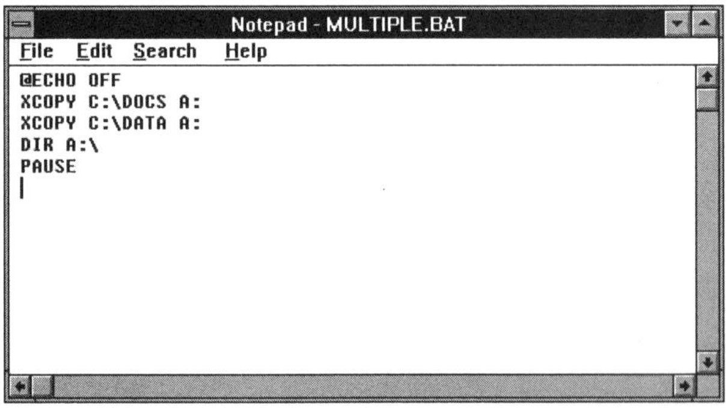

The Notepad screen with the batch file commands entered.

3. Save the file by pulling down the **F**ile menu and selecting **S**ave. The Save As dialog box appears. Enter a name for the batch file in the File **N**ame text box, making sure you use a .BAT extension, and select **OK**. (For example, I called my file MULTIPLE.BAT.)
4. Pull down the **F**ile menu and select E**x**it to return to Program Manager.
5. Load the PIF Editor and, in the **P**rogram Filename text box, enter **COMMAND.COM**. In the **O**ptional Parameters text box, enter **/C**, followed by a space, followed by the name of the batch file (for example, **/C MULTIPLE.BAT**).
6. Enter any other PIF options, save the PIF, and then exit PIF Editor.
7. Create a new Program Manager icon that runs the PIF you just created.

When you run this icon, Windows starts a DOS session and then runs the batch file. When it hits the PAUSE command, DOS displays a **Press any key to continue** message. After you've checked out how much room is left on the floppy disk (the last line of the DIR listing tells you that you have ***x* bytes free**, where *x* is a number), press any key to return to Windows.

DOS Deluxe: Customizing a DOS Session

If you prefer to display your DOS sessions in a window, you can check out a few customization options to make the window behave the way you want it to. To try out these options, follow these steps:

1. Start a DOS session and place it in a window by pressing **Alt+Enter**.
2. Pull down the window's **Control** menu and select the **F**onts command. (Recall that you display the Control menu by either clicking on the **Control-menu box** in the upper left corner or by pressing **Alt+Spacebar**.) The Font Selection dialog box appears, as shown on the following page.

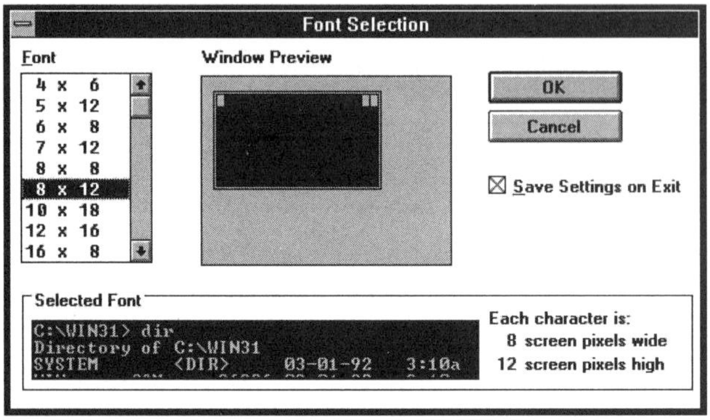

Use the Font Selection dialog box to customize your DOS session characters.

3. Use the Font list to select the size of the characters you want. The Selected Font box shows you what a typical DOS screen looks like.
4. Select **OK** to return to the DOS window.
5. Pull down the **Control** menu and select the Settings command.
6. In the dialog box that appears (see the following page), choose from the following options:

   Display Options Indicates whether the DOS session appears in a Window or Full Screen.

   Tasking Options The Exclusive and Background check boxes serve the same function as the PIF Editor's Exclusive and Background options, which we looked at earlier. The difference is that, unlike the PIF settings, these are only temporary; they last only as long as the current DOS session is active. This is handy if, say, you just need background multitasking occasionally (such as for an occasional print job).

   Priority These settings are supposed to control how much processing time is given to the application when it's either active (the Foreground value) or running in the background (the Background value). In theory, increasing these values should speed up the application; in practice, the actual speedup is negligible, and your other running programs may suffer as a result. My recommendation: ignore these settings.

   Terminate Use this button to shut down an unruly application that won't respond to your keystrokes, mouse clicks, or verbal abuse. Note that you'll lose any unsaved changes in the application, so this should always be a last resort.

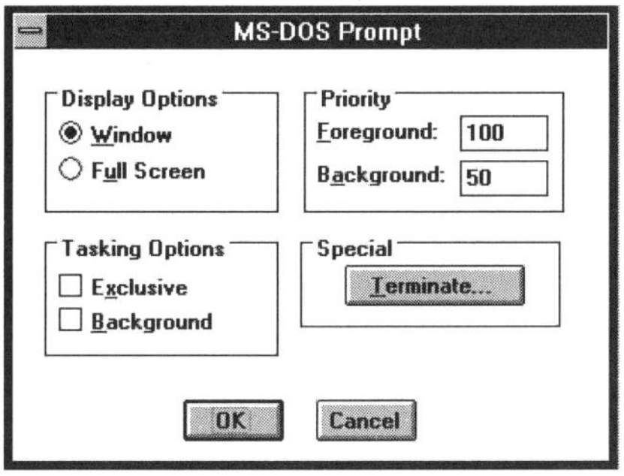

Use this dialog box to customize your DOS session settings.

7. Select **OK** to put the new settings into effect and return to the DOS window.

The Least You Need to Know

This chapter showed you how to soothe the savage DOS beast. The material we covered was, admittedly, a bit technical (with DOS was it ever thus), so just to help things sink in, here's a quick review:

- ☛ To start a DOS session, you can either run a DOS application, or you can run COMMAND.COM, the DOS command interpreter. In the latter case, you have two choices: select the **MS-DOS Prompt** icon in Program Manager's **Main** group; or pull down the **F**ile menu, select **R**un, enter **COMMAND.COM**, and select **OK**.
- ☛ If your computer is at least a 386, press **Alt+Enter** to toggle a DOS session between a window and full screen.
- ☛ To run a DOS command, add COMMAND.COM's **/C** switch, followed by the command. If you have DOS 6, the **/K** switch is better for some commands because it doesn't automatically shut down the DOS session when the command has finished its business.

continues

continued

- A program information file (PIF) tells Windows how to run a DOS session. You create and modify PIFs using the PIF Editor.
- Use the PIF Editor's **O**ptional Parameters text box to enter parameters for a DOS session. If you enter a question mark (**?**), Windows prompts you for the parameters before starting the session.
- To customize an active DOS session, place it in a window, pull down the **Control** menu, and then select either **F**onts or Se**t**tings.

Chapter 6
Hard Copy Hijinks: Getting the Most Out of Windows Printing

In This Chapter

- Installing your printer in Windows
- The basic printing steps for just about any Windows application
- Drag-and-drop printing
- Checking out the Print Manager
- Umpteen other tips and topics that will have you printing like a pro

Remember when all this high falutin' computer technology was supposed to result in the "paperless office" of tomorrow? Hah! Clearly tomorrow never came because we are, if anything, awash in more paper than ever since computers took over our lives.

I suspect one of the reasons for this plenitude of paper is that we all have a real need for hard copy. For one thing, it just feels good to create something tangible, something that we can literally get our hands on. For another, I don't think we trust our computers fully. Electronic files, with their unfortunate tendency to be wiped out by the merest power surge or the accidental push of a Delete key, seem so fragile. Printouts, on the other hand, seem hardier and, well, safer.

So I say, if we're going to be printing fools, we may as well be wise printing fools. Happily, as this chapter shows, such wisdom is fairly easy to come by thanks to Windows' easy and consistent approach to printing. You begin with some printing basics and then graduate to some intermediate and advanced techniques that help you get the most out of Windows printing.

Telling Windows About Your Printer

Windows is the control freak of the computer world. I mean it has to know absolutely *everything* about your machine and whatever peripherals—especially printers—are along for the ride. This isn't a bad thing, though, because it actually makes our lives easier. How? Well, in the anarchic world of DOS, every program has its own particular printing agenda. The down side to this digital individualism is that you and I have to perform the rigamarole of setting up our printers for every DOS program.

Windows, though, is different because it performs the printing drudgery itself. As a result, you only have to tell Windows what kind of printer you have, and then you're in business. Windows applications handle print jobs simply by passing the buck over to Windows, so there's no need to perform separate printer setups for all your programs.

So why do we even need to worry about setting up our printers? If you read Chapter 3, "Tweaking Windows with Setup," you recall that software and hardware can only communicate by means of special programs called device drivers. Printers are no exception. To translate the bits and bytes that make up your data files into something the printer can spit out, you need to install a *printer driver*. If you didn't do this during the Windows installation, or if you have a new printer to set up, you can use the Control Panel to do it from within Windows. Here are the steps you need to follow:

1. Open Program Manager's **Main** group and select the **Control Panel** icon.
2. In the Control Panel window that appears, select the **Printers** icon, or pull down the **S**ettings menu and select **P**rinters. Control Panel displays the Printers dialog box.

3. Select the Add button to expand the dialog box, as shown below. (If you haven't already installed at least one printer, the dialog box is already expanded, so you can skip this step.)

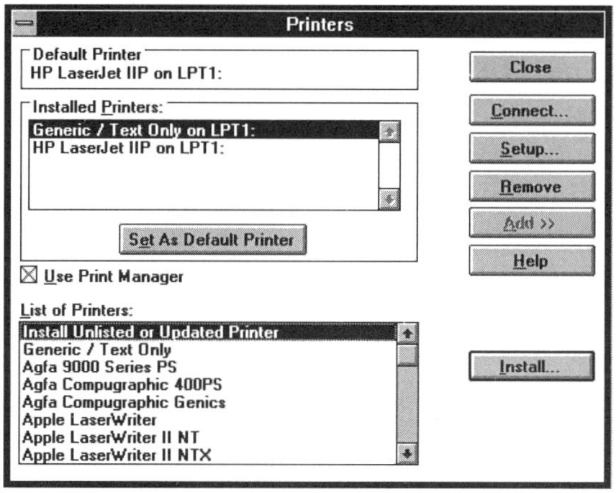

The expanded Printers dialog box.

4. Windows has the goods on dozens of different printers, all of which are shown in the List of Printers box. Find your printer in this list and highlight it. If your printer isn't in the list, you have three choices:

    - Check your printer manual to see whether the printer works like (or *emulates*) another printer. If it does, see whether you can find the emulated printer in the list.
    - Highlight one of the list's catch-all printers. For example, highlight **Generic/Text Only** for a dot-matrix printer or **PostScript Printer** for, of course, a PostScript printer.
    - If your printer comes with a disk, choose **Install Unlisted or Updated Printer** at the top of the list.

5. Select the Install button. One of the following things happens:

    - If the printer driver is already on your hard disk, the printer name appears in the Installed Printers list.
    - If the printer information isn't on your hard disk, Control Panel prompts you to insert one of your Windows installation disks. Place the disk in the appropriate drive (change the displayed drive letter if it's wrong) and select **OK**.

- If you selected **Install Unlisted or Updated Printer**, the Control Panel asks you to insert the disk that came with the printer. Insert the disk and select **OK**. Another dialog box appears that shows a list of the printer drivers on the disk. Highlight your printer and select **OK**.

Note: Depending on which printer you chose, you may be asked to insert another disk for font files or some such nonsense; just follow the directions on the screen. In the end, you return to the Printers dialog box.

6. Select the Connect button to display the Connect dialog box.
7. Use the Ports list to select your printer port, then select **OK**.

TECHNO NERD TEACHES...

A *port* is a connection where you plug in the cable for a device such as a mouse or printer. If you're not sure which port your printer uses, check the printer cable connection at the back of your computer. Some thoughtful computer companies actually label their ports, so look for something like LPT1 or COM2. If there are no labels, your computer manual should tell you. If you're still not sure, just choose LPT1—and cross your fingers.

8. Repeat steps 4–7 to install any other printer drivers you need.
9. If you've installed multiple drivers, you need to tell Windows which one to use as the default in your Windows applications. To do this, highlight the printer in the Installed Printers list and then select the Set As Default Printer button. The printer name appears in the **Default Printer** box.

TECHNO NERD TEACHES...

What happens if you want to use a printer other than the default printer in a Windows application? This isn't a problem. Any application that lets you print also lets you select which printer to use. How you do this varies from application

> to application. In some cases, a **Print Setup** command is in the **F**ile menu. In others, you have to select the **F**ile menu's **P**rint command, and then choose a button in the Print dialog box (it could be labeled **Printer** or **Print Setup** or just **Setup**). A list of the installed printers is in the dialog box that appears. Select the one you want to use and select **OK**.

10. Select **Close** to return to the Control Panel.

Windows Printing: Just the Facts

One of Windows' principal missions is to give all the applications we use a reasonably consistent look and feel. This means that the vast majority of Windows applications use the same dialog box controls, the same method for selecting text, the same command for saving a file, and so on. The printing process is a good example of this consistency. In most applications, with some relatively minor exceptions, the steps involved in printing a file are the same:

1. Make sure your printer is ready to go before you start printing. Check to see that the printer is turned on and is on-line, that the cables are plugged in properly, that there's enough paper for your printout, and so on.
2. In your application, open the file you want to print.
3. Pull down the **F**ile menu and select the **P**rint command. A Print dialog box appears, the layout of which varies from application to application. For example, the picture on the following page shows the Print dialog box from Windows' Write word processor.

> **OOPS!**
>
> If you pull down the **F**ile menu and see that the **P**rint command is dimmed, it means you haven't installed a printer yet. See "Telling Windows About Your Printer," earlier in this chapter.

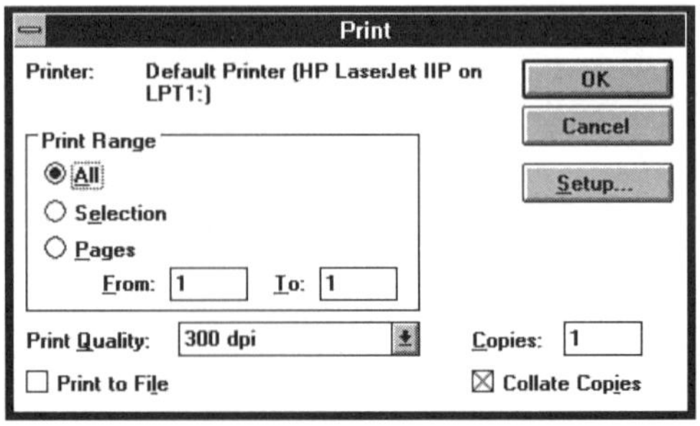

The Print dialog box, Write style.

4. Fill in the options you need for your printout. Although, like the proverbial snowflakes, no two Print dialog boxes are exactly alike, there are a few controls that are common to most. Here's a summary:

   Copies You usually see a text box or spinner for entering the number of copies you want.

   Print Range Most applications let you print some or all of a file. In a word processor, for example, you can usually print the entire document, a range of pages, or the current selection.

   Quality Many applications allow you to choose a range of print qualities. In general, lower quality settings don't look all that great, but they print much faster; higher quality printouts are good for presentations and reports, but they tend to print as slowly as molasses in January.

   Printer Setup You almost always see some kind of option for setting up the current printer. Write, for example, has a **S**etup button; in other applications, you might see a **Printer** button, a **Print Setup** button, or some variation on this theme. These options let you choose from various printer settings (such as selecting a paper tray), and they usually let you select a different printer as well.

5. When you're done, select **OK** to start printing (some Print dialog boxes have a **Print** button, instead). If the bottom of the screen is visible, the Print Manager icon appears while the printing is in progress. See "Managing Print Jobs with Print Manager" later in this chapter to learn how to use Print Manager to control your print jobs.

Using Drag-and-Drop to Print Files

Windows 3.1's drag-and-drop capabilities can be radically useful. (See Chapter 12, "Let's Do Launch: Interesting Ways to Start Applications," and Chapter 13, "Fiddling Around with File Manager," to check out all kinds of drag-and-drop fun.) But, to my mind, one of the coolest uses for drag-and-drop is to print a file without even opening the appropriate application! Here's how it works:

1. Start Print Manager by selecting the **Print Manager** icon from Program Manager's **Main** group.
2. Open File Manager and make sure you can see at least part of the Print Manager window.
3. Move the mouse pointer over the file name you want to print, hold down the left mouse button, and then drag the file until the mouse pointer is inside the Print Manager window.
4. Release the mouse button. Windows opens the appropriate application, invokes the Print command, and then closes the application. All you do is sit back and wait for your file to print. Pretty slick, huh?

Getting a "Soft" Copy: Printing to a File

Printing to a file? Who the heck would want to do that? Isn't getting a hard copy what this printing stuff is all about? Well, yes it is, but what if you don't have a printer? Or what if you only have a dot-matrix printer, and you really need to print your résumé on a laser printer? If you know someone else who has the printer you need, Windows lets you print your document to a file. You can then transport the file to the other computer and print it there. Amazingly, the other computer doesn't even have to have the same application.

It sounds like a lot of hocus-pocus, I know, but it works. Here are the steps you need to follow:

1. Start Control Panel and select the **Printers** icon to display the Printers dialog box.

2. In the Installed **P**rinters list, highlight the printer you'll eventually use to print the file. (You may need to install the printer if you haven't done so already. Note, however, that since you don't own the printer, you presumably don't have access to its printer driver disk. This means you have to select one of the existing printers from the list.)
3. Select the **C**onnect button. Control Panel displays the Connect dialog box.
4. In the **P**orts list, select **FILE** (see below), and select **OK**.

To print to a file, select the FILE "port" in the Connect dialog box.

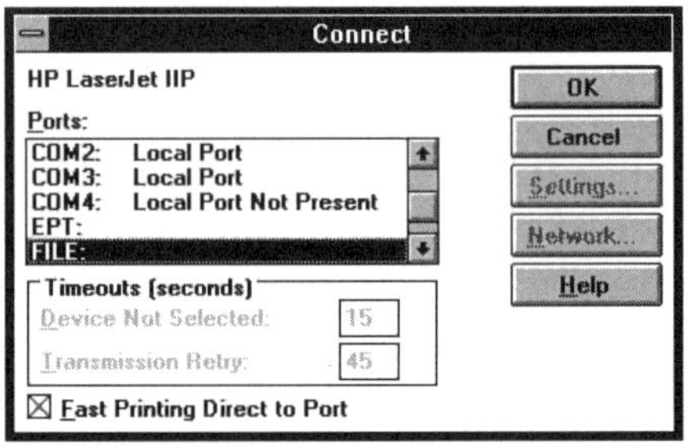

5. Select **Close**, then exit Control Panel by selecting Exit from the **S**ettings menu.
6. Return to the application and open the document you want to print to a file.
7. Pull down the **F**ile menu, select **P**rint, and then make your selections in the Print dialog box. In particular, make sure you choose the printer you want to print the file to. When you're ready, select **OK** (or **Print**). The Print To File dialog box appears, as shown below.

Use the Print To File dialog box to enter the name of the file to which you want to print.

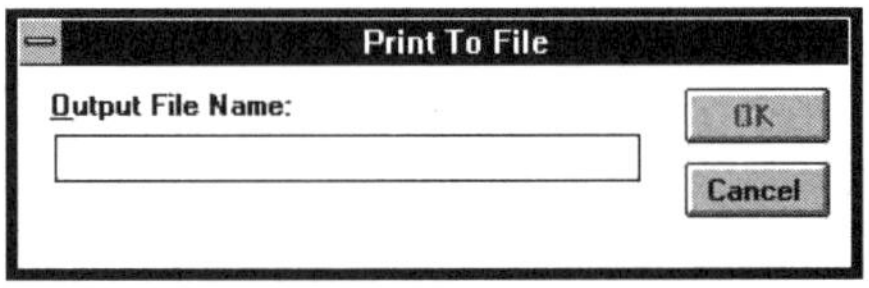

8. In the **O**utput File Name text box, enter a name for the file (including the drive and directory) and select **OK**. Windows prints the document to the file.

Okay, so now what? Now you copy the file to a floppy disk, truck on over to where the printer is located, and copy the file to the other computer. To print the file, you have two choices:

- If the other computer has Windows, start File Manager, highlight your file, pull down the **F**ile menu, and select **C**opy (or press **F8**). In the Copy dialog box, enter the name of the printer's port (for example, **LPT1**) in the **T**o text box. When you select **OK**, Windows asks if you want to replace a file named **LPT1** (or whatever port you entered). You can safely ignore this nonsense and select **Y**es. Windows prints the file.
- If the other computer doesn't have Windows, you need to print from DOS using the following generic command:

  COPY *filename port*

  Here, *filename* is the name of your file, and *port* is the port to which the printer is attached. For example, if your file is named PRINT.DOC, and the printer is attached to LPT1, you type **COPY PRINT.DOC LPT1** and press **Enter**. (I'm assuming the file is in the current directory. If it's not, you need to include the drive and directory with the file name.)

Managing Print Jobs with Print Manager

As I mentioned earlier, when you print from a Windows application, you see the Print Manager icon appear briefly at the bottom of the screen (if, that is, you can see the bottom of your screen; if you can't, trust me, the Print Manager icon shows up). What's that all about? Well, printing is a notoriously slow business. It's not unusual for even small documents to take a few minutes to wend their way through your printer. And large documents with lots of graphics? Forget about it!

To prevent users from wearing out their thumbs from excess twiddling while waiting for documents to print, Windows performs a nifty trick. When an application prints, Windows first calls Print Manager to the scene. Print Manager makes a temporary copy of the file (this is called *spooling* the file) and hands control back to the application. This allows you to keep working while Print Manager prints the copy in the background.

Print Manager is one of those unassuming applications that does its job quietly and without a lot of fanfare. In most cases, you can just let it go about its business, safe in the knowledge that your printing chores are in the hands of a competent professional. But what if you need to cancel a print job in progress, or pause the printing while you insert some paper? Ah, in these situations you have to disturb Print Manager's peace and quiet.

For starters, switch to Print Manager using one of the following techniques:

- If you can see the Print Manager icon at the bottom of the screen, double-click on it.
- If Print Manager is running, hold down **Alt** and press **Tab** until you see the Print Manager box.
- Select the **Print Manager** icon from Program Manager's **Main** group.

As you can see in the picture below, Print Manager lists each of your installed printers and any print jobs in progress or pending. Notice that you can fire more than one job at a time at Print Manager. If it's currently printing another document, Print Manager just calmly inserts any new work in the queue and prints each document in order.

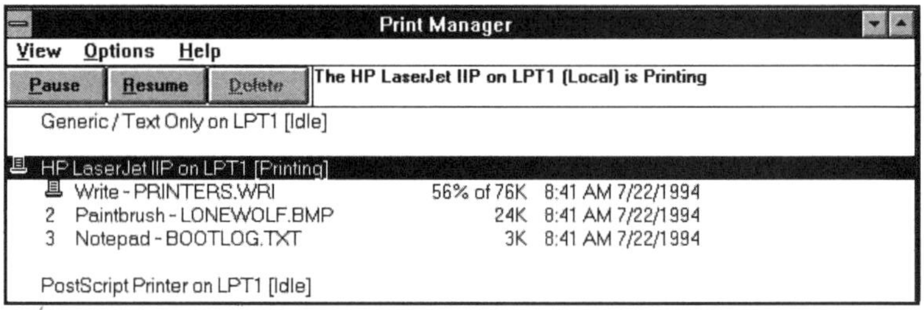

The Print Manager window shows each installed printer and the current print jobs for each one.

Here's a summary of the fun things you can do with Print Manager:

A pause for the cause If you need to add paper to your printer or change the ribbon, you can tell Print Manager to hold its horses. Just highlight the name of the printer that's printing (you can click on it with your mouse or use the up and down arrow keys) and select the **P**ause button. When you're ready to go again, select the **R**esume button.

Nuking print jobs If you accidentally print the wrong file, or if you simply change your mind, you can delete a file from the queue. Just highlight the appropriate file in Print Manager and select the **D**elete button. Print Manager plays it safe and displays a dialog box asking whether you're sure you want to stop printing the file. Select **OK** to remove the file from the queue.

Changing the print order In Print Manager—with the exception of the file currently printing—each file has a number beside it. This number tells you the print order for the jobs. This order is not set in stone, however. If you need to, you can move files up or down in the queue so they print sooner or later. With a mouse, all you do is drag the file to the new position. With your keyboard, highlight the file, hold down the **Ctrl** key, and use the up or down arrow keys to move the file.

Getting your print priorities in order Printing files in the background is a good example of Windows' multitasking capabilities. Once Print Manager has a copy of the file, you're free to get back to work. However, this luxury does come with a price. To process the print job, Windows has to divide its attention between the Print Manager and your application. This tends to make both the printing and your application a little slower than they would be on their own. Fortunately, you have some control over this. You can use Print Manager to tell Windows how much priority to give to your print jobs. Higher priority means that your printing will be faster, but your application will be slower. Lower priority speeds up your application, but slows down the printing. To set the priority, pull down Print Manager's **O**ptions menu and select **L**ow Priority, **M**edium Priority, or **H**igh Priority.

Tips for Saving Paper

As you've seen in this chapter, Windows and Print Manager make printing so easy that you now have yet another reason to print too many documents. To keep your paper costs down and to save a tree or two, here are some tips to help you cut down on the amount of paper you use:

- Only print a document when you have to. Too many people print intermediate drafts, or print whenever they make the slightest change. With Windows' WYSIWYG (What You See Is What You Get) display, you shouldn't have to print a hard copy until the document is finished.
- Take advantage of the Print Preview feature. Many Windows applications have a Print Preview command that lets you see exactly what your document will look like (including things like headers and footers, page numbers, and footnotes) when it's printed. A sneak peek at the document will save you many a reprint.
- Proofread your documents carefully before you print them. Most reprints are because of spelling and grammatical errors that aren't caught until you read the printout. You can avoid this by giving a document the once-over before you print it. And by all means use the built-in spell checker and grammar checker if your application has them.
- Try to maximize the print area on each page. You can do this by reducing the margins and by using smaller type sizes. Many word processors also have a feature that suppresses *widows* (single lines that appear by themselves at the top of a page).
- Print only what you need. Most applications let you print just a selection of text, a single page, or a range of pages. There's no point printing the entire document if you only need a small chunk of it.
- If you print a document and then discover a small mistake (such as a spelling gaffe) on one page, reprint only the offending page.
- Distribute your documents electronically if you can. Instead of sending a printout to someone, you can send the file over a network, as an e-mail attachment, or even via floppy disk.

- Reuse printouts you no longer need. If you're printing out an unimportant document that only you will see, turn your used pages around and print on the other side.

The Least You Need to Know

This chapter took you on a crash course in Windows printing. Here's a brief recap of some of the chapter's main points:

- To install your printer in Windows, select the Control Panel's **Printers** icon, select **A**dd, choose your printer from the list, and then select **I**nstall.
- Printing is more or less identical in most Windows applications. Pull down the **F**ile menu, select **P**rint, fill in the Print dialog box options, and select **OK** (or **Print**).
- Windows 3.1 users can print a file from File Manager by dragging the file and dropping it inside the Print Manager window.
- The Print Manager prints your files in the background by spooling the document and then returning control to the application. You can use Print Manager to pause your printer, delete print jobs, or change the queue order.

Chapter 7
Flexing Your Font Muscles

In This Chapter

- Getting a grip on basic font know-how
- Learning about TrueType fonts
- Activating TrueType on your system
- Adding and removing fonts
- A fountain of font fun

Windows has turned many otherwise ordinary citizens into avid amateur typographers. People at cocktail parties the world over are debating the relative merits of serif versus sans serif fonts and expounding the virtues of typefaces with names like Desdemona and Braggadocio.

Although most of us don't take fonts to that extreme, they certainly do jazz up our documents, spreadsheets, and graphics. This chapter takes a closer look at fonts to learn just what makes them tick. We'll begin with a two-part refresher course on font basics, and then build from there into topics that'll help you maximize your font fun.

Fontamentals Part I: What Is a Font?

In Chapter 19 of *The Complete Idiot's Guide to Windows,* I likened fonts to architecture. Architecture deals with the style and design of a building in the same way that a font deals with the style and design of a character. To a trained eye, certain characteristics of a building identify the architectural school from which it sprung (be it Rococo, Modernist, or what have you). In much the same way, letters, symbols, and even numbers boast a unique set of characteristics that define their font family. Here's a quick rundown of each of these characteristics:

Typeface The typeface is the design part of a font. It refers to a set of characters that share common features such as the width of the strokes that make up each character (this is sometimes called the font's *weight*) and whether the characters have *serifs*. Serif typefaces contain fine cross strokes at the extremities of each character that produce highly readable type. Typefaces that don't have these cross strokes are called *sans serif.* They have a clean look that's ideal for headlines and titles. (This book uses the traditional combination of these two kinds of typefaces: a sans serif typeface for the chapter titles and paragraph headings, and a serif typeface for the body text.)

TECHNO NERD TEACHES...

Just to be confusing, Windows and Windows applications often use the terms *font* and *typeface* interchangeably.

Size This is the height of the font. Specifically, it measures the distance from the top of a tall letter (such as t) to the bottom of a letter with a "tail" (such as y). Type sizes are expressed in *points,* where there are 72 points in an inch. (This book is set in a 10-point font.)

Font style This refers to certain variations of the font that produce a different look. Windows recognizes four different font styles: regular (also known as normal, or roman), **bold**, *italic*, and ***bold italic***. These font styles should not be confused with *font effects*, such as color, underlining, and strikeout (sometimes called "strikethrough") characters, which are available in many applications.

Character spacing This is the amount of space allotted to each character. A font's character spacing can be either *monospace* or *proportional*. Monospace fonts dole out the same amount of space for each character, so even skinny letters such as "i" and "l" take up as much space as wider letters, such as "y" and "w." Proportional fonts, on the other hand, vary the amount of space given to each character according to the actual width of the letter.

Fontamentals Part II: Font Types

Windows also categorizes fonts according to how they're produced on your screen or at the printer. There are three font types: raster fonts, vector fonts, and TrueType fonts.

In *raster fonts*, each character is represented by a pattern of dots, as shown in the following example. While these fonts display and print quickly, they have two major disadvantages:

- They're stored in files as graphic images or *bitmaps* (which is why they're also called *bitmapped fonts*). These files contain everything the system needs to know about the font (what styles it can display, what sizes are available, and so on). The problem is that to show even a single character from the font, Windows has to load the entire file into memory, which can really slow things down.
- The available representations of the font are set in stone according to what's in the font file. You only get a fixed number of font sizes (usually just 8-, 10-, 12-, and 14-point). You can try a different size, but it has to be a multiple of one of the supplied sizes, and the resulting text is decidedly ugly.

> **SPEAK LIKE A GEEK**
>
> In a **raster font**, each character is represented by a pattern of dots; in a **vector font**, each character is generated by a mathematical formula; in a **TrueType font**, each character is produced by a font management program.

Windows ships with five raster fonts: Courier, MS Sans Serif, MS Serif, System, and Terminal. (The System and Terminal fonts, by the way, are only available through Paintbrush. To access them, pull down the Text menu and select Fonts, and you'll see them listed in the Font dialog box.)

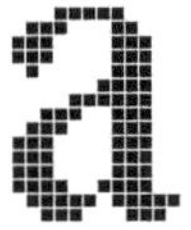

The characters in raster fonts are made up of a pattern of dots.

Vector fonts are created from an obscenely complex mathematical model that defines an outline for each character, which is then filled in with whatever the current text color is. The picture below shows an example. The big advantage to using vector fonts is that you can scale them to different sizes because all Windows has to do is make a slight adjustment to the formula (which is why these are also called *scalable* fonts). This scalability saves memory because you don't have to keep the full font family loaded.

However, vector fonts do have their disadvantages:

- The complexity of the math tends to slow things down a tad.
- You need separate fonts for your screen and printer.
- The character outlines tend to break down at smaller font sizes (anything smaller than 14 points or so), and they become virtually unreadable.

Windows comes with three vector fonts: Modern, Roman, and Script.

The characters in vector fonts are created from outlines defined by mathematical equations.

TrueType fonts (you need Windows 3.1 to get 'em) use a newer, more sophisticated outline technology. Instead of using a few hard-wired equations, TrueType fonts are displayed using a full-fledged *font management program* (called TrueType, which is where the fonts get their name). This program can produce great-looking characters at any size. But truly scalable characters are by no means the only advantage TrueType brings to the table. Consider these factors:

- TrueType uses the same fonts for both the screen and the printer, which makes your characters truly WYSIWYG (What You See Is What You Get).

- TrueType fonts use less disk space because you need only a couple of small files to create every size and style for each font.
- TrueType fonts will print on any printer—laser or dot-matrix—that Windows supports. Other fonts are often printer-specific, so if you switch printers, you have to switch fonts.
- You can exchange files with other Windows 3.1 users without hassle. When you use other types of fonts, you never know if someone else will be able to view or print your documents properly.
- Many companies have put together collections of TrueType fonts that you can get for as little as a dollar a font.
- TrueType doesn't cost a dime because everything you need is built right into Windows.

Windows comes with five TrueType font families: Arial, Courier New, Symbol, Times New Roman, and Wingding.

The following table shows you which types of fonts can be used for the four main varieties of printers:

Type of printer	Raster fonts	Vector fonts	TrueType fonts
Dot-matrix	Yes	No	Yes
Hewlett-Packard laser	No	Yes	Yes
PostScript	No	Yes	Yes
Plotter	No	Yes	No

Turning TrueType On (or Off)

TrueType comes with so many advantages that it should always be your font manager of choice. When selecting fonts in your Windows applications, look for the "double-T" TrueType logo beside the font name in the Font dialog box. For example, check out the Font dialog box from Write, shown on the following page.

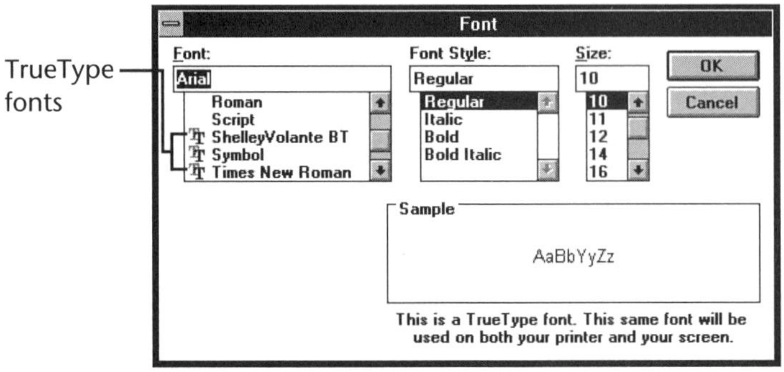

Look for TrueType's "double-T" symbol to pick out TrueType fonts in your Windows applications.

TECHNO NERD TEACHES...

Your Windows applications' Font dialog boxes enable you to format text with different typefaces, styles, sizes, and effects. But what about Windows' other fonts? For example, Windows uses a specific font for window title bars, menu bars, and icon titles. To learn how to change these *system* fonts, check out Chapter 9, "Learning to Love Those Strange INI Files."

If you don't see any TrueType fonts in your Font dialog boxes (and you're sure you're using Windows 3.1), you probably need to activate TrueType for your system. Alternatively, if you're using TrueType fonts and you find Windows is taking forever to display your text, you may need to turn TrueType off while you work. (This should only be a problem on older, less powerful systems.) To turn TrueType on or off, follow these steps:

1. In Program Manager's **Main** program group, select the **Control Panel** icon. Windows starts Control Panel.
2. Select the **Fonts** icon, or pull down the **S**ettings menu and select Fonts. The Fonts dialog box appears.
3. Select the TrueType button. Control Panel displays the TrueType dialog box shown on the following page.

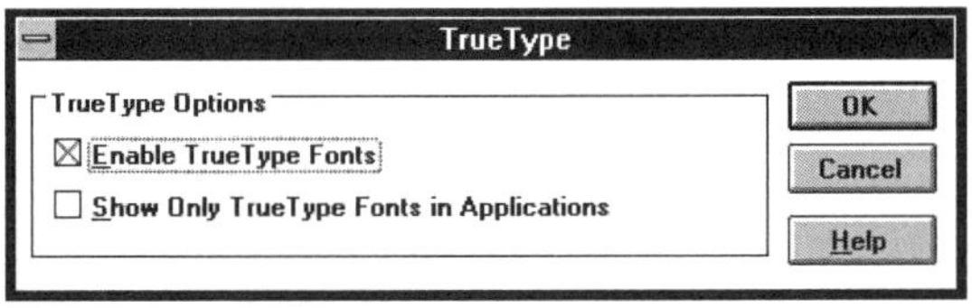

Use the TrueType dialog box to turn TrueType on or off.

4. To turn TrueType on, activate the Enable TrueType Fonts check box. If you want to disable TrueType, deactivate this check box.
5. If you think TrueType is so spiffy that you want to use it and nothing else, activate the Show Only TrueType Fonts in the Applications check box.
6. Select **OK** to return to the Fonts dialog box.
7. Select **Cancel** to return to the Control Panel, then select Exit from the Settings menu.

Going Font Crazy: Adding New Fonts to Windows

As I mentioned earlier, there are all kinds of TrueType font collections on the market nowadays. If you're feeling cramped by the paltry selection that comes with Windows 3.1, perhaps one of these packages can provide just the right typeface to give your documents that certain *je ne sais quoi*. Before you can use your new fonts, however, you need to add them to Windows. The following steps show you how it's done:

1. Start Control Panel and select the **Fonts** icon (or select Fonts from the Settings menu). Control Panel displays the Fonts dialog box.
2. Select the Add button. The Add Fonts dialog box appears.
3. Insert the disk containing the font files, then select the appropriate disk drive from the Drives list. (If the font files are in a different directory, use the Directories list to select the appropriate directory.) Windows reads the font names from the disk and displays them in the List of Fonts list box (see the following page).

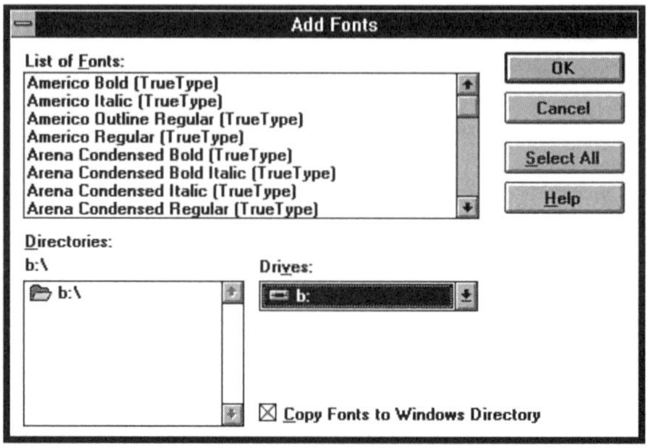

Use the Add Fonts dialog box to select the new fonts you want to add to your system.

4. Use the List of Fonts box to highlight the fonts you want to install. If you're using a mouse, hold down the **Ctrl** key and click on each font. From the keyboard, press **Shift+F8** and then highlight each font you want to add using the up and down arrow keys, and press the **Spacebar**. When you're done, press **Shift+F8** again.

   Alternatively, you can install all the fonts on the disk by choosing the Select All button.

5. Windows normally likes to see the font files copied to the Windows directory (technically, they're copied to Windows' SYSTEM subdirectory). So, in most cases, you should make sure the Copy Fonts to Windows Directory check box is activated. However, there are two exceptions to this rule:

   - If hard disk space is at a premium and the font files already exist elsewhere on the hard disk, there isn't much point in creating an extra copy of each file.

   - If you're loading the font files from a CD-ROM drive, it's usually impractical to load onto your hard disk the tens if not hundreds of megabytes of fonts that a CD-ROM disk can hold.

6. Select **OK**. Control Panel returns you to the Fonts dialog box and adds your selected fonts to the Installed Fonts list. If an existing font with the same name is already installed, Control Panel displays a dialog box to let you know. In this case, select **OK** to avoid installing the font.

7. Select **Close** to return to the Control Panel, and then select Exit from the Settings menu.

You may have problems sending files that use third-party fonts to other people because those people won't have the proper font files on their systems. The result is usually a mess, because Windows tries to convert the fonts into something like Courier. To avoid this, either stick with the standard fonts that come with Windows, or send the font files with your document (along with a note telling the recipient to install the fonts; he'll be very pleased, I'm sure).

Some applications (notably Microsoft PowerPoint and Microsoft Word for Windows 6.0) let you *embed* fonts in your documents. Embedded fonts make it possible for the other person to view the file properly without having to clutter their hard drive with your fancy-shmancy fonts. Over the next year or so, you'll likely see this feature included in most mainstream Windows applications.

Uninstalling Old Fonts

Although TrueType fonts take up considerably less disk space than the other font types, you're still looking at anywhere from 30K to 80K per font file. If you have hundreds of fonts, the numbers can add up to a big chunk of hard disk real estate in a hurry. Also, all your installed fonts take up memory, whether you use them or not. To keep a lid on both hard disk and memory usage, you should periodically clean out those font files you never use. Here's how to do it:

1. Crank up Control Panel and select the **Fonts** icon (or select Fonts from the Settings menu) to display the Fonts dialog box.
2. Using the Installed Fonts list, highlight the fonts you want to remove.
3. Select the Remove button. Control Panel displays the Remove Font dialog box, asking whether you're sure you want to remove the font (see below).

Control Panel displays the Remove Font dialog box to verify that you want to remove the font.

> **OOPS!**
>
> Do not, I repeat, *do not* activate the **D**elete Font File From Disk check box unless you're sure you have another copy of the font on a floppy disk or CD-ROM, or elsewhere on your hard drive.

4. Control Panel normally only removes the font from the list of installed fonts. If you also want the font file deleted from your hard disk, activate the **D**elete Font File From Disk check box.
5. Select **Y**es to remove the font. If you want to remove all the highlighted fonts, select Yes to **A**ll. Control Panel removes the fonts and returns you to the Fonts dialog box.
6. Select **Close** to return to the Control Panel, and then select E**x**it from the **S**ettings menu.

To learn how to move fonts from one directory to another, pop in on Chapter 9, "Learning to Love Those Strange INI Files."

Font Tips

Windows makes it easy to add unique and eye-catching fonts to all your documents. But have some restraint here. Nothing looks worse—or is as confusing—as a document with too many fonts crammed together on one page. Here are a few things to keep in mind when performing your font formatting chores:

- Try to restrict your fonts to no more than a couple per document. If you need various looks, use larger sizes or different styles of the same fonts.
- A good font combination is a sans serif font for titles and headings, and a serif font for the document's main body text.
- If you need to emphasize something, bold or italicize it in the same typeface as the surrounding text. Avoid using underlining for emphasis; it just looks amateurish.
- Only use larger sizes for titles and headings. I'd avoid anything smaller than 10 points; text that small is also too difficult to make out.
- Avoid using decorative or excessively narrow fonts for large sections of text. They're almost always hard on the eyes after a half dozen words or so.

A (Not So) Real-Life Example

Although it's best to avoid using lots of fonts in your documents, there is one time when it pays off: writing a ransom note! What drudgery that used to be—cutting out all those individual letters and pasting them onto the paper. Yuck! And if you made a spelling mistake? Well, it was start-over city! Computers, though, have changed all that. Now all you have to do is format each individual letter with a different font. It still takes awhile, but at least you don't get glue all over your fingers. The picture below shows an example ransom note. See how professional it looks!

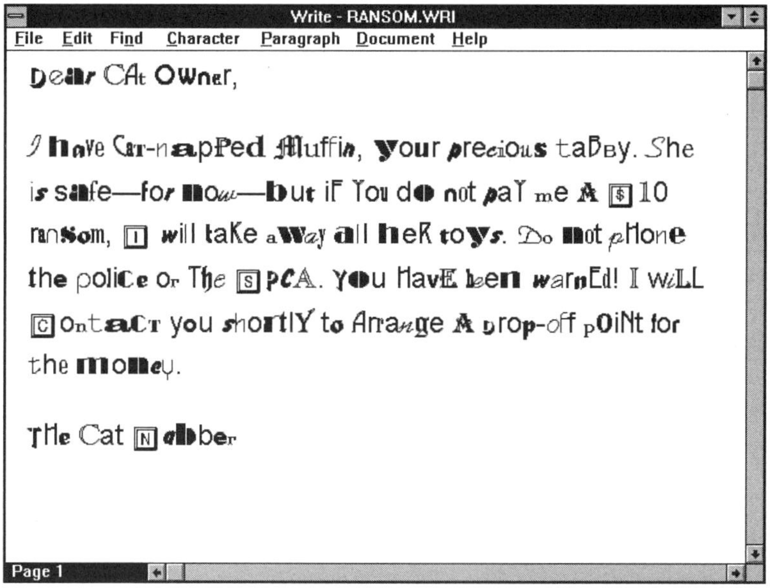

The plethora of fonts available today takes the drudgery out of creating ransom notes.

The Least You Need to Know

This chapter showed you how to flex your Windows font muscles. Here's a brief rundown of what was important:

- A font is a unique set of characters with a specific typeface and character spacing, and one or more type styles and type sizes.

continues

continued

- Windows fonts come in three flavors: raster, vector, and TrueType. For most applications, TrueType fonts are your best bet because they produce the best type, use the least disk space, and are scalable.
- To turn TrueType on or off, select the Control Panel's **Fonts** icon, and then select the **T**rueType button.
- To add fonts to your system, select the **Fonts** icon in the Control Panel, and then select the **A**dd button.
- To remove fonts from Windows, select the Control Panel's **Fonts** icon, highlight the font, and then select **R**emove.
- To keep your documents readable, stick to a couple of fonts, using sans serif fonts for headings and serif fonts for text, and using bold, italics, and large type sizes appropriately.

Chapter 8

Understanding the Mysterious Snake Oil of OLE

In This Chapter

- Data sharing without OLE
- What OLE is and how it can change your life
- Linking data between two applications
- Embedding data inside a document
- Figuring out the Object Packager thing
- A no-bull approach that emphasizes the practical side of OLE

Okay, let's get a couple of things straight right off the bat. First of all, OLE is pronounced *OH-lay* (now you get the bad pun in this chapter's title). Secondly, despite this pronunciation, OLE has nothing whatsoever to do with *olé*, the bullfight chant. It stands for *object linking and embedding,* which sounds scary but is just a method for sharing data between some Windows applications.

This chapter will attempt to knock some sense into this OLE business by keeping theory to a minimum, and by placing OLE in its most practical, hands-on light. The examples you'll see will show you how to harness the power of OLE to make your life easier, and to accomplish tasks you'd never have thought possible a few minutes ago.

Dividing the Spoils: Data Sharing Basics

Windows was foisted upon an unsuspecting computing public for many reasons—the fancy graphics, the easy interface, and the multitasking fun, for example. But one of Windows' biggest reasons for being is to share data between programs. Long gone are the days when our word processing documents were expected to contain only text, and our spreadsheets were expected to contain only numbers. Today's modern files often include alien elements such as images from a graphics program, or sound files from a library of sound clips.

Windows makes it easy to combine data from separate programs by acting as the middleman to make sure things go smoothly. Windows has a number of tricks up its electronic sleeve to accomplish this, but the two most common are the Clipboard and OLE. We'll examine the Clipboard in this section; the rest of the chapter will focus on the hocus-pocus of OLE.

Any time you cut or copy something in an application, Windows stores the data in a special place called the *Clipboard*. The data sits there, waiting patiently, until you issue a Paste command. Windows then copies the info from the Clipboard to the current cursor position in the application. The trick here is that, for the most part, Windows doesn't care which application sends out the paste message. In other words, you can cut or copy data from one application, then paste into something completely different.

For the sake of spelling all this out, let's go through the specific steps required to exchange data via the Clipboard:

1. Activate the application containing the data you want to share.
2. Select the data, pull down the **E**dit menu, and select either Cu**t** or **C**opy. Windows transfers the data to the Clipboard.
3. Switch to the application into which you want to place the data.
4. Move to where you want the data to appear, pull down the **E**dit menu, and select the **P**aste command. The data is pulled from the Clipboard and pasted into the application. A copy of the data remains on the Clipboard, however, so you can run as many **P**aste commands as you need.

TECHNO NERD TEACHES...

Selecting data is basically the same in most Windows applications. If you have a mouse, you just drag the pointer over the data. From the keyboard, position the cursor where the data starts, hold down the **Shift** key, and use the application's navigation keys (usually the arrow keys, Page Up, Page Down, and so on) to select the data. Some applications may require an extra step or two. (In Paintbrush, for example, you need to select the Scissors or Pick tool.)

The Clipboard sounds like some mysterious place, but it's actually just a special chunk of your computer's memory that Windows sets aside for all this cut-and-paste malarkey. You can view the current contents of the Clipboard by opening the **Main** group in Program Manager and selecting the **Clipboard Viewer** icon. The Clipboard Viewer window that appears shows your most recently cut or copied data. (The Clipboard can only hold the contents of a single Cut or Copy command.)

For example, take a gander at the figure on the following page. The Cardfile window at the top shows an address that I've copied from a card. The Clipboard Viewer window in the middle shows the copied data, intact and ready to paste. The Write window at the bottom shows the same data pasted into a document.

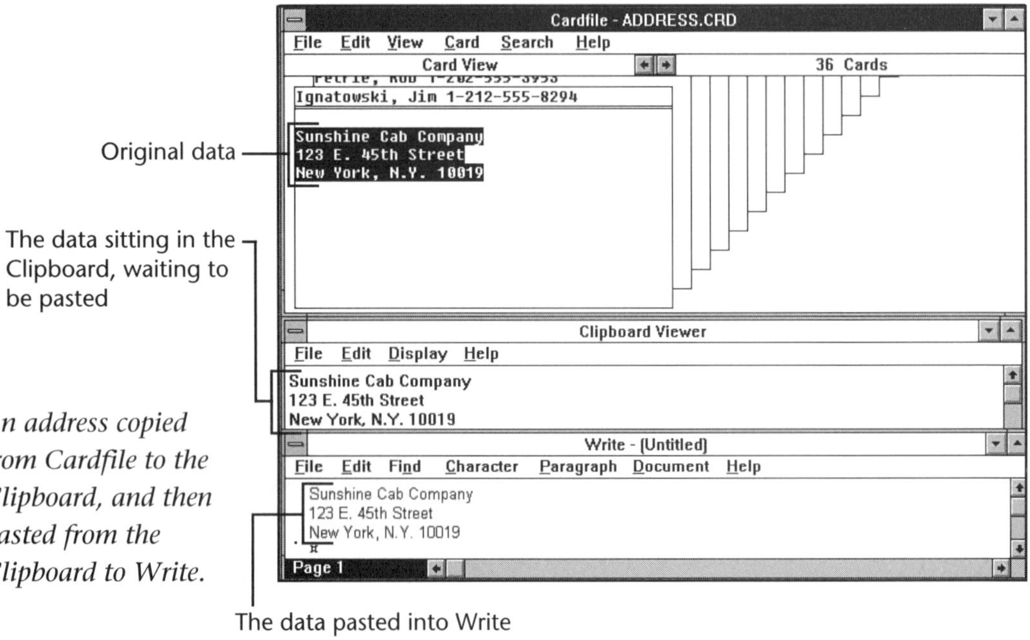

An address copied from Cardfile to the Clipboard, and then pasted from the Clipboard to Write.

OLE: Can You See?

The Clipboard method's greatest virtue is its simplicity, but it suffers from two major drawbacks. Firstly, if the data is changed in the original application, the document containing the copy becomes out of date. This has two consequences:

- If you know the copied data needs to be updated, you have to repeat the whole copy-and-paste procedure to get the latest version of the data.
- If you don't know the data needs to be updated (for example, if someone else changes the original data without telling you), you're out of luck because you'll be stuck with an old version of the info.

Secondly, what if you want to make changes to the copied data? You may be able to edit the data directly (if it's just text, for example), but more often than not you'll need to crank up the original application, change the data there, and then do the Clipboard thing again. However, you might run into problems if you're not sure which application to use, or if you're not sure which file contains the original data.

If you put together a shared data wish list, it would probably contain two items:

- If the data changes in the other application, I wish the copied data would be updated automatically.
- If I want to make changes to the copied data, I wish it were easy to find both the original application and the original data file.

Well, my friends, I'm here today to tell you that wishes can come true, because OLE addresses both of these issues. To see how, let's examine the three parts of OLE: objects, linking, and embedding.

The *object* is the data that is inserted into the receiving application. The basic Clipboard method just sends raw data, but OLE is more sophisticated because it also sends information that lets you easily update and work with the data.

> **SPEAK LIKE A GEEK**
>
> To get through the rest of this chapter, we'll need some terminology for the application that creates the original data, and for the application that gets the copy. The official terms are **server** and **client**, respectively, but most people can never remember which is which. Instead, I'll use the terms **source** and **destination.**

Linking is one of the OLE methods you can use to insert an object into a destination document. In linking, OLE sets up and maintains a link between the source application and the object so that if the original data is changed, OLE can update the object automatically. For example, suppose you insert a linked spreadsheet object into a word processor document. If you revise some of the numbers in the spreadsheet sometime down the road, the copy inside the document is automatically updated to reflect the new numbers.

Embedding is the other OLE technique you can use to insert an object into a destination file. In embedding, OLE copies not only the source data, but also all kinds of info about the source application. It's easy to make changes to the object because OLE knows where it came from and can start the source application for you automatically. For example, if you've embedded a spreadsheet object in a word processor document, you can make changes to the object simply by selecting it. (I'll show how to do this later on.) When you select the embedded object, OLE starts up the source application and automatically loads the object so you can make your changes.

Should I Link or Embed?

Ah, good question. This is perhaps the most confusing aspect of OLE: under what circumstances should you link your objects and under what circumstances should you embed them? The answer lies in how OLE treats the source data. When you link an object, OLE doesn't even bother to send the data to the destination; it just sends a reference that tells the destination application which file contains the source data. This is enough to maintain the link between the two applications. When you embed an object, however, the actual data is crammed into the destination document.

You should link your objects if the following statements are true:

- You want to keep your destination documents small. The destination just gets the link info, and not the data itself, so there's much less memory and hard disk overhead associated with linking.
- You're sure the source file won't be moved or deleted. To maintain the link, OLE requires that the source file remain in the same place. If it's moved or deleted, the link is broken.
- You need to keep the source file as a separate document in case you want to make changes to it later, or in case you need it for more OLE fun. You're free to link an object to as many destination files as you like. If you think you'll be using the source data in different places, you should link it to maintain a separate file.
- You won't be sending the destination file via e-mail or floppy disk. This is true because OLE expects the linked source data to appear in a specific place. If you send the destination file to someone else, that person might not have the proper source file to maintain the link.

You should embed your objects if the following statements are true:

- You don't care how big your destination files get. Embedding works best in situations where you have lots of hard disk space and lots of memory.
- You don't need to keep the source file as a separate document. If you only need to use the source data once, embedding it means you can get rid of the source file and reduce the clutter on your hard disk.
- You'll be sending the destination file and you want to make sure the object arrives intact. If you send a file containing an embedded object, the other person will see the data complete and unaltered.

Doing the Linking and Embedding Thing

Deciding whether you want to link or embed is actually the hardest part of OLE. Once you know what you want to do, the rest is straightforward. However, just to keep you all on your toes, OLE gives you a few different methods to use to link or embed an object:

- You can copy the object from the source application and paste it in the destination application as a linked or embedded object.
- You can insert a new embedded object from within the destination application.
- You can insert an existing file as an embedded object from within the destination application. (I'll hold off discussing this method until Chapter 13, "Fiddling Around with File Manager.")

Linking or Embedding an Object by Pasting

If the object you want to link or embed already exists, you can place it on the Clipboard and then paste it in the destination document. If you think this sounds like what we did earlier in the chapter, you're close. The difference, as the following steps will show, is that you paste not with the **P**aste command, but with the Paste **S**pecial command.

1. Activate the source application and open or create the document that contains the object.
2. Select the object you want to link or embed, pull down the **E**dit menu, and then select the **C**opy command to place the data on the Clipboard.
3. Switch to the destination application and move to where you want the object to appear.

OOPS!

If the destination application doesn't have a Paste **S**pecial command, it's bad news: it means the program doesn't support object linking and embedding.

4. Pull down the **E**dit menu and select the Paste **S**pecial command. A Paste Special dialog box appears, similar to the one shown below. (The appearance of the Paste Special dialog box varies from application to application.)

   Alternatively, some applications (such as Write and Cardfile) have a Paste **L**ink command on their **E**dit menus. If you want to link the object, you can use this command to bypass the Paste Special dialog box.

Use the Paste Special dialog box to select the type of object to paste and to optionally set up a link.

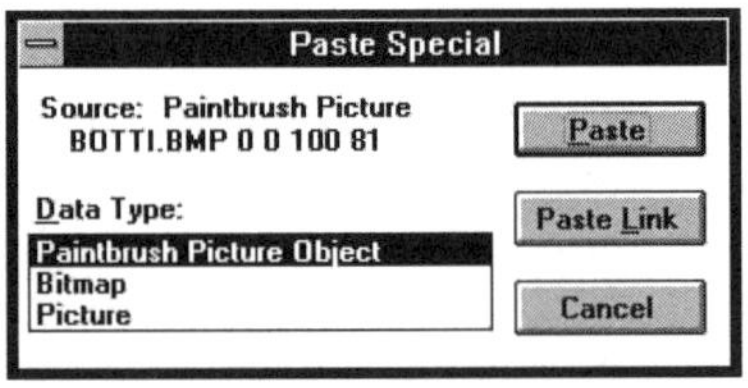

5. In the list of data types, select the one with "Object" in the name (such as **Paintbrush Picture Object**).
6. Select either Paste **L**ink (to paste the data as a linked object) or **P**aste (to paste the data as an embedded object). In some Paste Special dialog boxes, you select either the Paste **L**ink or **P**aste option, then select **OK**.

Inserting a New Embedded Object

If the object you want to embed doesn't already exist, and you don't need to create a separate file, OLE lets you create the new object directly into the destination application. Here's how it works:

1. In the destination application, move to where you want the new object to appear.
2. Either pull down the **E**dit menu and select **I**nsert Object or pull down the **I**nsert menu and select **O**bject. In either case, a dialog box appears, similar to the one shown below.

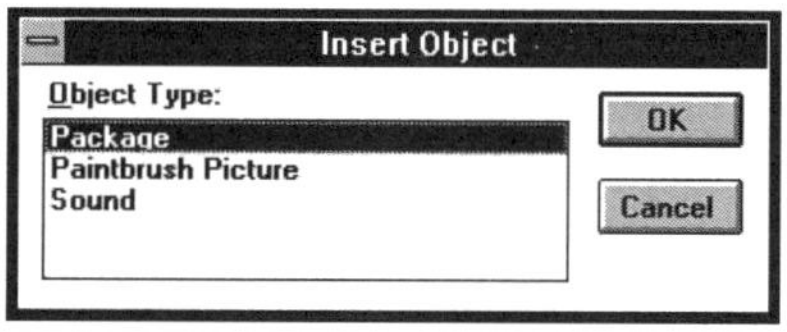

Use this dialog box to select the type of embedded object you want to create.

3. In the **O**bject Type list, select the type of object you want to create. (If you're wondering what a Package object is, see "Package Deals: Using the Object Packager," later in this chapter. To work with Sound objects, see Chapter 11, "Hopping on the Multimedia Bandwagon.")
4. Select **OK**. Windows starts the source application for the object type you selected.
5. Create the object you want to embed.
6. Exit the source application. In most cases, you'll do this by pulling down the **F**ile menu and selecting the Exit & Return to *document* command, where *document* is the name of the active document in the destination application. The source application asks whether you want to update the embedded object.
7. Select **Y**es. Windows embeds the object.

> **E-Z**
>
> In most source applications, you can embed the object without leaving the application by selecting the **F**ile menu's **U**pdate command. Since you won't be creating a separate file for the object, this is sort of like saving your work.

Editing a Linked or Embedded Object

If you need to make changes to a linked or embedded object, you can start the source application and load the object automatically by using any of the following methods:

- Double-click on the object.
- Select the object, pull down the **Edit** menu, and select the **Edit** *DataType* **Object** command, where *DataType* is the type of object you selected (e.g., Paintbrush Picture or Document).

Working with OLE 2 Applications

The latest version of object linking and embedding—version 2—includes many new features that make it even easier to create and maintain embedded objects. Dragging and dropping objects between applications, in-place inserting, and in-place editing are just a few of the features included.

Even though OLE 2 is built into Windows 3.1, you can't use it unless your applications have been specifically designed to handle it. As I write this, only a handful of applications support OLE 2, including Microsoft Word 6.0, Microsoft Excel 5.0, and Shapeware's Visio (although most in-the-know types expect that OLE 2 will become ubiquitous in 1995.) How can you tell whether a program is OLE 2-compatible? Unfortunately, there's no easy way. Either you can try some of the OLE 2 techniques discussed below, or you can ask the program's tech support department. (You could also try looking on the box the software came in, if you still have it.)

With the capability to drag and drop objects between applications, you can copy information between two open OLE 2 applications simply by dragging selected data from one application window and dropping it in the other. If you want to copy the data instead of moving it, you must hold down **Ctrl** while dragging.

When you insert a new OLE 2 object, Windows activates *in-place inserting*. This means that instead of displaying the source application in a separate window, certain features of the destination application's window are temporarily hidden in favor of the source application's features. For example:

- The title bar changes to tell you what kind of object you're now working with.
- The menu bar (with the exception of the **File** and **Window** menus) is replaced by the source application's menu bar.
- The toolbars are replaced by the source application's toolbars.
- Any other features you need to create the source object are also added to the window.

To exit in-place inserting and embed the object, click outside the object.

In-place editing enables you to edit an OLE 2 object. When you edit an OLE 2 object, the object remains where it is and the destination application's window changes as it does with in-place inserting. Make your changes, then click outside the object to complete the edit.

Let's look at an example to see OLE 2 in action. First off, the following figure shows the normal Microsoft Excel window.

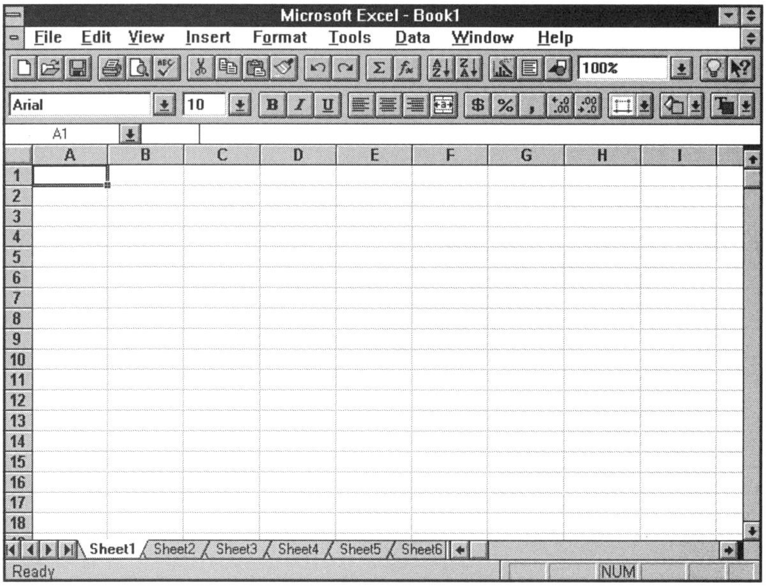

Yer basic Microsoft Excel window.

Now I'll insert a Microsoft Word for Windows 6.0 document into Excel. Word 6 is an OLE 2 application, so it supports in-place inserting. As the following picture shows, OLE 2 changes the menu bar and toolbars from Excel's to Word's.

Word's menu bar

Word's toolbars

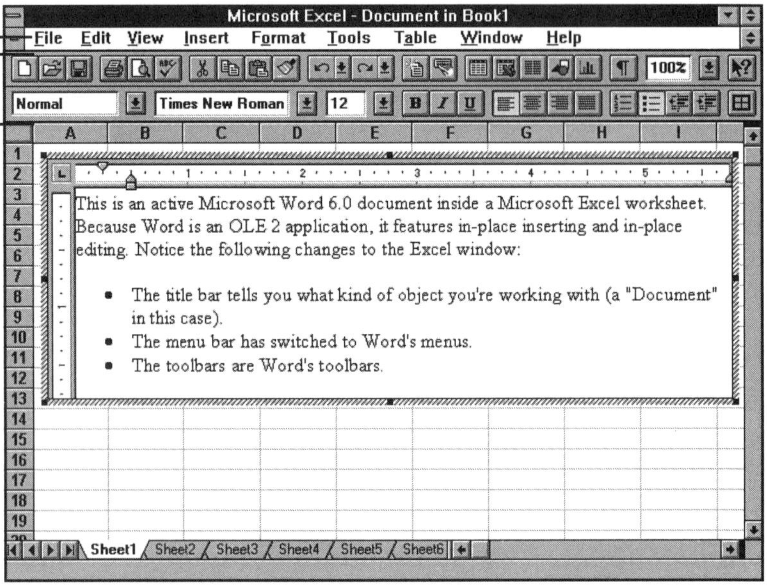

During in-place inserting, the Excel window assumes many features of the Word for Windows 6 window.

Package Deals: Using the Object Packager

One of the problems you'll encounter in your OLE adventures is that some objects like to hog lots of space in your destination documents. For example, you may have written a report summarizing some numbers from a spreadsheet, and then decided to embed the spreadsheet itself as backup. In this case, your readers will probably only want to check out the raw numbers occasionally, so it's overkill to have this huge spreadsheet sprawled all over your document.

To solve this problem, you can use an application called Object Packager to embed the spreadsheet as a *package*. A package is just a container for linked or embedded objects, but it appears in the destination document as a nice, neat icon (see the following picture). If your reader wants to see the spreadsheet, he only has to double-click the icon to display the contents of the package.

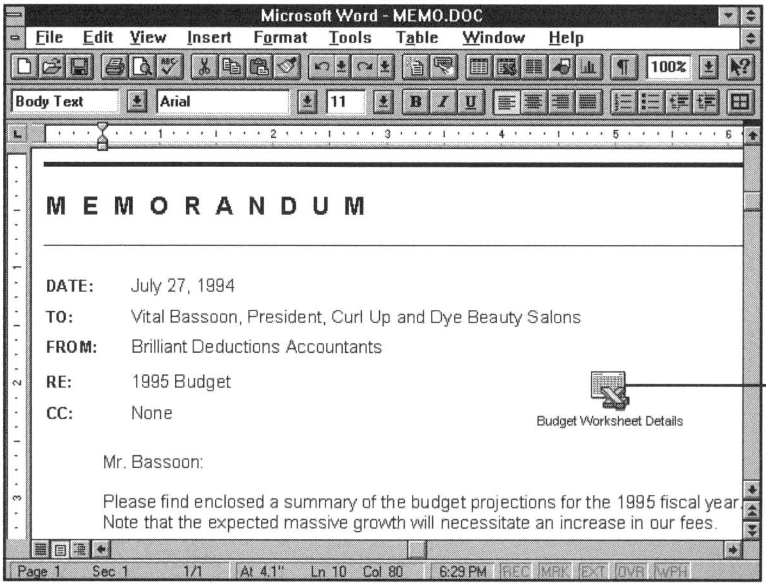

Packages are embedded in the destination file as an icon.

You can use Object Packager to package entire files, objects that you've copied to the Clipboard, or DOS commands. Here are the steps to follow:

1. Start Object Packager by opening Program Manager's **Accessories** group and selecting the **Object Packager** icon. The Object Packager window is divided into two areas: the left side is the **Appearance** window that shows you the package's icon and label; the right side is the **Content** window that shows you what's in the package (see the following figure).

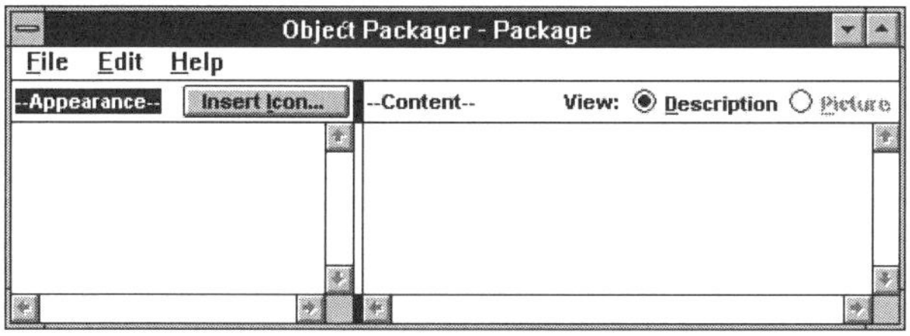

The Object Packager window.

2. Use one of the following techniques to package your data:

    - If you're packaging data from the Clipboard, pull down the Edit menu, and select either Paste (or press **Ctrl+V**) to embed the data or Paste Link to link it.
    - If you're packaging an entire file, pull down the File menu, select Import, highlight the file in the Import dialog box, and then select **OK**.
    - If you're packaging a DOS command, pull down the Edit menu, select Command Line, enter the command in the Command Line dialog box, and then select **OK**. For example, to copy all the files in the C:\DATA directory to drive A, you'd enter the following:

      COMMAND /C XCOPY C:\DATA A:

3. If you want to change the package's icon, select the Insert Icon button to display the Insert Icon dialog box. Select an icon from the Current Icon box (or select Browse and choose another icon file from the Browse dialog box), then select **OK**.
4. To change the icon label, select the Edit menu's Label command, enter the new label in the Label dialog box, then select **OK**.
5. Pull down the Edit menu and select Copy Package.
6. Switch to the application where you want the package to appear.
7. Move to where you want the package to appear, pull down the Edit menu, and select the Paste command. Windows pastes the package as an icon.

With your package safely in the destination document, you can view its contents at any time either by double-clicking on the icon, or by pulling down the Edit menu, selecting Package Object, and selecting Activate Contents.

To see a good example of Object Packager packages in action, turn to Chapter 14, "Improving Your Write Skills," to see how you can use packages to turn Write into a powerful program launcher.

A (Not So) Real-Life Example

The Windows manual says the number of cards you can add to Cardfile depends on how much memory your computer has. Wrong! In fact, you can only add a maximum of 1,260 cards to a single Cardfile file. So does that mean the world's extroverts with their thousands of friends and associates are out of luck? No way. All you have to do is create a separate file for your various categories of acquaintances (U.S. friends, European friends, first cousins, whatever). Still, loading all those separate files is a pain; isn't there an easier way to manage everything?

You bet there is: you can use the Object Packager and Cardfile's OLE capabilities to create a mega-Cardfile file that blows the normal 1,260-card limit to smithereens. Here's how it works:

1. In Cardfile, create separate files for your friends and associates.
2. Start a new file (by selecting the File menu's New command), and then pull down the Edit menu and select the Picture command.
3. Pull down the Edit menu, select Insert Object, select **Package** in the Insert New Object dialog box, and then select **OK**. The Object Packager window appears.
4. Select the Edit menu's Command Line command, type the name of one of your Cardfile files (include the drive and directory if you've stored the file somewhere other than your Windows directory), and select **OK**.
5. Select the Insert Icon button, select an icon from the Insert Icon dialog box, and then select **OK**. (If you want to use the Cardfile icon, type **CARDFILE.EXE** in the File Name text box and press **Enter**.)
6. Select the Edit menu's Label command, enter a label for the icon in the Label dialog box, and then select **OK**.
7. Select the File menu's Exit command, and then select Yes when Object Packager asks you about updating the Cardfile file. The package appears inside the card, as shown in the following figure.

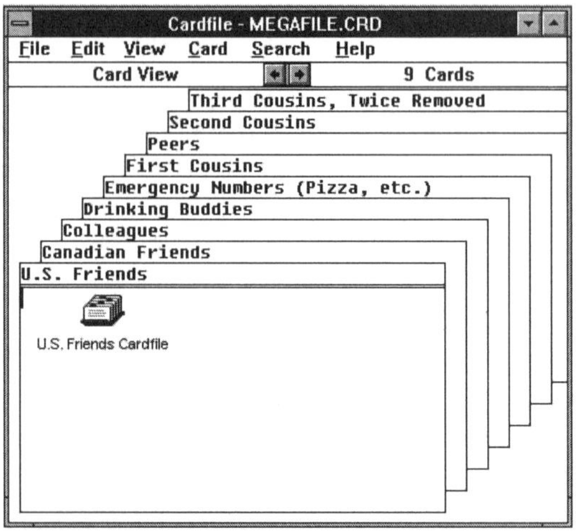

A Cardfile card with another Cardfile file embedded as a package.

8. Add a new card and then repeat steps 3–7 to add packages for your other Cardfile files.

The Least You Need to Know

This chapter took you on a tour of the strange and wonderful world of OLE. We covered a lot of ground, so I think a quick review is in order:

- The basic, non-OLE way to share data is to copy it to the Clipboard, activate the destination application, and then paste it.
- In OLE, an object is a chunk of data that gets inserted into the destination application.
- Linking an object doesn't insert the data into the destination document. Instead, only an image of the data is presented, and a link to the original file is maintained. This allows OLE to update the destination document automatically.
- To link an object, copy it to the Clipboard, select the destination application's Paste **S**pecial command, and then choose Paste **L**ink.

- Embedding an object places a stand-alone version of the data into the destination file. You don't need a separate file to hold the data because the object contains all the info OLE needs to edit the data directly from the destination application.
- To embed an existing object, copy it to the Clipboard, select the destination application's Paste **S**pecial command, and then choose **P**aste. To embed a new object, select either the **E**dit menu's **I**nsert Object command or the **I**nsert menu's **O**bject command.
- To embed an object as a package, select the **Object Packager** icon from Program Manager's **Accessories** group.

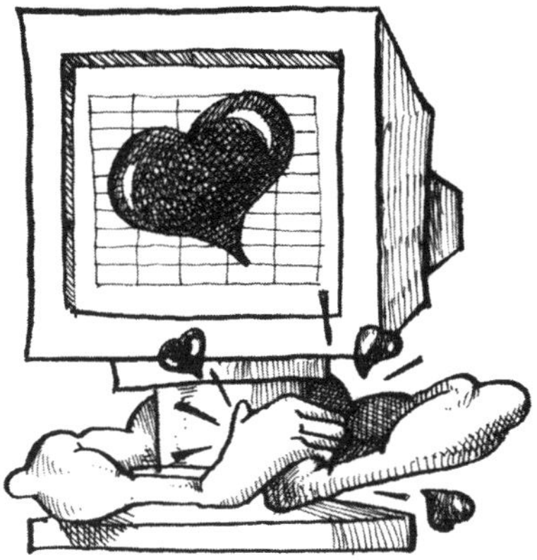

Chapter 9
Learning to Love Those Strange INI Files

In This Chapter

- What is an INI file?
- Getting around in an INI file
- How to edit an INI file
- Some INI examples
- The ins and outs of INI files

I know what you're thinking. You've heard rumors about INI files and now you're convinced they're complex, nearly impossible to decipher, and appeal only to hackers and propeller heads with no social life. Nothing could be further from the truth. If you can perform basic text maintenance such as typing characters and deleting them, you've already mastered the most complicated INI file skills! No lie.

So the next question is, what's in it for you? Why should you bother learning even the merest INI iota? I'll give you not one, but two good reasons. First, INI files are the royal road to Windows mastery. If you've ever been frustrated by something stupid in Windows (and who hasn't?), chances are that a quick tweak of an INI file will set things straight. Second, I'll be referring to INI files in many places throughout the rest of this book (especially in Part III, "When Windows Won't Work: A Troubleshooting Guide"). So even a quick perusal of this chapter will let you join in on the fun later.

An Initial Look at INI Files

Okay, first things first: just what the heck do I mean when I talk about an INI file? First of all, the name "INI files" comes from the fact that these files all end with the extension .INI (for example, SYSTEM.INI). INI is short for "initialization," so right off the bat you know we're dealing with files that do some kind of initializing.

What do they initialize? All kinds of things, really. The main INI file—it's called WIN.INI—sets up the Windows environment. For example, back in Chapter 2, "Dressing Windows for Success: Customization Fun," I showed you how to use Control Panel to change Windows' wallpaper. If, for example, you chose the wallpaper CHITZ.BMP, Windows made a note of this in WIN.INI by entering the following line:

Wallpaper=chitz.bmp

So whenever you start Windows, it goes through the settings in WIN.INI and sets itself up accordingly. If it sees that the wallpaper is supposed to be CHITZ.BMP, it covers the desktop with the CHITZ.BMP image. A typical WIN.INI file can have dozens or even hundreds of these settings, and they all serve to control how Windows works.

Why do we need to work with a file like WIN.INI directly when we can use Control Panel to change the settings? That's a good question. The answer is that Control Panel only affects some of the WIN.INI settings; the rest need to be tweaked by hand. And besides, WIN.INI isn't the only INI file in the world. Windows actually divides its initialization chores into several different files, as the following table shows:

INI File	What it initializes
WIN.INI	The Windows environment
SYSTEM.INI	How Windows works with your computer's hardware

INI File	What it initializes
CONTROL.INI	Control Panel settings not found in WIN.INI (color schemes, desktop patterns, printer drivers)
PROGMAN.INI	Program Manager
WINFILE.INI	File Manager

And that's not all: most of your Windows applications also have their own INI files that contain various program settings. For example, Minesweeper has an INI file named WINMINE.INI.

The Lay of the INI Land

To make INI files easier for us mere mortals to work with, they all have the same overall structure. Having at least a basic understanding of this structure will make your INI editing chores both faster and simpler.

First off, each file is broken down into various sections, where each section contains one or more related settings. The section names are always enclosed in square brackets ([ ]). For example, WIN.INI has a [Desktop] section.

Below the section name appear the settings, which always take the form *SettingName=Value*. Here, *SettingName* is—you guessed it—the name of the setting (e.g., Wallpaper) and *Value* is the current value of the setting (e.g., chitz.bmp). Here's what the [Desktop] section looks like in a typical WIN.INI file:

```
[Desktop]
Pattern=(None)
Wallpaper=chitz.bmp
GridGranularity=0
IconSpacing=75
TileWallpaper=1
IconTitleWrap=0
```

The picture below shows the Desktop dialog box for the Control Panel that produced these settings. Notice how the value of each setting can be either text (such as a file name or list box selection) or a number. For the latter, the number can be a real value (such as the setting of 75 for Icon Spacing), or it can represent true/false values. For example, if a setting is turned on (see the Tile option in the dialog box), it's represented by a 1 in the INI file (you'll also sometimes see the value True, Yes, or On). Similarly, if a setting is turned off (see the Wrap Title check box in the dialog box), it's represented by a 0 (or sometimes by the values False, No, or Off).

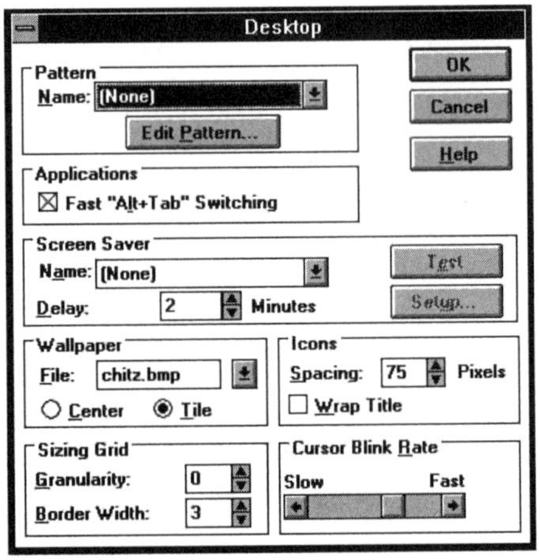

The Desktop dialog box controls that correspond to the WIN.INI settings shown earlier.

You may be wondering why WIN.INI doesn't have a [Desktop] setting for every control in the Desktop dialog box. Well, some settings can be found elsewhere (such as another part of WIN.INI), and some settings don't show up until they've been changed from their default values.

Editing INI Files

In the example I showed you in the last section, I used WIN.INI settings that you could modify using Control Panel. This is the preferred way to work with INI settings because the dialog boxes usually make it easy to select a value by giving you list boxes, spinners, and so on. However, as I've said, many INI settings don't have a corresponding dialog box control. For these cases, you need to edit the INI files directly.

Every INI file is a simple text file, so you can work with them using any text editor (such as Notepad, the text editor that comes with Windows). Here's a summary of the methods you can use to load an INI file into Notepad for editing:

- In Program Manager, open the **Accessories** group and select the **Notepad** icon. Pull down Notepad's File menu, select Open, and select the INI file with which you want to work. Note that, by default, Notepad's Open dialog box only shows files that end with TXT. If you know the name of the INI file, type it in the File Name text box and select **OK**. Otherwise, choose **All Files (*.*)** from the List Files of Type drop-down list, and then hunt down the file you want.
- In File Manager, find the INI file you want to edit, and double-click on it. (Or you can highlight the file and press **Enter**.)
- If you know the INI file lives inside your Windows directory (most do), pull down either Program Manager's or File Manager's File menu and select Run. In the Run dialog box, type the name of the INI file and select **OK**. If the file is in some other directory, you can still use the Run command, but you need to include the file's drive and directory in the Run dialog box.
- If you want to edit WIN.INI or SYSTEM.INI, select Run from Program Manager's or File Manager's File menu, type **SYSEDIT** in the Run dialog box, and select **OK**. Windows opens the System Configuration Editor, as shown in the following figure. This is just a version of Notepad that automatically opens WIN.INI and SYSTEM.INI (as well as a couple of other files).

> **OOPS!**
>
> It's possible, in a pinch, to edit an INI file in your favorite word processor. If you do, though, you need to be careful. First, always open and save the INI file as a pure text file. If you save the file in the word processor's own document format, Windows may not be able to read it. Secondly, don't add any kind of formatting to the file. Again, weird fonts and things may cause Windows to choke on the file.

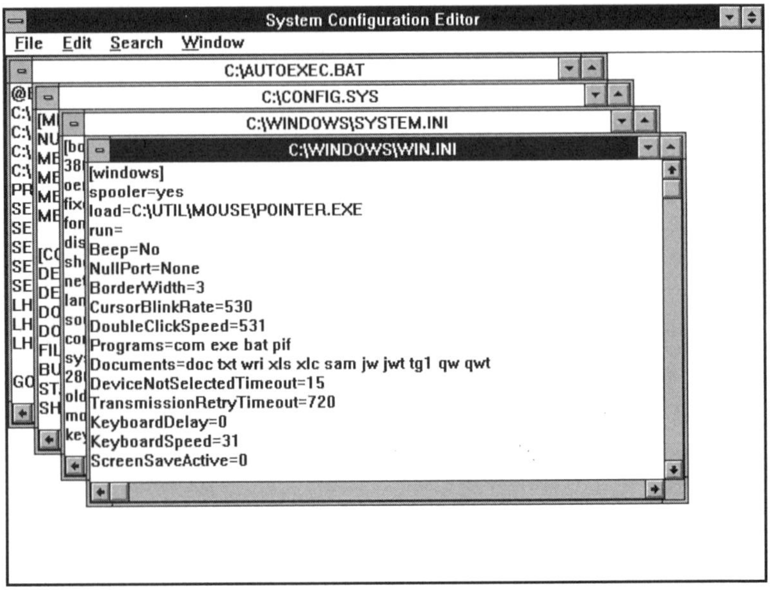

The System Configuration Editor automatically opens WIN.INI and SYSTEM.INI for your editing pleasure.

Once you have the INI file opened, you're ready to go. You can make whatever changes are necessary just as you would in any word processor. You'll mostly be typing in new data and using the Backspace and Delete keys to wipe out what you don't need. Here are a few other things to keep in mind when editing INI files:

- If you're using Notepad, the Find feature may come in handy for tracking down section names and such. To use it, pull down the Search menu and select Find. In the Find dialog box that appears, enter the text you want to locate, and then select the Find Next button until you find the text you want.
- If you want Windows to ignore a line in an INI file, you could just delete it, but that could cause problems later on if you decide you want to reinstate the setting. Instead, you can disable a line simply by placing a semicolon (;) at the beginning. Enabling the setting is as easy as deleting the semicolon.
- When you've finished editing, be sure to save the file and then exit Notepad (by selecting the File menu's Exit command). Because Windows only reads the INI file info at startup, you'll have to exit and restart Windows to put your changes into effect.

Exercises for the Anxious, Eager, and Adventurous

Okay, it's time to get under the hood and start tinkering with some INI settings. The next few sections show you various INI tricks that will help fine-tune your Windows configuration. Out of necessity, this selection won't be even remotely complete (there are, as I've said, hundreds of INI doodads to play with). Instead, I'll just try to whet your appetite with a few useful ideas. I'll assume you're familiar with INI files throughout the rest of the book, so we'll be looking at quite a few more examples as we go along.

For the Anxious: Simple Environment Tweaks

WIN.INI is chock full of settings that enable you to customize just about every aspect of the Windows environment. Here's a selection of settings that prove you *can* have Windows your way:

A different title bar and menu font Sick of the same old font in your window titles and menus? No problem. Head into WIN.INI and add the following line to the [Windows] section:

SystemFont=*Font*

Here, *Font* is the name of one of Windows' system font files (such as MODERN.FON and ROMAN.FON). To see a list of these fonts, look for files that end with .FON in your Windows SYSTEM directory, or find the .FON files in the [Fonts] section of WIN.INI. The following picture shows the rather interesting effect produced by setting SystemFont equal to SCRIPT.FON. To return to the default font, delete or disable the SystemFont setting.

> **OOPS!**
>
> As you'll see in the next few sections, INI files can turn your PC into a Windows dream machine. However, they can also become an absolute nightmare if you make mistakes editing a file. So before you muck about with any INI file, it's a good idea to make a backup copy of the file first. This way, if you make a mess of things, you can recover just by restoring your backup copy.

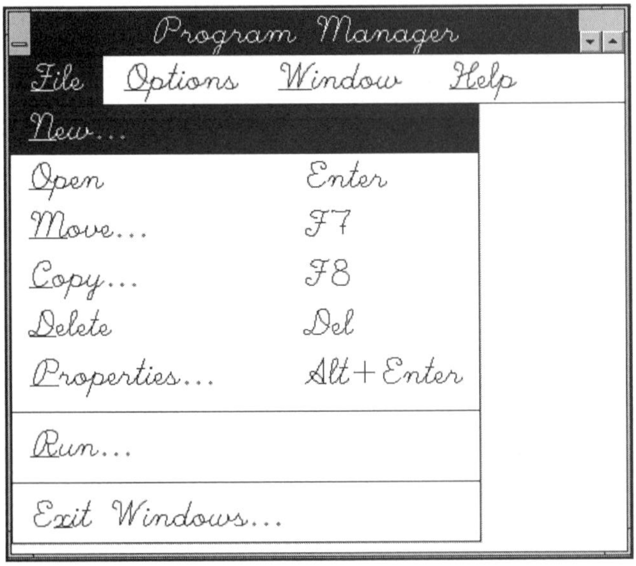

What happens when you add the line ***SystemFont= SCRIPT.FON*** *in the [Windows] section of WIN.INI.*

Icon see clearly now You can also use the system fonts (the ones with file names ending in .FON) and a couple of other options to improve the look of your Windows icons. Find WIN.INI's [Desktop] section and add the following lines anywhere in the section:

IconTitleFaceName=*Font*

IconTitleSize=*Size*

IconTitleStyle=*Style*

IconTitleFaceName controls the font of the icon label. Again, *Font* is the name of a .FON file. IconTitleSize specifies the size of the icon font, in points. The default size is 8 points, but a setting of 10 or 12 can make a big difference on a small screen. IconTitleStyle controls whether or not the icon label is bold. Set style to 1 for bold, or 0 for regular.

Giving icons their space Back in Chapter 2, "Dressing Windows for Success: Customization Fun," I showed you how to change the amount of space Windows allows to the left and right of each icon. You can also change the amount of space above and below each icon by adding the following line to WIN.INI's [Desktop] section:

IconVerticalSpacing=*Space*

Space represents the number of pixels you want between each icon. The default is around 75. To move the icons closer together, enter a smaller value; to move them farther apart, enter a larger value.

Uncentering your wallpaper Have you ever selected a wallpaper file and then groaned in disappointment when you saw some or all of it was hidden behind the Program Manager window? Well, you can specify exactly where Windows displays the wallpaper by adding the following two settings to the [Desktop] section of WIN.INI:

WallpaperOriginX=*FromLeft*

WallpaperOriginY=*FromTop*

WallpaperOriginX specifies the distance, in pixels, from the left side of the screen. WallpaperOriginY specifies the distance from the top of the screen. If you want your wallpaper to appear in the upper left corner, as shown in the following picture, use 1 for both the *FromLeft* and *FromTop* values.

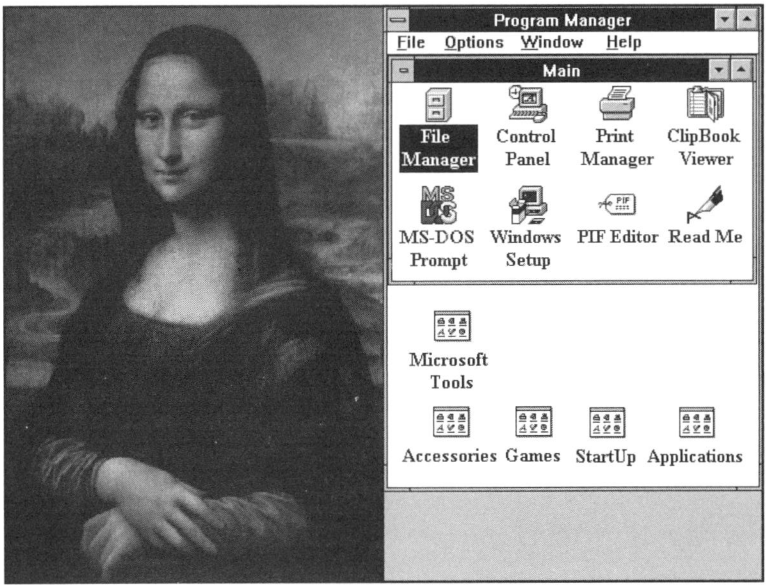

Wallpaper moved to the upper left corner of the screen and Program Manager icons where IconTitleFaceName is SERIFE.FON, the IconTitleSize is 12, and the IconTitleStyle is 1.

Menus for left-handers Some southpaws I know complain that pull-down menus are awkward to use because they pull down to the right. If you agree, you can exact your revenge by forcing the menus to pull down to the left. You just need to add the following line to WIN.INI's [Windows] section:

MenuDropAlignment=1

Changing this setting to 0 reverts the menus to their default behavior.

For the Eager: Helping Out the Help System

Back in Chapter 4, "Secrets of the Windows Help System," you learned how to use Help to get info quickly and easily. WIN.INI has a [Windows Help] section that lets you improve on certain aspects of the Help system.

One problem many people have with the Help screens is that the light green jump text is hard to read on some monitors. To fix this, you can specify a different color for the jump text by adding the following line to the [Windows Help] section:

JumpColor=*RedValue GreenValue BlueValue*

Here, the three values *RedValue*, *GreenValue*, and *BlueValue* determine the color. The following table lists the red-green-blue mixtures that produce some common colors:

Color	RedValue	GreenValue	BlueValue
Red	255	0	0
Green	0	255	0
Blue	0	0	255
Yellow	255	255	0
Magenta	255	0	255
Cyan	0	255	255
Dark Red	128	0	0
Dark Green	0	128	0

Color	RedValue	GreenValue	BlueValue
Dark Blue	0	0	128
Dark Yellow	128	128	0
Purple	128	0	128
Dark Cyan	0	128	128

For example, if you entered **JumpColor=128 0 0**, Windows would display the jump text in an easily readable dark red. With the following line, you can also change the color of the broken-underlined text that displays a definition:

PopUpColor=*RedValue GreenValue BlueValue*

One of the best ways to learn more about an application is to browse through the various Help topics. Unfortunately, most Help files make this difficult at best because they force you to jump around randomly from topic to topic. To overcome this limitation, add the following line to the [Windows Help] section:

SeqTopicKeys=1

With this setting enabled, you can press **Ctrl+Shift+right arrow** to move sequentially through the topics in any given Help file. To return to the first topic in the file, press **Ctrl+Shift+Home**.

For the Adventurous: Moving Your TrueType Fonts

If you like TrueType fonts as much as I do, you may end up with a hundred or more on your system. (See Chapter 7, "Flexing Your Font Muscles," to get the scoop on TrueType fonts.) One of TrueType's few problems is that each font requires not one, but two files: a TTF file (e.g., ARIAL.TTF) that contains the font itself, and an FOT file (e.g., ARIAL.FOT) that tells Windows where to find the TTF file. Instead of having all these files cluttering up your Windows SYSTEM directory, you may prefer to move them all to their own directory. The following steps show you how it's done:

1. Start Control Panel, and select the **Fonts** icon to display the Fonts dialog box.

2. Use the Installed Fonts list to highlight all the TrueType fonts, and then select the Remove button. Control Panel displays the Remove Font dialog box.
3. Make sure the Delete Font File From Disk check box is *not* activated, and then select Yes to All. When the operation is complete, don't exit the Fonts dialog box (you'll need it again in a sec).
4. Switch to Program Manager, start File Manager, and create the new directory for the TrueType files, if necessary.
5. Display Windows' SYSTEM directory, select all the .TTF files, and then move them to your new TrueType directory (either by dragging the files to the new directory, or by using the File menu's Move command).
6. Return to Control Panel's Fonts dialog box, select Add, and then use the Directories list to select your new TrueType directory. You'll see a list of the TrueType fonts in the List of Fonts box.
7. Choose the Select All button, deactivate the Copy Fonts to Windows Directory check box, and then select **OK**. Control Panel adds the fonts back into the Installed Fonts list.
8. Select **Close** to return to Control Panel, and then exit.
9. Switch back to File Manager, and this time move all the .FOT files in the SYSTEM directory to your TrueType directory. Exit File Manager when the operation is complete.

TECHNO NERD TEACHES...

Why do we need to move the TTF and FOT files in two separate operations? Can't we just move everything at once? Unfortunately, we can't, because the FOT files tell Windows where to find their corresponding TTF files. When you move the TTF files and then reinstall them, Windows updates the FOT files to make a note of the new TTF location. We have to wait until after this update to move the FOT files to their new home.

10. Open WIN.INI, find the [Fonts] section, and add the drive and directory where the FOT files are now stored to the beginning of

each FOT file name. For example, the [Fonts] entry for Arial originally should look something like this:

Arial (TrueType)=ARIAL.FOT

If your TrueType files are now in a directory named TRUETYPE, you'd edit this line to look like so:

Arial (TrueType)=C:\TRUETYPE\ARIAL.FOT

A search and replace feature would make this chore a breeze, but unfortunately, Notepad doesn't have one. You might consider using a word processor—such as Write—to make these changes. In the above example, you'd search for, say, **(TrueType)=** and replace it with **(TrueType)=C:\TRUETYPE**.

11. Save the file, exit the text editor you're using and Windows, and then restart Windows to put the new settings into effect.

The Least You Need to Know

This chapter showed you how to work with INI files from the inside out. Here's a summary of just a few of the amazing things you learned:

- INI files contain the initialization settings that Windows (and many Windows applications) uses to get itself up and running.
- Many INI settings are produced by dialog box controls in the Control Panel and other applications. The rest you either have to edit or add yourself.
- All INI files have the same structure: several sections with names in square brackets (such as [Desktop]) followed by settings that take the general form SettingName=*Value*.
- To edit an INI file, use Notepad, SYSEDIT, or any other text editor. If you use a word processor, be sure to save the file as pure text.
- WIN.INI is the most common INI file, but chapters later in this book will also delve into SYSTEM.INI (for hardware), PROGMAN.INI (for Program Manager), WINFILE.INI (for File Manager), and more.

Chapter 10

A Few of My Favorite Windows Things

In This Chapter

- My favorite Windows tips and tricks
- A Windows Easter egg hunt
- Windows screen savers that I know and love
- Windows shareware to die for
- An exercise in Windows self-indulgence

This chapter presents a treasure trove of Windows stuff. You'll find tips, tricks, arcana, utilities, shareware, even strange but fascinating animations called "Easter eggs." They're all things I've come across in my years of wandering the Windows landscape, and I've collected them all in one place for your browsing pleasure.

Twelve Transcendental Tips and Tricks

There's no doubt that Windows is a complicated, arcane, and sometimes just plain weird program. To survive over the long haul, you'll need to develop your own arsenal of shortcuts and handy techniques that will smooth your Windows work and get you out of jams. As a starter kit, here's a list—in no particular order—of 12 of my favorite tips and tricks.

Note that several of these tips and tricks require you to edit an INI file of one kind or another. If the very thought of doing this gives you the willies, truck back to Chapter 9, "Learning to Love Those Strange INI Files," to find out how easy it all is.

1. Cheating at Solitaire

Many people I know count themselves as devoted Windows fans only because they've become addicted to Solitaire! While this little gem of a game is certainly one of the world's great time wasters, it can be frustrating if you don't win as often as you like. (The card "waterfall" that appears at the end of each successful game is, I'm sure, something we all enjoy seeing as much as we can.) To help out, Solitaire has a couple of built-in "cheat" features you can use to put a few more in the win column (how well you'll sleep at night is up to you):

- I'm sure many a Solitaire savant has pulled out a hair or two when, during a Draw Three game, the card you've been dying to get is drawn underneath one or two cards in the pile. To get at that pesky devil, pull down the Game menu and select Undo to reverse the draw. Now hold down the **Ctrl**, **Alt**, and **Shift** keys and click the deck. Solitaire draws only one card this time! Keep clicking until you turn over the card you want, and then resume the game normally.
- The quickest road to Solitaire defeat is to miss adding a drawn card to the row stacks. To prevent this from happening, pull down the Game menu and select Options. In the Options dialog box, activate the Outline dragging check box, and then select **OK**. Now drag each card you draw over the bottom card in each row stack. If one of the bottom cards turns black, you know you've found a match.

2. Cheating at Minesweeper

Minesweeper is a game that'll give anyone's logic circuits a workout (especially that maddening Expert grid). If you're hitting more mines than you're missing, you can exact your revenge by, of course, cheating. Here's how: start Minesweeper and press **XYZZY**. Now press **Enter** and then **Shift**. When you move your mouse pointer over the squares, watch the pixel in the upper left corner of the screen. If the pointer is over an unmined square, the pixel turns white; if the pointer is over a mined square, the pixel turns black. (To see this properly, you may need to minimize any other running applications, and you might try coloring the desktop a neutral gray.)

3. Minesweeper Sounds Off!

To make your Minesweeper games more of a multimedia experience, add the following line to the end of the file WINMINE.INI (you'll find this file in your Windows directory):

Sound=10

The next time you start Minesweeper, you'll hear a cheerful song when you win or a siren-like wail when you lose.

4. Starting Windows Automatically

If you use Windows every day, why not force your computer to start Windows every time you boot up. It's easy. In Program Manager or File Manager, pull down the **F**ile menu and select **R**un. In the Run Dialog box, type **SYSEDIT** and then select **OK**. In the System Configuration Editor window that appears, select the C:\AUTOEXEC.BAT window, and then enter **WIN** on a separate line at the end of the file (see the next picture).

TECHNO NERD TEACHES...

AUTOEXEC.BAT is a file that DOS runs every time you turn on or reboot your computer. Each line in AUTOEXEC.BAT is a command, so entering WIN at the end of the file tells DOS to run Windows when it's completed its other chores. One caveat though: if AUTOEXEC.BAT already runs a program (such as the MS-DOS Shell), Windows won't run until you exit that program. Therefore, unless you really want to run the other program, I'd suggest deleting it from AUTOEXEC.BAT.

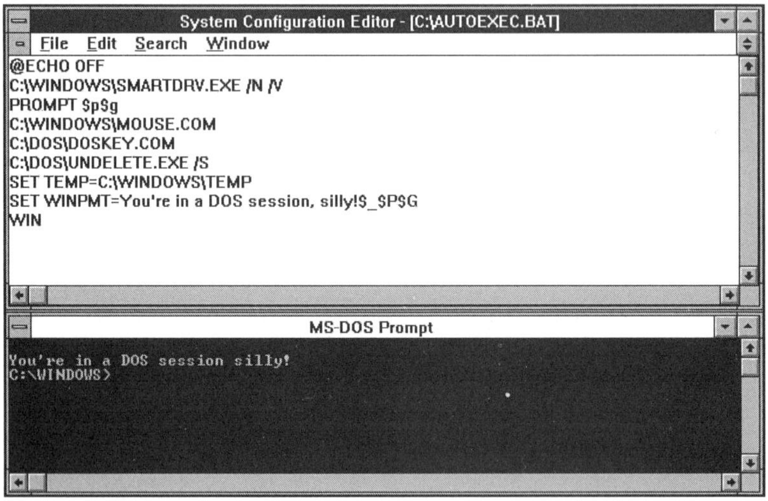

To start Windows automatically each time you boot your computer, add ***WIN*** *to the end of AUTOEXEC.BAT.*

5. A Windows Reminder

While you're in AUTOEXEC.BAT, there's another line you can add that will tell you when you're in a Windows DOS session (see the picture above). This handy reminder will prevent you from trying to start Windows, or from trying to load a DOS program that you may have running in a separate DOS session. Just add the following line anywhere in AUTOEXEC.BAT (but before the WIN command, if you have one):

SET WINPMT=You're in a DOS session, silly!$_$P$G

Actually, the part between the equals sign (=) and the first dollar sign ($) is optional: you can write whatever you like (up to a maximum of 120 characters).

6. Putting the Kibosh on Windows' DOS Instructions

Speaking of DOS sessions, if you shell out to DOS frequently, you're probably mighty sick of seeing Windows' instructions each time. (The ones that tell you to type EXIT and press Enter to quit the DOS session, and a couple of other things.) To banish this text from your future DOS sessions, add the following line to the [386Enh] section of your SYSTEM.INI file:

DOSPromptExitInstruc=No

7. The Fast Way to Maximize a Window

If you find that the Maximize button in Windows' windows is too small a target, there's an easier way to max out a window: just double-click on its title bar.

8. More Icon Bang for Your Buck

Although some DOS applications come with their own Program Manager icon, most don't. The result? You end up with Windows' boring MS-DOS icon for all your DOS programs. You don't have to stand for this! First, open the icon's Program Item Properties dialog box by holding down **Alt** and double-clicking the icon, or by highlighting the icon and pressing **Alt+Enter**. Select the Change Icon button, enter **MORICONS.DLL** in the File Name text box, and press **Enter**. The Current Icon box displays a whole bunch of cool icons. (You can also try entering **PROGMAN.EXE** in the File Name text box to see a smaller icon collection.) Highlight the icon you want, and then select **OK**.

9. A Shortcut for Program Manager

As you may know, you can use the Program Item Properties dialog box to assign a shortcut key to an application. But the application many of us use the most is Program Manager itself, so it would be nice to be able to switch to it with a simple key combination. Well, you can. First, in any Program Manager group, add a new program item for Program Manager (in the Command Line text box, enter **PROGMAN.EXE**), and specify a shortcut key. (For example, if you move to the Shortcut Key text box and press **P**, you get the key combination **Ctrl+Alt+P**.) Exit and then double-click on the new Program Manager icon. Nothing happens, of course, because Program Manager is already running. However, your shortcut key will now be in effect.

10. Icons for Control Panel Stuff

I use the Control Panel constantly to muck around with my Windows setup. Instead of starting Control Panel each time, however, I bypass the middleman by starting some Control Panel modules directly. How do I do it? Well, I created icons in Program Manager, and in their Program Item Properties dialog box, I used the following for the Command Line text:

CONTROL.EXE MAIN.CPL *module*

Here, *module* is the name of the Control Panel module you want to run. You can use any of the following: Color, Fonts, Ports, Mouse, Desktop, Keyboard, Printers, International, Date/Time.

11. An Easy Way to Save Your Settings

Like most Windows users, you've probably spent at least a little time setting up Program Manager and File Manager to suit your tastes. To preserve their settings in both programs, most people activate the Save Settings on Exit command in the Options menu, exit the program, start it again, and then deactivate the Save Settings on Exit command. If you later make a slight change, however, you have to go through this whole hassle again just to save your settings. Forget that. Instead, hold down the **Shift** key, pull down the File menu, and select the Exit command. This doesn't exit either program; it just saves your settings so you can continue working.

12. Don't Forget the Task List!

If you regularly have lots of applications running at the same time, it can be a pain to **Alt+Tab** your way through all the programs to find the one you want. In most cases, you're probably better off using the Task List to switch applications. Just press **Ctrl+Esc** (or double-click on the desktop, if you can see it) to display the Task List (see below), highlight the program you want, and then select the Switch To button.

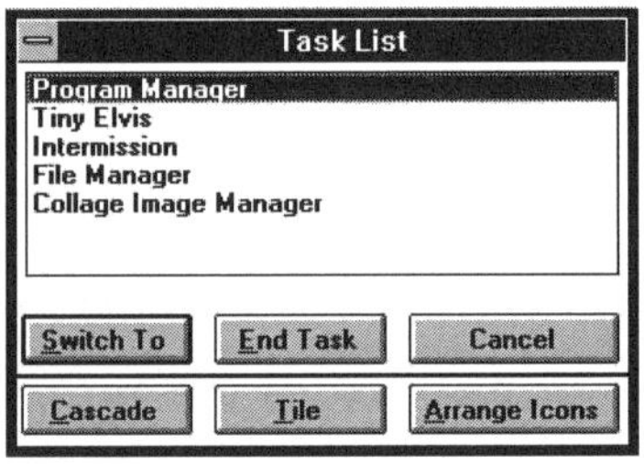

Use the Task List to quickly switch between your running programs.

A-Hunting We Will Go: Searching for Windows Easter Eggs

Programmers usually toil thanklessly in obscurity, and I'm sure most prefer it that way. However, we all like to get at least a little recognition in our lives, and programmers are no exception. To that end, many Windows applications include *Easter eggs*—animated boxes that display cute characters and list the names of the programming wizards who created the program. (These animations are also called *gang screens*.)

The Windows Easter Egg

Windows has its own Easter egg, and as a diversion from our labors, here are the steps to follow to display it.

1. Pull down the **H**elp menu and select the **A**bout Program Manager command. The About Program Manager dialog box appears.
2. With the **Ctrl** and **Shift** keys held down, double-click on the Microsoft Windows logo.
3. Select **OK**.
4. Repeat steps 1–3. When you double-click on the logo this time, you'll see a waving flag and a message.
5. Repeat steps 1 and 2. Now when you double-click on the logo, a box appears, and the names of all the people who worked on Windows 3.1 scroll by (actually, you only see their first names and one or two letters from their last names). You'll also see one of four Microsoft characters "presenting" the names. (If you see a guy with glasses, that's Bill Gates, the chairman and co-founder of Microsoft; the balding guy is Steve Ballmer, co-president of Microsoft; the bearded fellow is Brad Silverberg, vice-president of Microsoft's Personal Systems Group; the bear is some sort of bizarre Microsoft mascot.)
6. When you've seen enough (the list keeps repeating), select **OK**.

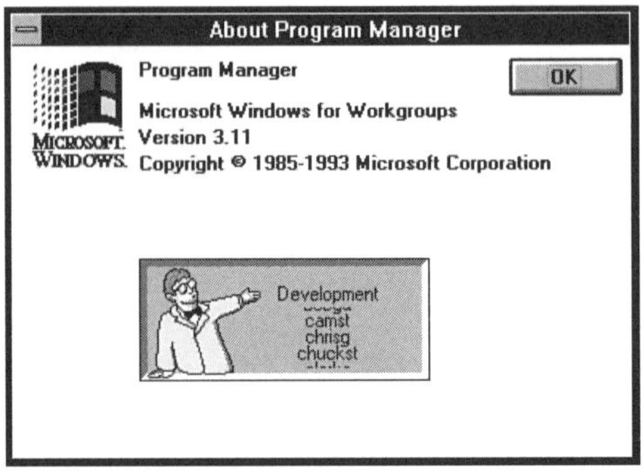

The Windows Easter egg.

More Easter Eggs

These Easter egg things must be something of a tradition with Windows programmers because most programs have them. And many of these truly live up to the name "Easter egg" because you really have to hunt high and low to find them. As a public service, here are the instructions for finding Easter eggs in some popular Windows applications:

Word for Windows 6.0 Type the characters **T3!** and then select them. Click on the **Bold** button, click on the **AutoFormat** button, and then pull down the **Help** menu and select About Microsoft Word. In the dialog box that appears, click on the Word for Windows logo.

Excel 5.0 Load Excel with a blank workbook, right-click on a toolbar, and select **Customize** from the menu. In the Customize dialog box, select the **Custom** category, and then drag the Solitaire icon onto the workbook. Click on **Cancel** in the Assign Macro dialog box, and then click on **Close** to return to the workbook. Hold down **Ctrl**, **Alt**, and **Shift** and click on the Solitaire icon.

CorelDraw 4.0 Pull down the **Help** menu and select About CorelDraw. In the dialog box that appears, double-click on the hot-air balloon. Hold down the left mouse button to make the balloon rise, and then click the right mouse button a couple of times. Watch out for the flying Elvises!

Quicken 2.0 or 3.0 While holding down either S, R (version 3.0 only), or V, select the **Help** menu's About Quicken command (ignore the beeps your computer will make). Depending on which letter you're holding down, you'll see a brief animation on the screen.

PageMaker 4.0 or 5.0 Hold down **Shift** (for version 5.0) or both **Ctrl** and **Shift** (for version 4.0), and then select the **Help** menu's About PageMaker command.

Stunning Screen Savers

Back in Chapter 2, "Dressing Windows for Success: Customization Fun," I showed you how to use Windows' screen savers to reduce the wear-and-tear on your monitor and provide you with a little diversion during your busy day. With screen savers, though, the emphasis is always on the diversion side of the equation. So all kinds of companies have come out with increasingly wild screen saver effects that may be, in the end, *too* diverting. That's a risk we all have to take, however, so here's a list of my fave rave screen savers:

After Dark One of the first—and still one of the best—collections of screen savers. The Flying Toasters are the most famous, but there are all kinds of equally amazing animations in this package. $49.95. Berkeley Systems Inc., 2095 Rose St., Berkeley, CA 94709; (510) 540-5535.

Berkeley Breathed's Opus 'n Bill Screen Saver Displays sounds and animation using various characters from the Bloom County comic strip (see below). Most of the 16 animations are hilarious, and at up to 3 minutes in length, are truly time-wasting. $44.95. Delrina Corp., 6830 Via Del Oro, #240, San Jose, CA 95119; (800) 268-6082.

A sample screen from Berkeley Breathed's Opus 'n Bill Screen Saver.

3DPC Wow! Stunningly real 3-D images that are downright mesmerizing. $19.99. Forté, 2141 Palomar Airport Rd., #100, Carlsbad, CA 92009-9788; (619) 431-6400.

Marvel Screen Posters Relive your wasted youth with images of the Hulk, Captain America, Spiderman, and over 30 other images of heroes and covers from Marvel Comics. $32.25. Available from Berkeley Systems.

Microsoft Scenes This is more of a highbrow approach. You can choose from the Sierra Club collection (mountains, forests, and other outdoorsy stuff), the Outer Space collection (planets and NASA stuff), or the Impressionists collection (paintings from the likes of Monet, Renoir, and Degas). $29.95. Microsoft Corp., One Microsoft Way, Redmond, WA 98052; (800) 426-9400.

Shareware: Cool Software That's Cheap (and Sometimes Free!)

Between the behemoth professional programming jockeys (like the wizards who created Windows) and the people young and old who use their programs, there's an entire community of computer enthusiasts. These hobbyists genuinely enjoy computers (as hard as that may be for some of you to believe), and for them there's no higher expression of this enjoyment than programming.

Now obviously, one guy hacking out code in his den can't hope to match the sophistication of a hundred people slaving away in some corporate hive. So amateur programmers can't justify charging outrageous prices for their creations. Instead, most just make their programs available as *shareware*: you can try it out for free, but if you decide to use it regularly, you need to send in a small registration fee (generally between $1 and $25). Some programs (like the ones included on this book's disk) are actually *freeware*—yup, they're absotively, posolutely, free of charge!

There are, as you might imagine, thousands and thousands of shareware programs available. They range in quality from the execrable to the excellent, and in usefulness from the indifferent to the indispensable. To get you started, here's a list of my 10 all-time favorite Windows shareware programs.

WinZip If you'll be grabbing your shareware from computer bulletin boards and online information services such as CompuServe and America Online, most of your downloads will come in compressed format. Uncompressing these files is a snap with WinZip 5.0. It works with all the popular compression formats, and it'll even compress files so you can save yourself some hard disk space. $29. Nico Mak Computing Inc., P.O. Box 919, Bristol, CT 06011-0919; (800) 242-4775.

More Control In Chapter 9, "Learning to Love Those Strange INI Files," I showed you how to edit Windows' INI files directly. More Control is a program that lets you set some popular INI settings with intuitive dialog box controls (see the picture below). It even has a Restart Windows button that will automatically restart Windows for you. $12.50. Sloop Software, 6457 Mesedge Lane, Colorado Springs, CO 80919; (719) 260-0433.

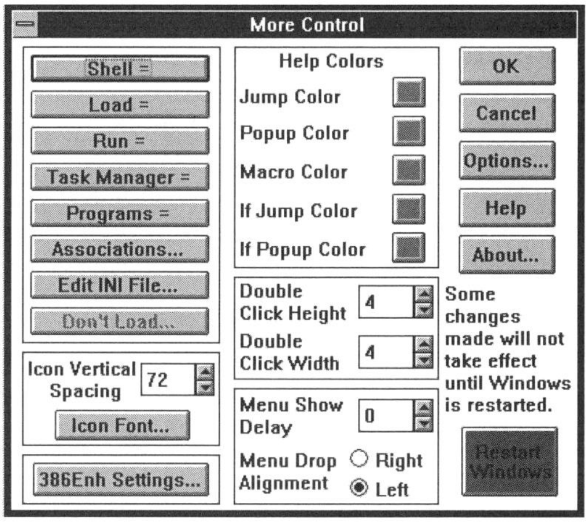

The More Control window.

Text Manager If you need to edit text files in Windows, Notepad is barely functional. Text Manager is much better because you can perform search and replace operations, open multiple windows, undo actions, and more. $20. Digital Software, 13620 98th Ave. N.E., Kirkland, WA 98034.

Roadways PC If you're planning any driving trips in the near future, this program's for you. Roadways PC can actually figure out the best route between any two points. It spells out the highways to take, how many miles between major cities, and even the total driving time. $10. Doug Fitler, P.O. Box 25424, Scott AFB, IL 62225.

Plug-In This little application (see the picture below) augments Program Manager by enabling you to do things like activate and deactivate groups, change group icons, and use alternative mouse cursors. You also get an enhanced Run command, a Save Settings Now command, and much, much more. A must! $20. Plannet Crafters Inc., 2580 Runic Way, Alpharetta, GA 30202; (404) 740-9821.

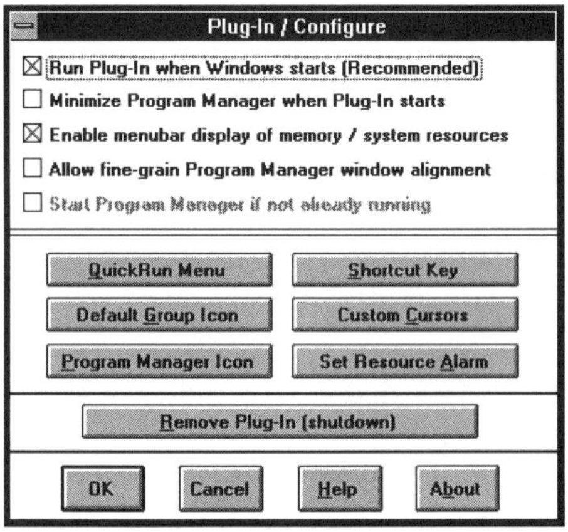

The Plug-In/Configure screen.

FontSpec If you use lots of fonts, put this program on your gotta-have-it list. FontSpec lets you view and print samples of your fonts, but its real power comes from FontManager—a powerful utility that lets you easily add and delete fonts, as well as create groups of fonts that you can install and remove as a unit. $25. UniTech Corporation, 2697 McKelvey Road, Maryland Heights, MO 63043; (314) 770-2770.

Cleanup for Windows Hungry for hard disk space? This program seeks out and displays hard disk detritus such as duplicate file names, BAK files, and empty files. You then have a choice of deleting these files. You'd be surprised how much hard disk real estate you'll be able to reclaim. $29.95. Foley Hi-Tech Systems, 185 Berry St., San Francisco, CA 94107; (415) 882-1730.

WizManager This is an add-on that beefs up File Manager to superhuman proportions. The utilities you get include a DOS command line box, a powerful file viewer, a program launcher, the capability to print a directory listing, and even a snappy toolbar that puts everything a mouse click away. $39.95. Mijenix, 6666 Odana Road, Suite 326, Madison, WI 53719; (608) 277-1971.

Mack's Tavern This one's not for teetotalers! Mack's Tavern gives you the ingredients and recipes for nearly 1,000 drinks. As an added bonus, you even get a picture of the perfect glass to serve the drink in. Don't plan your next party without it. $12. Ronnie Odom, 3227 Suncrest Drive, Jackson, MS 39212.

On This Day for Windows Most of the shareware I've listed here has been designed to improve your Windows productivity. (I did this, I suppose, as a counterbalance to the generally silly stuff on the disk.) On This Day for Windows, however, makes no claims to productivity enhancement. It's a simple calendar that tells you what happened in the world on a particular day. You get births, deaths, inventions, religious holidays, and more. $25. Software Construction Co., P.O. Box 160, N. Billerica, MA 01862.

Chapter 11
Hopping on the Multimedia Bandwagon

In This Chapter

- How to install multimedia drivers
- Using a CD-ROM drive with Windows
- Playing with sounds
- Trying out the Media Player
- Learning what this multimedia mania is all about

There was a time when our computers—big, dim-witted brutes that they were—would just sit there quietly and passively, letting out only an occasional beep to let us know someone was home. Now, however, our computers have turned into full-fledged entertainment centers capable of making realistic burping noises, showing videos, and even playing the latest audio CD from The Tragically Hip.

If you've heard about this multimedia stuff, but you didn't know how to become part of the show yourself, just step right up. This chapter gives you the basics of Windows' multimedia capabilities.

First Things First: Installing Multimedia Drivers

As I mentioned back in Chapter 2, "Dressing Windows for Success: Customization Fun," Windows can't communicate with your system's hardware until you install itty-bitty programs called *device drivers*. Well, Windows needs drivers to communicate with your multimedia devices (sound cards, CD-ROM drives, and such) too.

When you finish installing your equipment (and taking inventory of the extra gray hairs you probably now have), you can install the device's driver by following the steps below. As an example, I'll show you how to install Microsoft's PC Speaker driver. (This driver lets you play sounds on your machine without the added expense of a sound card. To find out how to get your mitts on this file, fire up Chapter 17, "Getting Wired with Terminal." The steps below assume you've gone through Chapter 17's instructions for downloading and extracting the file.)

Before you embark on the following instructions, check to see if it's necessary on your system. Some devices (such as the Microsoft Windows Sound System) come with their own setup programs that'll handle all these chores for you automatically. The instruction manual that comes with the hardware will let you know.

1. In Program Manager, select the **Control Panel** icon from the **Main** program group.
2. When Control Panel appears, select the **Drivers** icon or select the Drivers command from the **S**ettings menu. Control Panel displays the Drivers dialog box.
3. Select the Add button. The Add dialog box appears, as shown below.

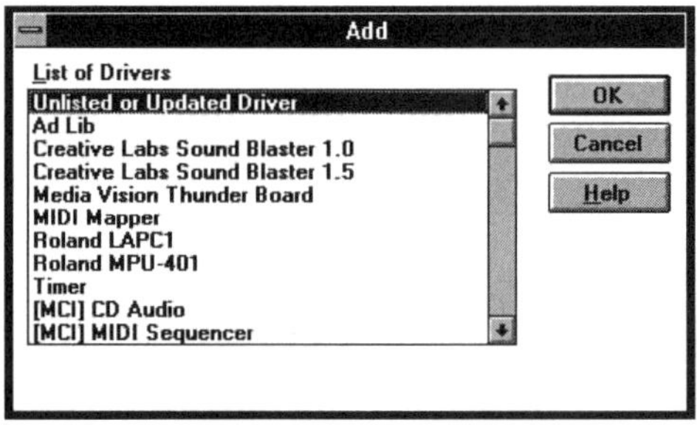

The Add dialog box lists the drivers that come with Windows.

4. In the List of Drivers, highlight the driver for the multimedia device you installed. If your device isn't one of Microsoft's chosen few, highlight the **Unlisted or Updated Driver** option. (Select the latter if you're installing the PC Speaker driver.)

5. Select **OK**. Depending on which option you chose, one of three things will happen:

   - If by some fluke the driver file is already lurking somewhere in your system, Windows will let you know and ask if you want to use the current driver or install a new one. Select the Current button, and then skip to step 8.
   - If you chose a driver that Windows recognized, the Install Driver dialog box appears and tells you to insert one of your original Windows disks. Insert the disk, change the displayed drive letter if necessary, and then select **OK**. Windows installs the driver. Go ahead and skip to Step 7.
   - If you chose the Unlisted or Updated Driver option, Windows asks you to insert the disk containing the driver. Pop in the disk, change the displayed drive letter if necessary, and then select **OK**. For the PC Speaker driver, type **c:\windows\system** and select **OK**.

6. Windows checks out the disk and displays a list of the drivers it found. (The picture below shows the dialog box that appears for the PC Speaker driver.) Highlight the driver you want (if there's more than one) and select **OK**.

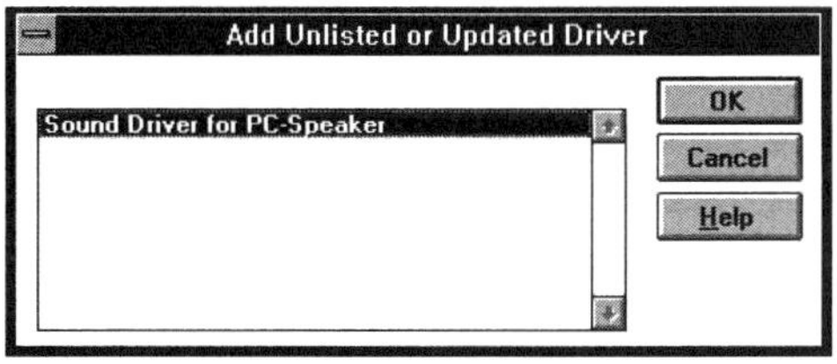

Use this dialog box to select the driver you want to install.

7. If the driver needs to be set up, you'll see a Setup dialog box something like the one shown on the following page. Enter the settings you want (the defaults are usually fine) and select **OK**. (In particular, there may be a Test button you can select to make sure your device is working properly.) Otherwise, you may just see a dialog box telling you that the driver has been installed successfully. Again, select **OK** to continue.

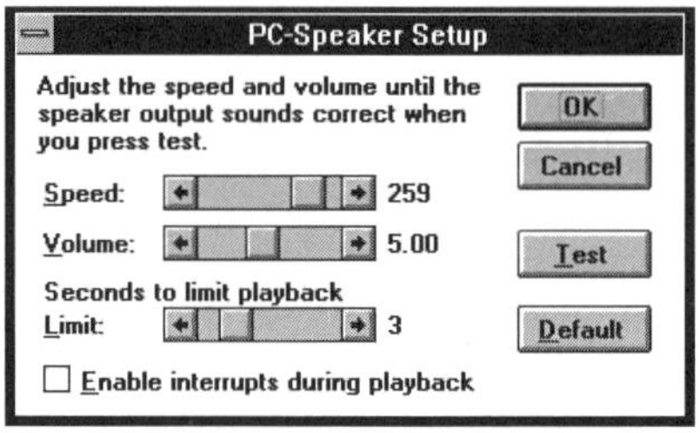

If the device driver needs to be set up, you'll see a dialog box similar to this.

8. In some cases, you'll need to restart Windows to get the new driver to work. If so, you'll see a dialog box telling you so. Select the **R**estart Windows button.

Windows and CD-ROM Drives

If you've plugged a CD-ROM drive into your system, I've got some good news: unless you want to play audio CDs, there's nothing, I repeat *nothing,* you have to do to make Windows recognize the drive. That's right: nothing to install, nothing to set up, nothing to edit. As long as your computer recognizes the CD-ROM okay (and it should once you've run the CD-ROM's installation software), Windows is happy to fall right into step. (If you have an external CD-ROM drive, make sure you turn on the drive before you turn on your computer. If you don't, the device driver that looks for the CD-ROM will fail, and Windows won't know the drive exists.)

So how do you access the stuff on a CD-ROM disk from Windows? Easy—just open File Manager and select the CD-ROM drive. (The CD-ROM installation software will have assigned a new drive letter to the CD-ROM; for example, if your system has only a single hard drive—drive C—your CD-ROM will likely be drive D.) As you can see in the picture below, the drive icon for a CD-ROM has a little CD sticking out. The drive will look and act just like any other drive on your computer. (Well, it doesn't act quite like a regular drive; for example, you can't move or copy files to a CD-ROM, and you can't delete files from a CD-ROM.)

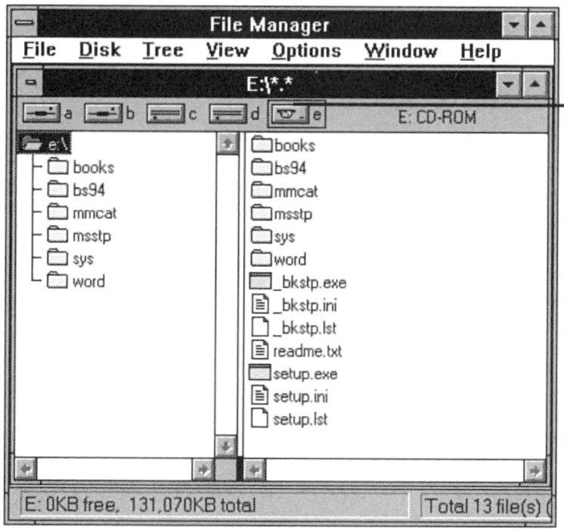

You access your CD-ROM drive just by clicking on the CD-ROM icon in File Manager.

Many CD-ROM disks have setup programs that will automatically install icons in Program Manager for easier access. Look for files named SETUP.EXE or INSTALL.EXE.

Later in this chapter, I'll show you how to use your CD-ROM drive to play audio CDs. Before you can do that, however, you have to install the appropriate driver. Follow the instructions in the previous section and, when you come to the List of Drivers in the Add dialog box, select the **[MCI] CD Audio** option.

OOPS!

Once you've installed a CD-ROM program, make sure the disk is in the drive each time you try to run it. If it's not, the least that will happen is that you'll get an error message. In the worst case, you may crash Windows or hang your computer (i.e., it freezes up).

Sound Advice: Working with Sounds in Windows

Take a stroll through any office these days and you're bound to hear all manner of boops, bips, and beeps emanating from most cubicles and work areas. Today's modern Windows user is truly wired for sound.

If you're sick of carrying on a one-way conversation with your computer (if the yelling, cursing, and threatening that most of us direct at our digital domestics can be considered conversation), you can get into the sound thing in one of these ways:

- Buy a sound card. This is a circuit board that you attach to your computer's innards. Popular examples include the Windows Sound System and the Sound Blaster. Many sound cards not only play sounds, but also let you record your own. (I'll show you how to record stuff later on.) For the best sound, you should also spring for a pair of external computer speakers. Also, make sure the sound card is "MPC-compatible" (MPC stands for Multimedia PC Marketing Council; look for an MPC logo on the sound cards' box). This ensures that the card can do things like play music and handle the sophisticated sounds found on many CD-ROM disks.
- If you don't want to shell out any bucks, you can still play sounds by picking up a copy of Microsoft's PC Speaker driver. Contact Microsoft or, if you have a modem, read Chapter 17, "Getting Wired with Terminal," to find out how to download this file from Microsoft's bulletin board.

The next few sections assume you have some sort of sound set up on your system, and they show you how to play sounds, assign sounds to Windows events, and record your own sounds.

Sounding Off: Playing Sounds

Sounds you play in Windows come packaged as WAV files (you pronounce WAV as *wave*), which (for our purposes, anyway) just means these files all end with a .WAV extension (e.g., CHIMES.WAV). (To be accurate, Windows also recognizes special sound files called MIDI files; I'll talk about these later.)

Windows comes with a measly collection of four WAV files (CHIMES.WAV, CHORD.WAV, DING.WAV, and TADA.WAV, all of which are in your main Windows directory), but there's no shortage of sound libraries available that contain dozens of sound effects and clips from old cartoons and movies.

To play a sound, follow these steps:

1. Open Program Manager's **Accessories** group and select the **Sound Recorder** icon. The Sound Recorder window appears, as shown in the following figure.

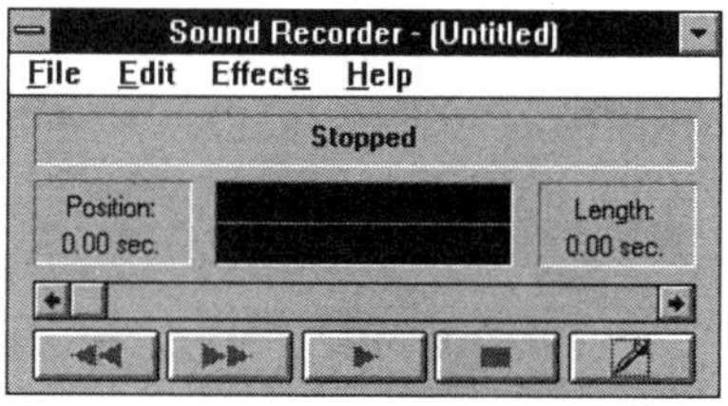

The Sound Recorder window, ready for action.

2. Pull down the **File** menu and select **Open**. Sound Recorder displays the Open dialog box.
3. Highlight the WAV file you want to hear and select **OK**.
4. Select the Play button to play the sound. For long files, you can also use the scroll bar to move to any position in the sound file and then start from there.

E-Z

You can roll steps 1–3 into one easy operation by double-clicking on the WAV file in File Manager.

For reference, here's a table of the Sound Recorder buttons:

Button	Name	What it does
	Play	Plays the sound
	Rewind	Moves the sound back to the beginning
	Forward	Moves the sound to the end
	Stop	Stops the sound in midstream
	Record	Records your own sounds (discussed later)

Giving Windows a Voice: Assigning Sounds to Events

If you're looking for some cheap thrills, you can assign sounds to different Windows events. For example, you can make Windows play a sound whenever it starts, or when certain dialog boxes appear on your screen. Windows recognizes no less than seven events, as shown in the following table:

Event	Dialog box icon	Occurs when
Asterisk		A dialog box is asking you for more info.
Critical Stop		A dialog box is warning you that something bad could happen if you proceed.
Exclamation		A dialog box is asking you to confirm your last action.
Question		A dialog box is asking you something or presenting you with a set of choices.
Default Beep	None	You do something silly like press an invalid key while a menu is pulled down.
Windows Exit	None	You're bailing out of Windows.
Windows Start	None	You're cranking Windows up to speed.

To try out this fun, follow these steps:

1. Start Control Panel by selecting the **Control Panel** icon from Program Manager's **Main** group.
2. Double-click on the **Sound** icon, or pull down the **S**ettings menu and select **S**ound. The Sound dialog box appears, as shown below.

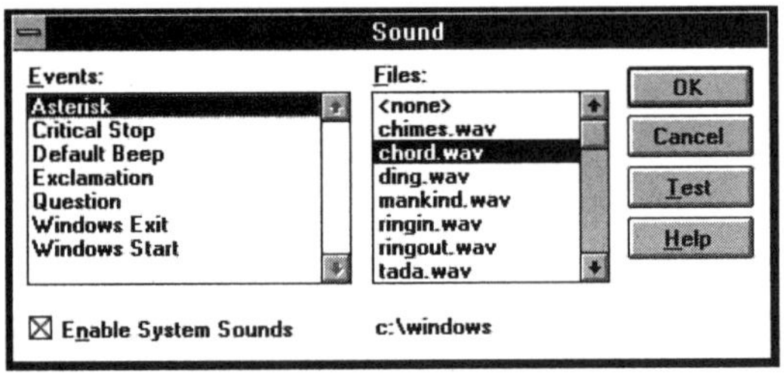

Use the Sound dialog box to assign sounds to Windows' events.

3. In the **E**vents list, highlight the event to which you want to assign a sound.
4. In the **F**iles list, highlight the WAV file you want to play whenever the selected event occurs. (If you want to check out a sound, highlight it and select the **T**est button.)

5. Repeat steps 3 and 4 to assign sounds to other events.
6. Make sure the Enable System Sounds check box is activated.
7. Select **OK** to return to Control Panel.

Rolling Your Own: How to Record Sounds

If you have a sound card capable of recording sounds (and you have a microphone attached to the sound card), you can have hours of mindless fun creating your own WAV files. Preserving silly sounds for posterity is the most fun, of course, but you can also create serious messages and embed them in business documents. (Chapter 8, "Understanding the Mysterious Snake Oil of OLE," tells you how to embed stuff in documents.)

To record a WAV file, follow these steps:

1. Start the Sound Recorder, as described earlier.
2. If Sound Recorder already has a WAV file opened, and you want to start a new file, select the File menu's New command. If you'd prefer to add sounds to an existing file, open it and find the position in the sound file where you want your recording to start.
3. Grab your microphone, clear your throat, get your script, and do whatever else you need to get ready for the recording.
4. Select the Record button.
5. Speak (yell, groan, belch, whatever) into the microphone. Sound Recorder shows you the length of the file as you record. Note that you have a maximum of 60 seconds to do your thing.
6. When you're done, select the Stop button.
7. If you're happy with your recording (select Rewind and then Play to hear how it sounds), select the File menu's Save command, enter a name for the file in the Save As dialog box (don't bother

> **OOPS!**
>
> Don't go off half-cocked and start recording every little thought that enters your head. WAV files, unfortunately, like to gobble up huge chunks of your precious hard disk real estate. For example, a 20-second recording will set you back almost a full megabyte! Only record what you have to, and be sure to delete any WAV files you no longer need.

adding the .WAV extension; Sounder Recorder is happy to add it for you automatically), and then select **OK**.

As if letting you record your own sounds isn't enough, Sound Recorder also comes with a host of cool options for creating some really wild effects. For example, you can mix WAV files, change the volume, alter the playback speed, reverse a sound, or add an echo—just to name a few.

You can mix two or more WAV files so they play at the same time. For example, you could combine one WAV file that contains narration with another that has some soothing music. To try this out, open one of the WAV files and move to where you want the second file to start. Pull down the Edit menu, select Mix with File, highlight the other WAV file in the Mix With File dialog box, and then select **OK**.

If you record your WAV file and then decide it's too loud or too soft, you can change the volume. To do so, simply pull down the Effects menu and select either Increase Volume (to make the sound louder by 25%) or Decrease Volume (to make the sound quieter by 25%).

> **OOPS!**
>
> If you make a mess of your WAV file, you can get back to square one by pulling down the File menu and selecting the Revert command. This returns the file to the state it was in when you last saved it.

You can make your voice recordings sound like either Alvin and the Chipmunks or Darth Vader by adjusting the speed of the playback. Pull down the Effects menu and choose either Increase Speed (to double the speed) or Decrease Speed (to halve the speed). Likewise, you can play a sound file backwards to produce some real mind-blowing effects. To check it out, pull down the Effects menu and select the Reverse command.

Adding an echo ... echo ... echo is easy. If you select the Effects menu's Add Echo command, Sound Recorder creates a neat echo effect that makes your WAV files sound like they're being played in some cavernous location.

A (Not So) Real-Life Example

What's that? Your office manager has made it *verboten* to hang around the water cooler? If you're dying to trade office gossip and rumors with your cronies, why not use Sound Recorder to pass along juicy tidbits on the sly?

All you have to do is record the latest hearsay to a WAV file, copy the file to a floppy disk, then just exchange disks with your friends. This way, you can keep up with all the news—and your boss will think you're working! (If you're worried about the disk falling into the wrong hands, use some of the effects I described earlier to disguise your voice.)

Checking Out the Magical Media Player

One of Windows' best kept secrets is the Media Player application. Depending on the hardware you've crammed into your system and the devices you've installed, this little gem can play sounds, MIDI files (they have an .MID extension), audio CDs, video files (they have an .AVI extension), and even videodiscs.

To see what's what, follow these steps to use Media Player:

1. Open Program Manager's **Accessories** group and select the **Media Player** icon. You'll see the Media Player window, as shown below.

> **TECHNO NERD TEACHES...**
>
> Instead of the Media Player, you might see a dialog box telling you there are "no MCI drivers installed on your system." Bummer. In this case, you'll need to run Control Panel's **Drivers** icon and install the appropriate drivers (as described earlier in this chapter). In particular, install the **[MCI] Sound** driver to play sounds, **[MCI] CD Audio** driver to play audio CDs, and the **[MCI] MIDI Sequencer** driver to play MIDI files. Other MCI (Media Control Interface) devices will come with their own drivers.

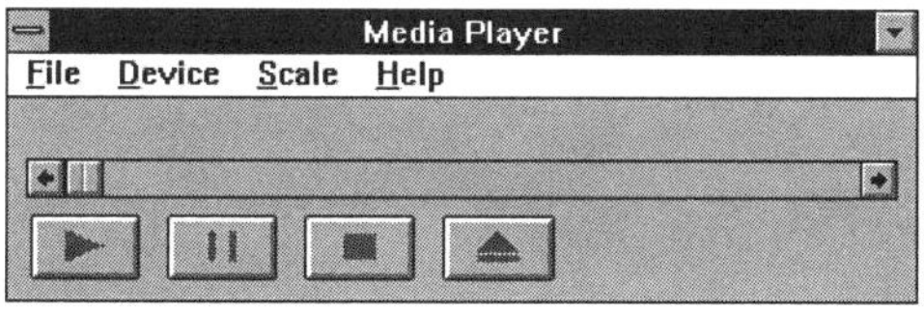

The Media Player window.

2. Set up Media Player by doing one of the following:
   - If you'll be playing a device that doesn't require a file, (such as an audio CD or a videodisc), pull down the **D**evice menu and select the type of device you'll be using (CD Audio, for example).
   - For devices that require files (such as a sound card or MIDI device), select the **F**ile menu's **O**pen command, highlight the file you want to play in the Open dialog box, and then select **OK**. In this case, Media Player automatically selects the appropriate device.
3. If necessary, prepare the device for playing. For example, if you'll be playing an audio CD, insert the disk in the CD-ROM drive.
4. Select the Play button to start playing. Here's a summary of Media Player's buttons. (As with the Sound Recorder, you can also use the scroll bar to move to any position in the media.)

Button	Name	What it does
	Play	Plays the media
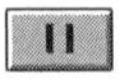	Pause	Pauses the media (you can select either Pause or Play to resume)
	Stop	Stops the media (select Play to resume)
	Eject	Ejects the media (this feature is only supported by some devices)

Many of today's multimedia PCs are being shipped with what's called a *runtime* version of Microsoft Video for Windows. ("Runtime" means it's a stripped down version of the real thing.) If this is the case with your machine, you'll also get the jazzed up version of Media Player shown on the following page.

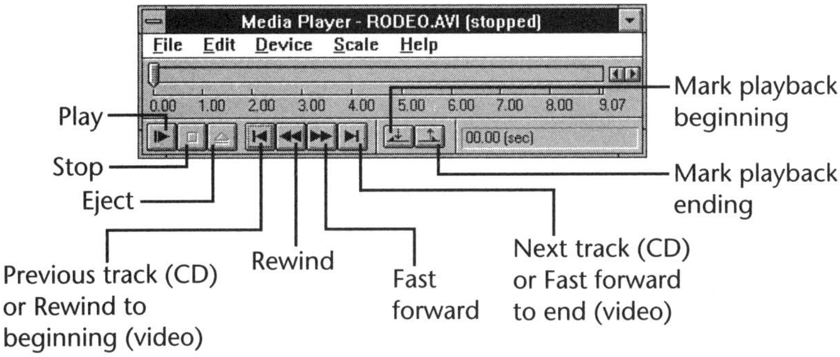

The new, improved Media Player that comes with the runtime version of Video for Windows.

The Least You Need to Know

This chapter took you on a magical multimedia mystery tour. Here's a rehash of some of the sights we saw along the way:

- Before you can play with any multimedia equipment, you need to install the appropriate device drivers. You do this by selecting Control Panel's **Drivers** icon.
- Once you've installed and set up a CD-ROM drive, Windows will recognize it with no questions asked. You can access the CD's contents by selecting the drive in File Manager.
- You can play sound files in Windows by installing either a sound card or the PC Speaker driver.
- To play sounds, start the Sound Recorder, open a WAV file, and play it.
- To assign sounds to Windows' events, select Control Panel's **Sound** icon.
- To record your own sounds, load Sound Recorder and press the Record button.
- The Media Player can play sounds, MIDI files, video files, audio CDs, and more. To try it out, select the **Media Player** icon in Program Manager's **Accessories** group.

Part II

Neat Things You Can Do with Windows Applications

In Part II, we turn our attention from the general Windows stuff we looked at in Part I to some application-specific topics. We'll be spending time with programs such as File Manager, Program Manager, Write, Paintbrush, Terminal, and Recorder. Again, you'll either be extending your existing knowledge of an application (the stuff you would have learned in The Complete Idiot's Guide to Windows*) or you'll be treading on new ground. In either case, there's lots to learn, and it's all designed to make your day-to-day Windows life a little easier—and a little more pleasant.*

Chapter 12
Let's Do Launch: Interesting Ways to Start Applications

In This Chapter

- Setting up icons for documents
- Assigning shortcut keys to icons
- Running programs from File Manager
- Starting an application as the Windows shell
- Loading applications from WIN.INI
- More ways to start programs than you can shake a stick at

Program Manager, as you know by now, does one thing and one thing only: start applications. You can't use it to write notes, crunch numbers, draw pictures, or any of the other drudgery for which you normally use your computer. In this era of specialists, Program Manager is the shining example.

This chapter celebrates Program Manager's single-mindedness by investigating all the different ways you can start applications. If you thought that pointing at an icon and double-clicking was all there was to it, think again. Not only does Program Manager have another trick or two up its sleeve, but Windows also provides an extra smorgasbord of methods for getting an application's show on the road. We'll tackle them all in this chapter.

A Recap of the Basics

Before moving on to some of the more esoteric (but still decidedly useful) methods for launching programs, let's take a fond look back at some basic stuff. The next few sections recap the procedures we checked out in *The Complete Idiot's Guide to Windows* or earlier in this book.

"Icon Start That Program with Two Mouse Clicks"

By far the most straightforward way to put a program's nose to its digital grindstone is to open the program group that contains its icon, and then double-click on the icon. If you prefer the keyboard, first open the program group by pulling down the **W**indow menu and selecting the group name from the list at the bottom of the menu. (If you have more than nine groups, you'll see a **M**ore Windows command. Choose this command to display the Select Window dialog box, use the up or down arrow keys to highlight the group, and then select **OK**.) With the group now open, use the arrow keys to highlight the icon and press **Enter**.

That's all well and good, but we should also review how you add groups and icons to Program Manager. First off, here are the steps to follow to create a new program group:

1. Pull down Program Manager's **F**ile menu and select the **N**ew command. Program Manager displays the New Program Object dialog box, as shown below.

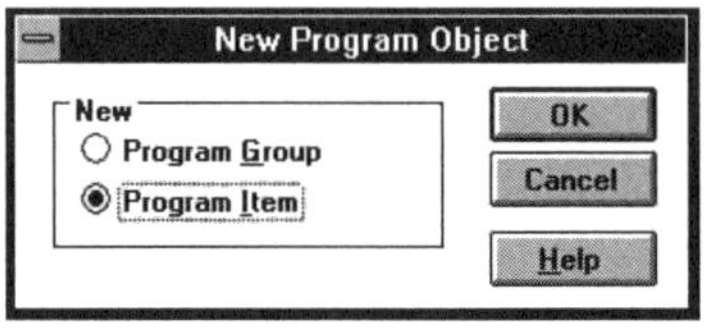

The New Program Object dialog box appears when you select the **F***ile menu's* **N***ew command.*

2. Activate the Program **G**roup option and select **OK**. The Program Group Properties dialog box appears, as shown in the following figure.

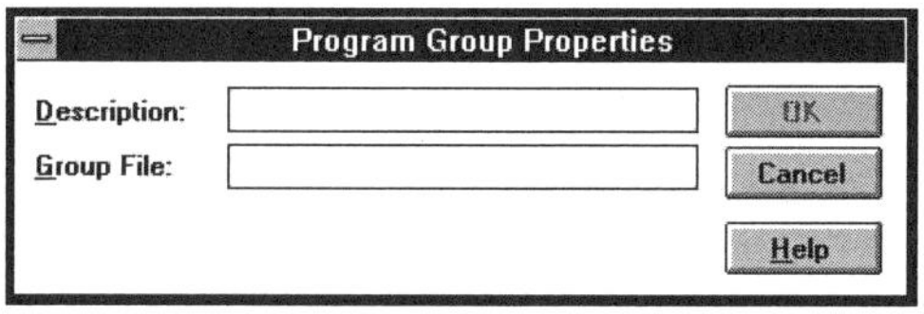

Use the Program Group Properties dialog box to define your new program group.

3. Enter the name of the group in the **D**escription text box and select **OK**. Program Manager obligingly creates the new group.

Although you'll rarely have to create new groups, creating new icons will be a regular task, and you should know how to do it in your sleep. Follow these steps:

1. Select the **F**ile menu's **N**ew command to display the New Program Object dialog box.
2. Select the Program **I**tem option and select **OK**. The Program Item Properties dialog box appears.

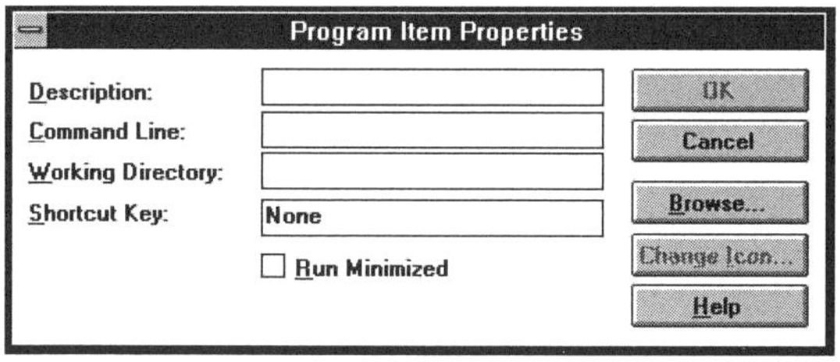

You use the Program Item Properties dialog box to enter all the pertinent info for starting your application.

3. In the **D**escription text box, enter the text you want to appear below the icon.
4. Use the **C**ommand Line text box to enter the name of the file that starts the program, including the appropriate drive and directory. In general, the **C**ommand Line takes the form *drive:\directory\filename*, where *filename* is the name of the file that loads the application (including its extension), *directory* is the directory where the file is stored, and *drive* is the letter of the disk drive where the directory is located. For example, the **C**ommand Line for Quicken for Windows is c:\quickenw\qw.exe.

   If you're not sure about any of this, select the **B**rowse button, hunt down the file in the Browse dialog box, and then select **OK**.

TECHNO NERD TEACHES...

A file that starts an application is called an *executable file.* You can always tell an executable file by its extension: EXE, COM, BAT, or PIF. EXE files are the most common, and COM files are smaller versions of EXE files. BAT files are *batch files* (text files that contain one or more DOS instructions; see Chapter 5, "Taming the DOS Beast," to eyeball a batch file example). PIF files represent the Program Information Files that start DOS programs (we also looked at these files in Chapter 5).

5. By default, Program Manager starts the application in whatever directory you spelled out in the **C**ommand Line box. If you'd like the program to begin in a different directory (for example, the directory where you store the program's data files), enter both the drive and directory name in the **W**orking Directory text box.
6. Select **OK**. If all is well, Program Manager creates the icon. Otherwise, you may see a message telling you that the "path" you entered in the **C**ommand Line is "invalid." In this case, select **Cancel** to return to the Program Item Properties dialog box, and then make whatever changes are necessary to set things right.

Running Programs with the Run Command

If you only use an application sporadically, it's probably not worth the hassle of creating an icon. For that reason, both Program Manager and File Manager have a **R**un command on their **F**ile menu. Selecting this command produces the Run dialog box, shown in the following figure. Enter the name of the file that starts the program (including the appropriate drive and directory where it can be found), and then select **OK**.

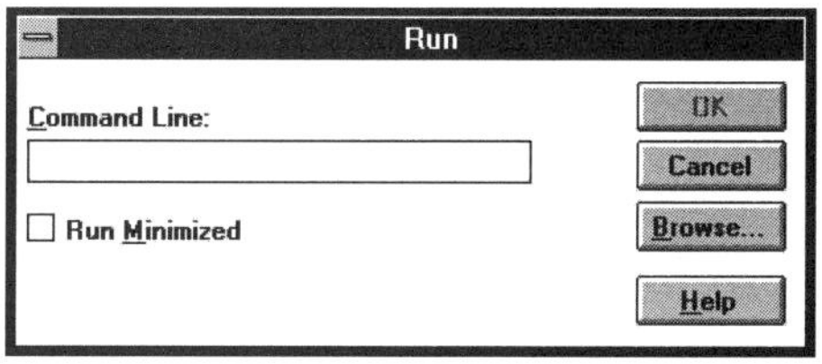

Use the Run dialog box to crank up programs you use only occasionally.

Using the Handy Startup Group

Windows 3.1 introduced a slick new feature that makes starting programs a breeze: the Startup group. The programs whose icons you stuff into this group will load automatically each time you start Windows. This is great for applications you use every day, such as File Manager, or personal information managers (PIMs), such as Lotus Organizer. You can either create your icons in this group directly, or you can copy existing icons from other groups using the following techniques:

- Hold down the **Ctrl** key and with your mouse, drag the icon from its current group into the Startup group.
- Highlight the current icon and select the **F**ile menu's **C**opy command (or press **F8**) to display the Copy Program Item dialog box (see below). Select **Startup** in the **T**o Group list, and then select **OK**.

Select Startup in the Copy Program Item dialog box to copy an icon to the Startup group.

Running Applications from File Manager

If you happen to be in File Manager, you don't have to head back to Program Manager to fire up an application. Instead, select the drive and directory that contains the program's executable file, and then either double-click on the file, or highlight the file and press **Enter**.

Starting a DOS Program from a DOS Session

The methods we've looked at so far apply equally well to both Windows and DOS applications. However, if you don't mind working with the DOS prompt, you can also load DOS programs while you're in a DOS session. Here are the steps:

1. Start a DOS session by selecting the **MS-DOS Prompt** icon from Program Manager's **Main** group.
2. At the DOS prompt, activate the drive that contains the directory you'll be using (if you're not there already). You do this by typing the drive letter followed by a colon (:), and then pressing **Enter**.
3. Change to the directory where you want to start the program (this could be either a data directory or the directory that contains the program's executable file). You do this by using the CD (Change Directory) command. For example, to change to the directory WP, you'd type **CD\WP** and press **Enter**.
4. Enter the name of the file that starts the program (include the drive and directory if the file doesn't reside in the current directory), and then press **Enter**.

Starting Applications Using OLE

Chapter 8, "Understanding the Mysterious Snake Oil of OLE," told you everything you need to know about object linking and embedding (OLE). I won't go into the details, but here's a summary of the ways you can use OLE to start applications:

- You can double-click on a linked or embedded object.
- You can insert a new object into a document (Windows starts the appropriate application so you can create the object).
- In Object Packager, you can add a command that starts an application to a package.

Document Exercises for the Anxious, Eager, and Adventurous

The usual *modus operandi* for most people is to launch an application and then open whatever file they want to work with. This is fine if you use different documents every day, but what if, like many Windows users, you crack open the same document each time you start an application? For example, you might have a "To-Do" list in your word processor that you update daily. In this case, it's possible to cut out a step and tell Windows to start the application and load the document all in one shot. The next few sections take you through some exercises that explain how this works.

In this section (and throughout most of this book, in fact), I use the word *document* in its most generic sense: to signify any kind of data file. So a "document" can refer to a spreadsheet, a graphic file, a database, or of course, a word processing document.

For the Anxious: Starting Documents

The easiest way to launch an application and have it load a document automatically is to specify the document's file name as part of the program's command line. For example, suppose you have a file named TODO.WRI and you store it in your C:\DATA directory. To start Write and have it load TODO.WRI, you'd enter the following command in the Command Line of either the Program Item Properties dialog box or the Run dialog box:

WRITE.EXE C:\DATA\TODO.WRI

(Note: WRITE.EXE is stored in the main Windows directory, so you don't have to specify a drive and directory for it.) Now that you know how to start a document, you can easily create Program Manager icons for documents. Follow the steps I outlined earlier for creating an icon, and be sure to make the following modifications in the Program Item Properties dialog box:

- In the **D**escription text box, enter a description of the document. Note that this provides you with a second significant advantage for this method: you no longer have to decipher cryptic 8-letter

DOS file names to figure out what a document contains. You can cram up to 40 characters in the Description text box, so you have lots of space to ramble on.

- In the Command Line text box, enter the application's executable file, followed by the document file name.

You can make your life a little easier by taking advantage of a little-known, but extremely powerful trick. You and I know that certain extensions are usually associated with certain applications. For example, if you see a file with the extension .WRI, you know right away it's a Write file. Similarly, a .CRD file is from CardFile, a .CAL file is from Calendar, and so on.

The trick is that Windows also knows these things. Therefore, you don't even have to specify which application you want to start. You can just tell Windows to start the data file, and it'll know the appropriate application to crank up. Neat, huh? Here are three ways you can take advantage of this:

- When creating an icon, just specify the document's file name (including the drive and directory) in the Command Line text box.
- If you're in File Manager, double-click on the document's file name.
- You can easily create an icon for a document by dragging its file name from File Manager into a Program Manager group. (This technique is called *drag-and-drop*, and I cover it more thoroughly in Chapter 13, "Fiddling Around with File Manager.")

For the Eager: Making Sure Windows Can Start Any Document

In the last section, I told you that Windows "knows" that certain applications are associated with certain extensions. This may seem like pretty smart behavior, but Windows, like everything related to computers, only knows what it's been told. For example, if you install Microsoft Excel, the installation program makes a point of telling Windows that files with the extension .XLS are associated with Excel.

If Windows hasn't been told about a particular extension, it won't know what to do. If you try to start such a document, you'll end up seeing the unfriendly message **There is no application associated with this file.**

Does this mean you're out of luck? Not even close. It just means you have to expand Windows' mind and tell it which application to associate with the extension you're trying to use. As an example, let's teach Windows how to handle files with a .ZIP extension. Here's what you do:

> **TECHNO NERD TEACHES...**
>
> A ZIP file contains one or more files that have been compressed to save space. If you download files from a bulletin board (as explained in Chapter 17, "Getting Wired with Terminal"), they'll usually arrive as a ZIP file. To decompress these files, you use a DOS program called PKUNZIP (which is available on almost every bulletin board on the face of the earth). For example, to decompress a file named DOWNLOAD.ZIP, you'd type **PKUNZIP DOWNLOAD.ZIP** and press **Enter**.

1. In File Manager, pull down the File menu and select the Associate command. The Associate dialog box appears.
2. In the Files with Extension text box, type the extension you want to work with (don't include the period). In our example, type **ZIP**.
3. Use the Associate With text box to specify the executable file for the application. You can do this in one of three ways:
    - Type the name of the executable file (including the drive and directory).
    - Select the Browse button, highlight the executable file's file name in the Browse dialog box, and then select **OK**.

- Choose one of the existing applications in the Associate With list. (Why would you want to do this? Well, many applications can handle different kinds of files. For example, Notepad can handle most any text file, no matter what the extension. So you could set up associations for common text file extensions such as PRN, ME—as in the READ.ME files that come with many programs—BAT, and so on.)

The next figure shows the completed Associate dialog box for the ZIP example. (If you're following along, be sure to enter the correct drive and directory for your copy of PKUNZIP.EXE.)

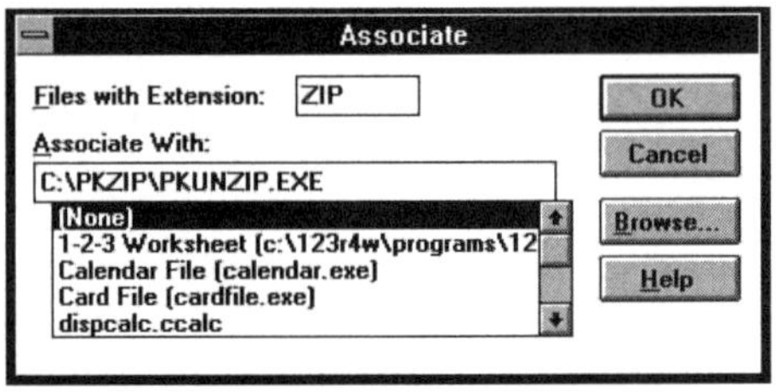

The Associate dialog box all set up to associate ZIP files with the PKUNZIP.EXE program.

4. Select **OK**. Windows sets up the association.

You can also use the Associate dialog box to change an existing association. For example, suppose you were once a Lotus 1-2-3 user, but now you've switched over to Excel. Ideally, you'd like to be able to launch one of your old Lotus files and have it open up in Excel. No problem. In the Associate dialog box, first type the extension for your Lotus worksheets (for example, WK1 or WK3) in the Files with Extension box. The Associate With box will probably display **1-2-3 Worksheet** or something. Now just highlight the appropriate Excel item (it'll either be **Microsoft Excel Worksheet** or **Microsoft Excel 5.0 Worksheet**, depending on which version you're using), and then select **OK**.

For the Adventurous: Creating Advanced Associations

While working in the Associate dialog box, you may have noticed a peculiar thing. When you create your own associations, the Associate With list just shows the drive, directory, and file name of the file that starts the application. The predefined entries, however, have both the file name *and* a plain-English translation, like this:

Paintbrush Picture (pbrush.exe)

This sure makes it easy to pick out the right application, but how can we set things up that way when we create associations? The answer lies in an obscure Windows feature called the *registration database*. Using this database, you can specify a *file type* (for example, "Paintbrush Picture") to go with an executable file (for example, PBRUSH.EXE). The following steps show you what to do:

1. In Program Manager or File Manager select the **F**ile menu's **R**un command, enter **REGEDIT.EXE**, and then select **OK**. The Registration Info Editor window appears.
2. Pull down the **E**dit menu and select the **A**dd File Type command. The Add File Type dialog box pops up.
3. In the **I**dentifier list, enter a name for the type of files you'll be dealing with. (Don't use any spaces; for example, **zipfile** will do for the ZIP files example.)
4. In the **F**ile Type text box, enter a short description for the type of files associated with the application. (This is the name that appears in the Associate dialog box.) For example, enter **Zip Files** for the ZIP example.
5. In the **C**ommand text box, enter the name of the executable file (including, as usual, the drive and directory), followed by a space, followed by the characters **%1**. In our example, you'd enter the following:

   C:\PKZIP\PKUNZIP.EXE %1

6. Deactivate the **U**ses DDE check box.
7. Select **OK** to return to the Registration Info Editor, pull down the **F**ile menu, and select E**x**it.
8. In File Manager, use the **A**ssociate command to associate the extension to the new entry you just created.

Saving Time with a Shortcut Key

I'm always on the lookout for ways to cut down on the number of keystrokes or mouse clicks I have to plow through to complete a chore. So I was very happy to learn that the Program Item Properties dialog box lets you assign a shortcut key to an icon. Pressing this shortcut key performs two actions that save wear and tear on the fingers. When you're in Program Manager, it launches the icon. And, once the application is running, it immediately switches to the icon from whatever other program you happen to be in.

> **OOPS!**
>
> If you press the wrong key by accident (or if you decide you don't want a shortcut key after all), press either **Delete** or **Backspace** to wipe out the key combo.

To assign a shortcut key combo to an icon, first open its Program Item Properties dialog box, and then move the cursor into the Shortcut Key text box. Now simply press a letter or number, and Windows creates a key combination in the form **Ctrl+Alt+*character*** (where *character* is the letter or number you pressed). If you like, you can hold down the **Shift** key when pressing the character; this creates a key combination in the form **Ctrl+Alt+Shift+*character***.

Starting a Program as a Replacement to Program Manager

A typical Windows session goes something like this:

1. Start Windows and end up in Program Manager.
2. Use Program Manager to start other applications.
3. Exit the applications to return to Program Manager.
4. Exit Program Manager to exit Windows.

In other words, we can think of Program Manager as the outer layer of Windows, which we use to move to the inner layers by launching programs and such. This notion of looking at Program Manager as an "outer layer" is exactly why Windows mavens call it a *shell*.

The surprising thing is that Program Manager doesn't have to be the Windows shell. In fact, you can designate just about any Windows application as the shell, and Windows won't mind a bit. For example, you could use Write as the shell. This means that Write would appear when you started Windows, and that you'd exit Windows when you exited Write. The downside to this arrangement, of course, is that you can't launch programs from Write, so you can't work in any other applications. But many people only use a single Windows application anyway, so why should they bother with Program Manager at all? Beats me.

To change the Windows shell, first open the file SYSTEM.INI. (Unsure about INI files? Toddle back to Chapter 9, "Learning to Love Those Strange INI Files," to get all the INI info you need.) The first section is called [boot], and in it you'll find a line that looks something like this:

shell=progman.exe

Delete the **progman.exe** part and type in the name of the executable file you want to use as your shell (including—you guessed it—the drive and directory if it's not in the Windows directory). For example, if you wanted to use Microsoft Word for Windows as your shell, the line would look like this:

shell=c:\winword\winword.exe

Save the file, exit the editor, and then exit and restart Windows to put the new setting into effect.

Using Run= and Load= in WIN.INI

The WIN.INI file we looked at back in Chapter 9, "Learning to Love Those Strange INI Files," is chock full of handy settings that let you set up Windows the way you want. In this section, we'll look at two more settings: Run= and Load=.

You use both of these lines to specify programs that Windows should launch automatically at startup. Now wait a minute, I know you're asking, "Isn't that what the Startup group is for?" Right on. But there are times when these lines come in handy:

- People who are still using Windows 3.0 don't have a Startup group.
- As you may know, you can bypass the Startup group by holding down the **Shift** key while Windows is loading. But this all-or-nothing arrangement may not be convenient. For example, you may have one or two programs that you definitely need to load at startup every day, and a couple more that you can live without one or two days a week. To solve this dilemma, you could take the definite ones out of your Startup group and use Run= or Load=, instead. By doing this, you can bypass the Startup group when you need to.
- If you've changed your Windows shell to File Manager (as explained in the last section), you don't have access to the Startup group. (Note: if you've changed the shell to a program that can't launch applications, you won't be able to use the Run= and Load= lines anyway.)

To try out these settings, first load WIN.INI. The first section is called [Windows], and it contains the Run= and Load= lines. Use Run= when you want to launch a program full-screen; use Load= when you want a program to start off as an icon. All you do is type in the executable file name of the application you want to start. As an added bonus, you can enter multiple file names, as long as you put a space between files, like this:

Load=C:\MOUSE\POINTER.EXE C:\ORGANIZE\ORGANIZE.EXE

The Least You Need to Know

This chapter introduced you to a thousand and one ways to launch applications in Windows. Here are a few of the highlights:

- You normally start applications by selecting a Program Manager icon, using the **R**un command, putting icons in the Startup group, or double-clicking an executable file in File Manager.
- To start a program and load a document, include the document's file name in the icon's command line. Alternatively, most applications let you specify just the document file name.
- If Windows doesn't know how to deal with a document, use File Manager's **A**ssociate command to set things up.
- You can launch your applications quickly by assigning a shortcut key in the Program Item Properties dialog box.
- To designate a program as the Windows shell, modify the Shell= line in SYSTEM.INI.
- As an alternative to the Startup group, enter executable file names in the Run= and Load= lines of WIN.INI.

Chapter 13
Fiddling Around with File Manager

In This Chapter

- Customizing the look and feel of File Manager
- A comprehensive catalog of drag-and-drop's capabilities
- Reclaiming wasted disk space with File Manager
- Oodles of tips and tricks that'll make File Manager—gasp!—useful

I used to *loathe* File Manager. Not dislike; not detest; not even hate. No, I'm talking about out-and-out loathing. Why the strong feelings? Because File Manager's default, right-out-of-the-box configuration is just plain dumb. It makes performing even the simplest task both frustrating and unnecessarily slow. I am, however, too cheap (or *thrifty*, as those of us of Scottish descent prefer to say) to shell out any bucks for one of the umpteen File Manager enhancements and replacements now available. Instead, I just decided to give File Manager an overhaul using its existing options. As you'll see in this chapter, a simple nip here and tuck there are all it takes to make File Manager a truly useful tool.

Giving File Manager a Facelift

When you start File Manager (by selecting the **File Manager** icon from Program Manager's **Main** group), you probably see a window that looks something like the one shown below. Ugh. This section explores a number of options you can exploit to give File Manager a much-needed makeover.

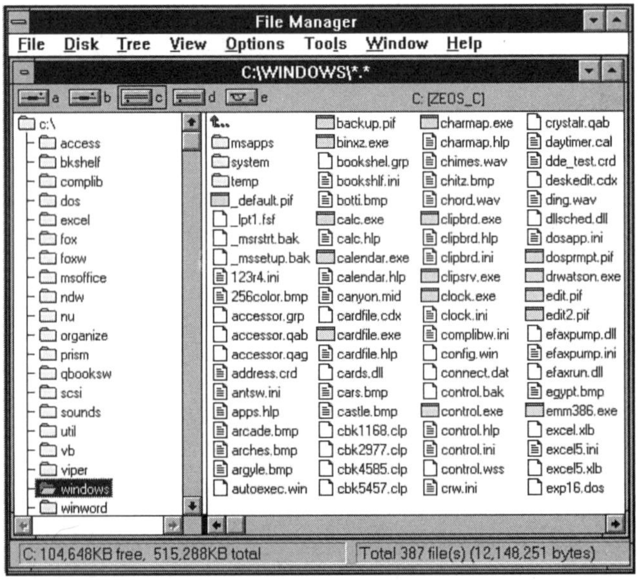

File Manager's default plain vanilla configuration.

TECHNO NERD TEACHES...

Before you dive into the deep end of File Manager's customization pool, we should talk briefly about saving your configuration. If you pull down the **O**ptions menu, you'll likely see a check mark beside the Save Settings on **E**xit command. This means that File Manager will save its current configuration each time you exit the program. However, you want to establish your own personalized configuration that appears every time you start File Manager. To accomplish this, first select the Save Settings on **E**xit command to turn it off (you don't have to do this if there's no check mark beside the command). Once you've set up File Manager to your satisfaction, hold down the **Shift** key, pull down the **F**ile menu, and select the E**x**it command (or you can press **Alt+Shift+F4**). This saves your current configuration without exiting the program.

File Manager Bonsai: Shaping the Directory Tree

As you know, each File Manager window is divided into two parts: the left side, the *directory tree*, shows the available directories on the currently selected drive; the right side, the *file list*, shows the contents (i.e., the subdirectories and files) of the currently selected directory. The following table shows the Tree menu commands you can use to manipulate the directory tree, as well as their shortcut keys.

Select	Or press	To
Expand One Level	Plus (+)	See the subdirectories immediately below the current directory. (You can also double-click on the directory.)
Expand Branch	Asterisk (*)	See all the subdirectories below the current directory.
Expand All	Ctrl+Asterisk (*)	See all the subdirectories below every directory.
Collapse Branch	Minus (–)	Hide the subdirectories below the current directory. (Again, you can also double-click on the directory.)

One of my pet peeves with the default File Manager setup is that you have no immediate way to tell which directories have subdirectories. To fix this, pull down the Tree menu and select the Indicate Expandable Branches command. File Manager adds a plus sign (+) to the folder icon of each directory that has subdirectories. When you expand one of these directories, a minus sign appears inside the folder (see the following figure).

E-Z

Whenever you select a different drive, you can expand all the branches by holding down the **Shift** key while you click on the drive letter.

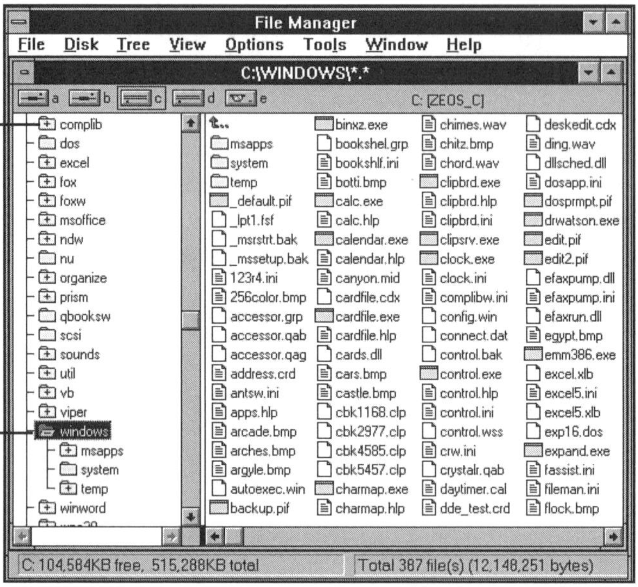

File Manager's directory tree becomes instantly more comprehensible with the **Indicate Expandable** *Branches command turned on.*

One of the most common File Manager chores is moving or copying files from one directory to another (possibly on a different drive). By far the easiest way to do this is with drag-and-drop (see "The Compleat Drag-and-Drop," later in this chapter for details), where you drag the selected files from one directory and drop them in another. For this to work, though, you have to see both directories on-screen at the same time. Because this isn't always possible, most people just head back to the boring old **C**opy command. Forget that. The solution is to select the **W**indow menu's **N**ew Window command, select the destination directory in the new window, and then arrange things neatly by selecting **T**ile from the **W**indow menu or by pressing **Shift+F4**. (File Manager tiles the windows horizontally, one on top of the other. If you'd prefer your windows tiled vertically, side-by-side, hold down **Shift** while selecting the **T**ile command.)

If you often move or copy files to a particular directory, there's an even easier way to do the drag-and-drop thing. First minimize the destination directory's window, and then select the **T**ile command. File Manager arranges the windows as shown in the following picture. As you can see, you get a lot more room to maneuver in the original window, and you move or copy your files simply by dropping them on the icon.

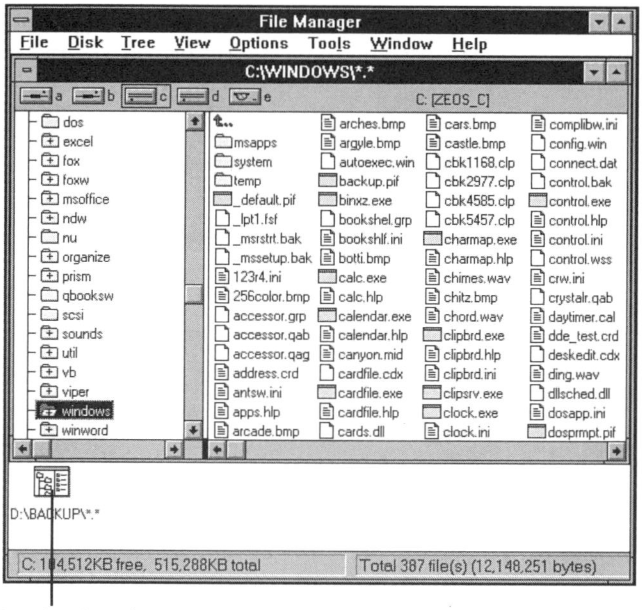

Destination directory icon

If you have a directory you use all the time, minimize its window to an icon.

Fixing the File List

The default file list is designed to show the maximum number of files possible. The trade-off is that all you see for each file is its name; you don't see other useful info such as the size of the file or the date and time it was last modified. One way to check out this data (and more) is to highlight a file name and select the File menu's Properties command. (You can also either hold down **Alt** and double-click on the file, or press **Alt+Enter**.) File Manager displays a Properties dialog box similar to the one shown below.

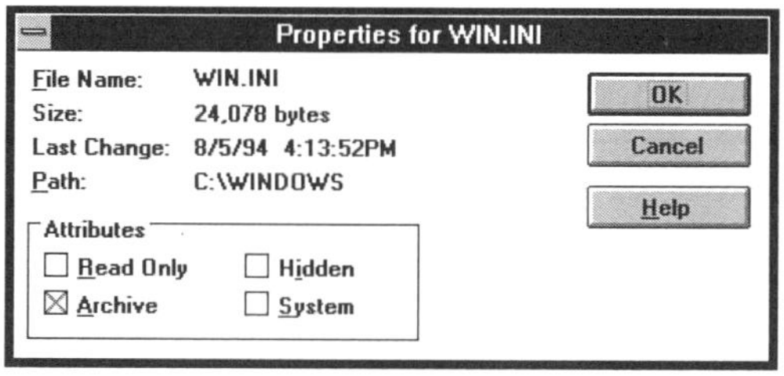

The Properties dialog box shows you some vital statistics for the selected file.

If, like me, you think this is a hassle, you can tell File Manager to display more file data in the file list. If you want to see all the available file info, pull down the View menu and activate the All File Details command. If you only want to see some of the info, select the **V**iew menu's **P**artial Details command to display the Partial Details dialog box shown below. Activate the appropriate check boxes, and then select **OK**.

Use the Partial Details dialog box to select the file info you want to see in the file list.

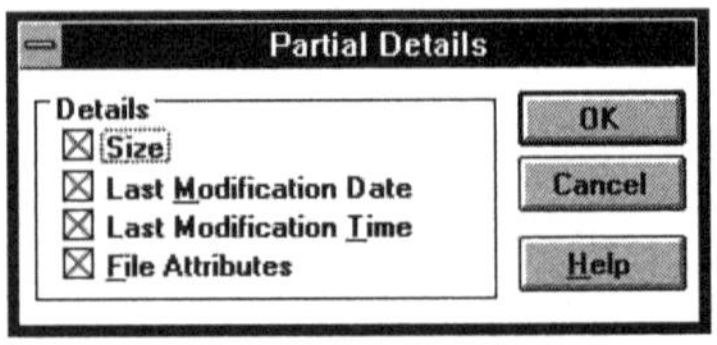

The file list normally displays your files in alphabetical order by file name. This makes it easy to find the file you want, but it's not always the most convenient order. The **V**iew menu has several commands that'll give you different arrangements:

Sort **b**y Type This command sorts the file list by each file's extension so that the .EXE files appear together, the .BMP files appear together, and so on. This is useful for basic file maintenance chores. For example, sorting by type puts all your INI and GRP files together, which makes it easy to select them for a backup.

Sort by S**i**ze This command sorts the file list by file size in descending order. I use this sort when I'm looking for a quick way to reclaim some hard disk space. Because the biggest files in each directory appear at the top of the file list, it's easy to pick out a few large files I no longer need and delete them.

Sort by **D**ate This command arranges the file list by date and time in descending order. This sort is handy if you're using File Manager to back up a few important files. The most recently modified files appear at the top of the file list and, since these are the ones you're most likely to back up, it's a snap to select the ones you want.

Sort by Name This command returns the file list back to its normal file name sort.

As a final file list tweak, if you've expanded a directory, it's redundant to have the subdirectories displayed in both the directory tree and the file list. You can remove them from the file list (and give yourself room to display more files) by selecting the **V**iew menu's By File **T**ype command, deactivating the **D**irectories check box in the By File Type dialog box, and then selecting **OK**.

Trying Different Fonts On for Size

Back in Chapter 7, "Flexing Your Font Muscles," I told you all about fonts and showed you how to use them to beautify your documents. Not many people know that you can apply this knowledge in File Manager as well. You can display both the directory tree and file list in a different typeface or a different type size, and you can even toggle the characters between uppercase and lowercase. Here are the steps to follow:

1. Pull down the **O**ptions menu and select the **F**ont command. The Font dialog box appears, as shown below.

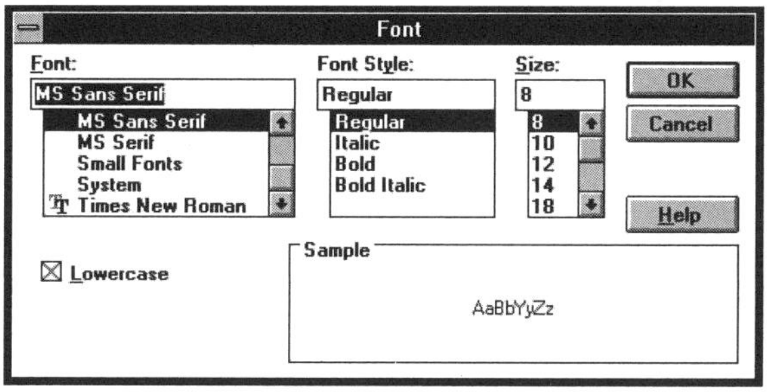

Use the Font dialog box to select your File Manager font.

2. Use the **F**ont, Font St**y**le, and **S**ize lists to select your font.

> **TECHNO NERD TEACHES...**
>
> If you'd like to move to a smaller font so you can see more directories and files in each window, I'd suggest the **Small Fonts** typeface. This typeface displays nicely in 6- or 7-point type (which size you choose depends on how well your eyesight is holding up).

3. If you'd like to see the characters in uppercase, deactivate the **L**owercase check box.

4. Select **OK**.

The Compleat Drag-and-Drop

Drag-and-drop is one of those features that, once you've used it, you wonder how in the world you ever got along without it. It really is amazing just how much it can simplify all kinds of everyday tasks. To celebrate this indispensable feature, this section presents a complete review of all the different tricks you can make drag-and-drop do.

Before we get to that, however, let's recap the basic drag-and-drop dance steps. And-a-one, and-a-two:

1. You begin by highlighting whatever it is you want to work with (some files, a directory, whatever).
2. Position the mouse pointer over one of the highlighted objects, and then hold down the left mouse button.
3. Move the mouse (this is the dragging part) and position the pointer over the destination.
4. Release the mouse button (this is the dropping part).

Moving and Copying Stuff

The most common drag-and-drop chores involve moving and copying directories and files. It's a great way to work because you avoid the Move and Copy dialog boxes, *and* you avoid having to type in a destination. Here are some notes to keep in mind when using drag-and-drop to move or copy files. (Note: In the following list, I use the term *object* as shorthand for all the things you can move or copy with drag and drop: a directory, a file, or a selection of files.)

- The rules File Manager uses to determine whether a drag-and-drop is a move or a copy are hopelessly confusing. To avoid mistakes, hold down **Ctrl** whenever you want to copy an object, and hold down **Alt** whenever you want to move an object.
- Another way to tell whether a drag-and-drop is a move or a copy is to check out the document icon. If you're copying, a plus sign (+) appears inside the little document icon that's attached to the mouse pointer; if you're moving, the object's icon disappears.

- If you drop one directory onto another, the directory you're dropping becomes a *subdirectory* of the destination directory. For example, if you drop a directory named DOCS onto a directory named WINWORD, the dropped directory becomes WINWORD\DOCS.
- File Manager doesn't let you select multiple directories in the directory tree. If you need to drag-and-drop two or more subdirectories, select them in the file list instead. (This is the one time when it's worthwhile to display subdirectories in the file list.)
- If you drop an object on a drive icon, File Manager moves or copies the object to the current directory in the drive. Suppose you display drive D, select the BACKUP directory, and then return to drive C. If you then drop some files on the drive D icon, File Manager will copy them to drive D's BACKUP directory.

Creating Program Manager Icons

Creating icons in Program Manager can take awhile, especially if you're not sure of the proper command line and you have to Browse around for it. However, drag-and-drop can relieve you of this drudgery.

The hardest part is arranging the File Manager and Program Manager windows so you can see both at the same time. To make this easier, I display the Task List (by pressing **Ctrl+Esc**) and click on the Tile button. Once that's done, you just drag the application's executable file (or a data file that has an association with an executable file; see Chapter 12 for details) from File Manager, and drop it on the group you want to use for the icon. A quick edit of the icon title, and you're done!

Starting Applications

We looked at all kinds of ways to get programs going in Chapter 12, "Let's Do Launch: Interesting Ways to Start Applications." If you liked the idea of loading a document automatically when you start an application, you'll really like what drag-and-drop can do. In the file list, just drag a data file and drop it on the application's executable file. You may see a dialog box asking you to confirm that you want to start the application and load the data file. If so, select **Yes**.

You can also use drag-and-drop to load a data file into an application that's already running. Again, you drag the data file from the file list and drop it either inside the application window or on the icon (if the program's minimized).

> This is a fast way to check out sound files. Start Sound Recorder or Media Player, minimize it, and then drag WAV files onto the icon. They'll play right away—and you never have to choose the Play button.

Drag-and-Drop Does OLE, Too!

Not many people know that you can use drag-and-drop to embed or link files in OLE applications. (If you need a refresher course in OLE—or if you just want to know what the heck I'm talking about—head directly to Chapter 8, "Understanding the Mysterious Snake Oil of OLE.") First, start the OLE application and open whatever document you want to embed the file in or link the file to. To embed a file in the document, just drag the file from File Manager and drop it in the document. To link a file to the document, hold down **Ctrl** and **Shift**, drag the file from File Manager, drop it in the document, and then release the keys.

Printing Documents

Last, but certainly not least, you can also use drag-and-drop to print documents. To begin, start Print Manager (by selecting the **Print Manager** icon from Program Manager's **Main** group) and minimize it. (Minimizing Print Manager is optional, but it's usually easier than arranging the windows.) Now drag the file you want to print from the file list and drop it on the Print Manager icon. Print Manager automatically loads the appropriate application, issues a Print command, shuts down the application, and merrily prints away.

File Manager Secrets, Shortcuts, and Showstopping Shenanigans

The techniques we've looked at certainly cast File Manager in a new light. Our feelings have changed from scorn and derision to something approaching respect and even admiration. To complete the transformation, we need to check out some handy techniques designed to knock a few mouse clicks and keystrokes off our day-to-day file management drudgery.

- You'll spend lots of time selecting multiple files in the file list, so it pays to know the speediest mouse methods. If you're selecting several files in a row, click on the first file, hold down the **Shift** key, and then click on the last file. If the files you need are scattered willy-nilly throughout the directory, click on the first file, hold down **Ctrl**, and then click on each of the other files you need.
- If you need to select every file in a directory, select one and press the **Slash** (/) key. To deselect all the files except the current one, press **Backslash** (\).
- The Tree menu's Expand All command displays every directory and subdirectory on the current drive. Unfortunately, File Manager doesn't have a "Collapse All" command to reverse the mayhem. Fortunately, there are a couple of easy workarounds: either double-click on the root directory (e.g., **C:**) twice, or move to the root directory and press minus (–) and then plus (+).
- Need to create a directory and a subdirectory? Don't waste time running two Create Directory commands, because File Manager lets you create both in one fell swoop. For example, suppose you want to set up the directory C:\DATA and a subdirectory called C:\DATA\DOCS. Move to the root directory (i.e., C:\), select the File menu's Create Directory command, and enter the following in the Create Directory dialog box:

  DATA\DOCS

  Now select **OK**. Presto! File Manager adds both directories to the tree.

> **SPEAK LIKE A GEEK**
>
> The topmost directory for any drive is called the **root directory**.

- The Select Files command is a handy way to highlight files with similar names. Until now, if you needed to select two or more file specifications, you probably entered one, chose the Select button, entered another, chose the Select button again, and so on. *Way* too much work. Instead, the Select dialog box is more than happy to accept multiple file specifications. For example, suppose you want to select all of Windows' INI and GRP files. From your WINDOWS directory, choose the File menu's Select Files command and enter the following in the Select Files dialog box:

  *.INI *.GRP

  (Notice there's a space between the two specifications.) Now just click on the Select button, and File Manager highlights all the files at once.

- As you read this, your hard drive is probably teeming with duplicate files. To find out, move to the root directory, and run the File menu's Search command for each of the following files: SMARTDRV.EXE, HIMEM.SYS, EMM386.EXE, RAMDRIVE.SYS, VBRUN100.DLL, VBRUN200.DLL, VBRUN300.DLL, COMMDLG.DLL, and BWCC.DLL. If the Search Results window shows multiple files, delete them all except the file that has the latest date (see below). In my case, I was able to trim a good 2MB of fat from my hard drive.

If Search reports multiple files, keep only the one with the latest date.

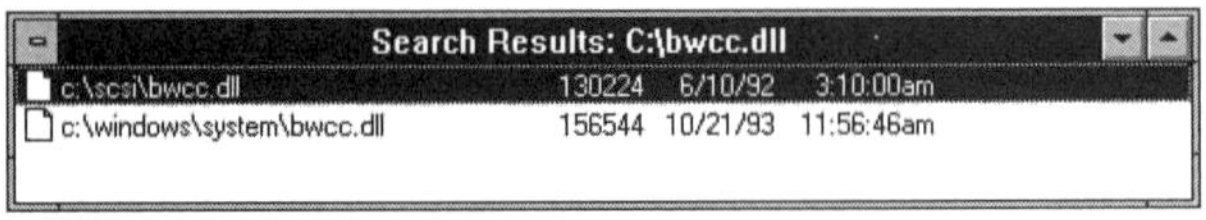

The Least You Need to Know

This chapter had you fooling around with File Manager in a quest to make the darn thing at least usable. Here are some of the hoops you made File Manager jump through:

- To save your current File Manager settings instantly, hold down **Shift** and select the **F**ile menu's E**x**it command.
- You can make the directory tree make sense by selecting the **T**ree menu's **I**ndicate Expandable Branches command. This adds plus signs (+) to the folder icons of directories that have subdirectories.
- Don't forget to take advantage of multiple windows to make tasks like dragging files between directories easier.
- The **V**iew menu's **A**ll File Details and **P**artial Details commands enable you to see more file info than just the name. You can also use the **V**iew menu's various Sort commands to order the files by name, type, size, or date.
- Using the **F**ont command on the **O**ptions menu, you can select a different typeface, style, and size for your File Manager font.
- The nifty drag-and-drop feature lets you move or copy files and directories, create Program Manager icons, load data files, print, and more.

Chapter 14
Improving Your Write Skills

In This Chapter

- Searching for and replacing text
- Taking advantage of Write's handy Ruler
- Adding headers and footers to your documents
- Working with pictures in Write
- Neat things you can do with Write even if you use another word processor
- Lots of Write stuff designed to prove that, yes, sometimes the best things in life *are* free

Unless you're cranking out big-time newsletters or your latest Great American Novel, Write—the little Windows word processor that could—can probably handle most of your word processing needs. No, it doesn't have all those shiny, high-tech features you get with the top-of-the-line programs, but at least in Write you don't have to have a PhD to figure out how to do anything (and it doesn't cost a gazillion bucks, either). To prove it, this chapter checks out a few of Write's more interesting features: Find and Replace, the Ruler, headers and footers, OLE capabilities, and much more. So get Write fired up (select the **Write** icon from Program Manager's **Accessories** group), and let's get to it.

Finding and Replacing

In a small Write document, finding the text you want is usually not a problem. But as your documents grow, you can waste all kinds of time hunting down bits of text. To make this chore easier and faster, Write has a Find feature that'll do your searching dirty work for you. Here's how it works:

1. Pull down Write's Find menu and select the Find command. You'll see the Find dialog box, as shown here.

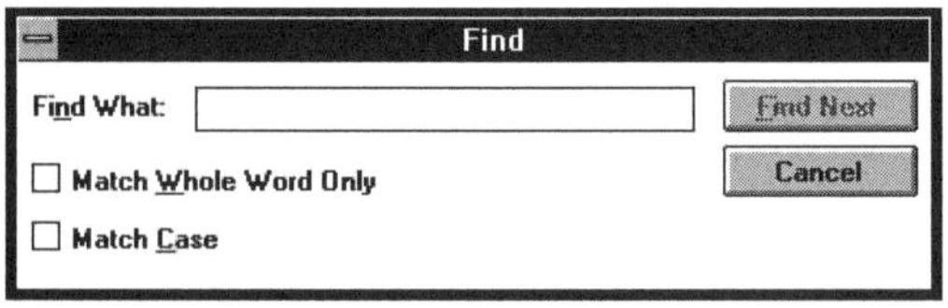

Use the Find dialog box to scope out text in a Write document.

2. In the Find What text box, enter the word or phrase you want to find. (Even though Write lets you enter up to 255 characters, I suggest you keep the search text short for best results.)
3. If you entered a single word as your search text, activate the Match Whole Word Only check box. If you keep this check box turned off, Write will find partial matches. For example, if you enter **bag** as the search text, Write will find not only the word *bag*, but also words that include the letters *bag*, such as *rutabaga* and *dirtbag*.
4. If you want Write to find a particular combination of uppercase and lowercase letters, check the Match Case check box. For example, if you search for **Bill** with this option turned on, Write will find only *Bill*, and not *bill* or *BILL*.
5. Select the Find Next button. Write highlights your text if the search is successful or displays a message telling you the text was not found. You have three ways to proceed:
   - If the search was successful and the highlighted text is the instance you want, select **Cancel** to return to the document.
   - If the search was successful and the highlighted text is not what you want, select Find Next to resume the search.
   - If Write didn't find your text, select **OK** to return to the Find dialog box. You can either repeat steps 2–5 to try again or select **Cancel** to bail out.

Instead of merely finding bits of text, you may need to find text and replace it with something else. This may not seem like a big deal for a word or two, but if you have to replace a dozen instances of *alright* with *all right*, the task suddenly seems a little more daunting. Not to worry, though. Write eats this kind of stuff for breakfast, and can handle even the most complex replacements in no time flat. The following steps spell everything out.

> **E-Z**
>
> If you need to redo your last search, don't bother with the Find dialog box. Instead, select the Find menu's Repeat Last Find command, or press **F3**.

1. Select the Find menu's Replace command. Write displays the Replace dialog box shown below.

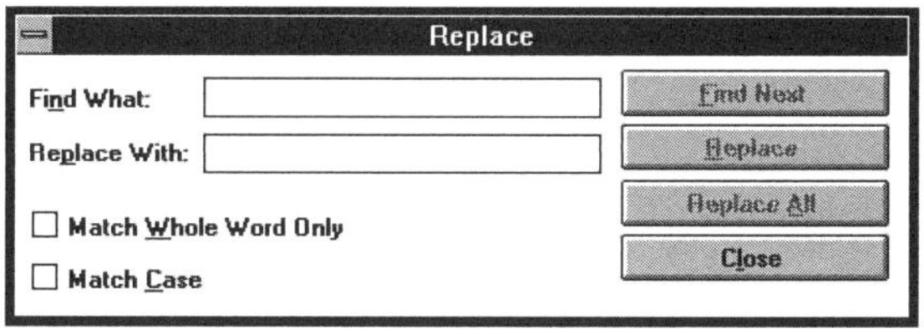

Use the Replace dialog box to seek out and replace Write text.

2. Use the Find What text box to enter the word or phrase you want to replace.
3. Use the Replace With text box to enter the replacement text.
4. As with Find, you can refine your search with the Match **W**hole Word Only and Match **C**ase check boxes.
5. Write gives you two methods to perform the replacement:
   - If you want Write to go crazy and just replace everything, select the Replace All button.
   - If you only want to replace some instances of the search text, select the Find Next button. When you see an instance of the search text you want to replace, select the **R**eplace button. You can keep repeating this until you're done.
6. When you're finished, select the Close button to return to the document.

Easy Formatting with Write's Ruler

In *The Complete Idiot's Guide to Windows*, I showed you how to do things like align paragraphs, set the line spacing, indent text, and set tab stops. These formatting tasks are crucial if you hope to create good-looking documents, so you'll probably use them regularly. The Ruler lets you perform all of the above-mentioned formatting chores with a simple click or two of the mouse.

To begin, you can display the Ruler by pulling down the **D**ocument menu and selecting the **R**uler On command. The Ruler appears below the menu bar, as shown here.

Write's Ruler puts many formatting tasks a mere mouse click away.

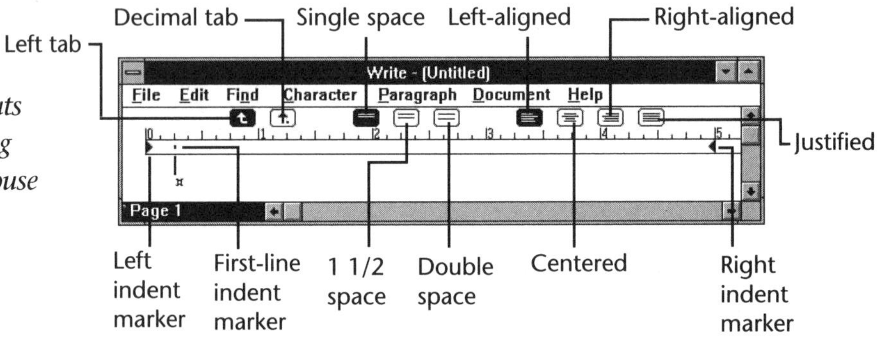

The numbers you see represent the distance, in inches, from the left margin. Here's a summary of what you can do once you've displayed the Ruler:

- To set a tab, click on either the left tab icon or the decimal tab icon, and then click inside the Ruler at the spot you want to set the tab. (Be sure to click in the white strip below the numbers.)
- To move a tab stop, drag it to the left or right. To remove a tab stop, drag it off the Ruler.
- To change the line spacing of the current paragraph, click on a line spacing icon in the Ruler (single space, 1 1/2 space, or double space).
- To align the current paragraph, click on one of the Ruler's alignment icons (left, centered, right, or justified).
- To indent the current paragraph, drag either the left or right indent marker. To indent only the first line of the paragraph, drag the first-line indent marker.

Dealing with Headers and Footers

Take a peek at the top of this page. Above the line that runs across the page you'll see a page number and some kind of text. (You'll see the chapter number and chapter title on odd-numbered pages, and the part number and part title on even-numbered pages.) These are called *headers*, and you can add them to your Write documents, just like the pros. (Well, not quite like the pros; Write only lets you add a single header in a document, so you can't do different headers for odd and even pages. It's no great loss, though.) You can also add a *footer* to a document. A footer is a section of text that appears at the bottom of every page.

The following steps show you how to add a header or footer to your Write documents.

1. Pull down the **D**ocument menu and select either the **H**eader or **F**ooter command. If you choose **H**eader, Write displays the HEADER window and the Page Header dialog box (see below). For a footer, you get the FOOTER window and the Page Footer dialog box.

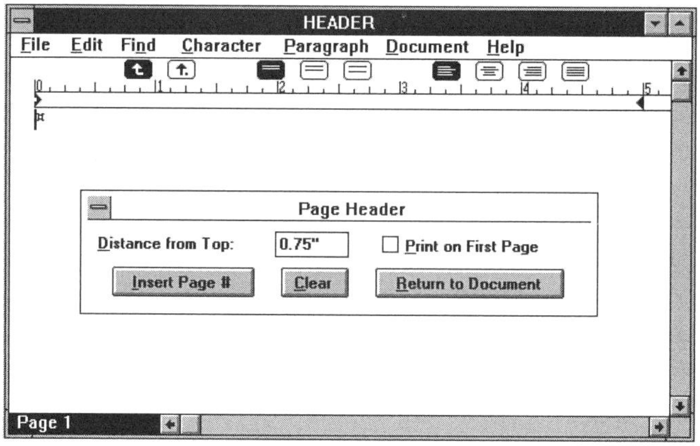

When you select the Header command, you get both the HEADER window and the Page Header dialog box.

2. Use the HEADER or FOOTER window to type in the text that you want to appear in the header or footer. You can add, edit, and format the text just like regular document text.
3. To work with the Page Header dialog box, click on it or press **Alt+F6**. You have the following options:

   Distance from Top (header) or **D**istance from Bottom (footer): The value in this text box controls how much space Write reserves either between the header and the top of the page or between the footer and the bottom of the page.

Print on First Page: Most manuscripts don't print a header or footer on the first page. If you prefer to ignore this convention, activate this check box.

Insert Page #: Select this button to insert a special page number code at the current cursor position.

Clear: Select this button to wipe out the existing header or footer so you can start with a clean slate.

4. When you're done, select the Return to Document button.

Don't panic if you don't see your header or footer when you get back to the document. It's still there, but Write isn't sophisticated enough to show it on-screen. You won't actually see the header or footer until you print the document.

Sprucing Up Write Documents with Pictures

Write supports object linking and embedding (OLE), so you can link or embed any kind of OLE data into a Write document. To do this, just follow the instructions we trudged through back in Chapter 8, "Understanding the Mysterious Snake Oil of OLE." When you use OLE, remember that if you want to link an object, it's faster to use the Edit menu's Paste Link command than to use Paste Special. In addition, you should make sure the cursor is positioned where you want the object to appear before you insert your object.

OOPS!

If you decide you don't want to size the picture after all, press **Esc** to cancel the operation.

Write works particularly well with graphic objects such as BMP files created with Paintbrush. Once you've pasted the picture, use the following techniques to work with it:

Selecting the picture To select your picture, either click on it or press the up and down arrow keys until it's highlighted.

Sizing the picture If you need to change the size of the picture, select it, and then select the Edit menu's Size Picture command. The mouse pointer changes to a square with a smaller square in the lower left corner (see below). Here's how you use this pointer to change the size:

- To change the width with your mouse, move the pointer so it rests on either the picture's left or right border, and then move the mouse to the left or right. To change the height, move the pointer so it rests on the picture's bottom border, and then move the mouse up or down. In either case, a gray line shows you what the new size will be (see below).

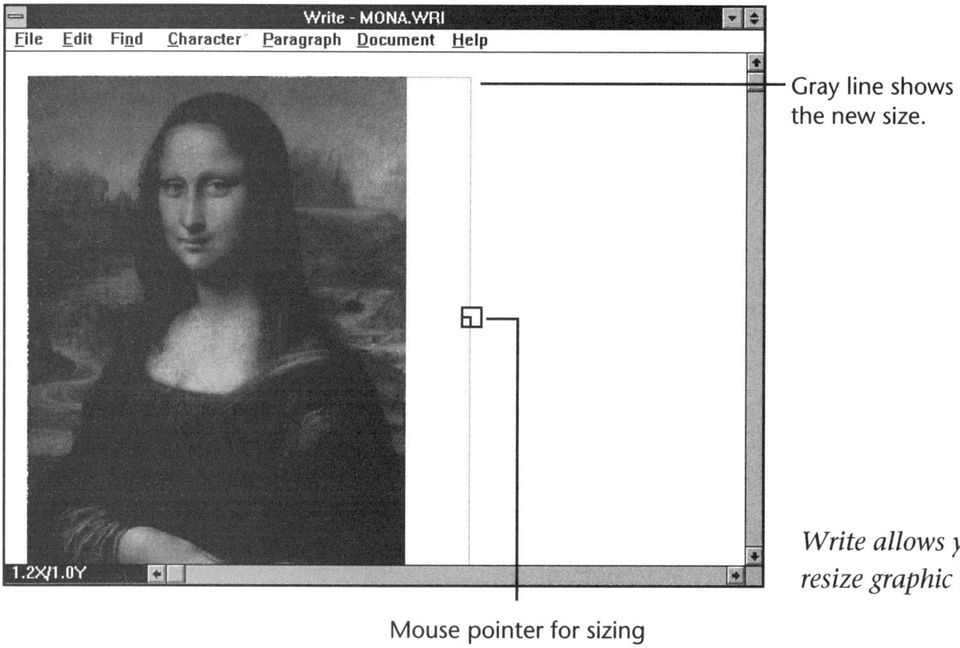

Write allows you to resize graphic objects.

- To change the width with your keyboard, press either left arrow (to select the left border) or right arrow (to select the right border), and then use left arrow or right arrow to adjust the border. To change the height, press down arrow, and then use up arrow or down arrow to adjust the border.

Moving the picture To move the picture to a new location, select it, and then select **Move Picture** from the **Edit** menu. Again, the mouse pointer changes to the square. Now either slide the mouse left or right to move the picture, or use the left and right arrow keys.

Exercises for the Anxious, Eager, and Adventurous

To finish our Write ruminations, I'll take you through three exercises that show off Write's versatility. Even if you're wedded to some other word processor for your writing, these tasks will prove that you don't have to write off Write completely.

For the Anxious: Printing Screen Shots

You've probably noticed your keyboard has a Print Screen key. If you used DOS applications before switching to Windows, you may remember that Print Screen's purpose in life was to take a picture of your screen and send it to your printer. This was useful for creating screen shots to include in manuals and training documents.

If you've tried pressing Print Screen in Windows, you were probably disappointed when nothing happened. That's not quite the case, however. Something did happen, but Windows prefers to keep such things to itself. What happened was that a picture of the screen was sent to the Clipboard, the storage location Windows normally reserves for cut and copied data. In a logical universe, we could just open the Clipboard Viewer and print the Clipboard's contents. Unfortunately, this is Windows we're dealing with, so logic isn't an option. That's right. There's no way to print directly from the Clipboard. Sigh.

> You can move the picture by selecting the Paragraph menu's Left, Centered, or Right commands.

All is not lost, however. Write rides to our rescue by making it a snap to print out screen shots. Here's the full procedure for capturing and printing screen shots:

1. Arrange your screen the way you want it.
2. If you want a shot of the entire screen, press **Print Screen**. If you only need a shot of the active window, press **Alt+Print Screen**.
3. Start Write.
4. Pull down the Edit menu and select the Paste command. Your screen picture appears in the Write document.

5. With your printer fired up and ready to go, pull down the **F**ile menu, select **P**rint, and select **OK**. Write prints the screen shot.

For the Eager: Turning Write into a Program Launcher

In Chapter 12, "Let's Do Launch: Interesting Ways to Start Applications," I showed you how to add a document icon in Program Manager that would start a program and load the document automatically. This is a great way to work, but Program Manager has two limitations that cramp this particular style:

- Your icon titles are limited to 40 characters. This is fine for application names, but it doesn't let you describe a document in detail.
- You can't "nest" one group inside another. For example, it would be handy to create a "Documents" group that included icons for other groups (for example, "Letters," "Spreadsheets," and so on).

This exercise shows you how to turn Write into a program launcher that doesn't have either of these limitations. As an example, I show you how to add an icon to Write that launches Notepad and loads the WIN.INI file. (The following steps assume you're familiar with the Object Packager doohickey. If you're not, this might be a good time to review the Object Packager stuff from Chapter 8, "Understanding the Mysterious Snake Oil of OLE.") Open a new Write document and then follow these steps:

1. Select the **E**dit menu's **I**nsert Object command. Write displays the Insert Object dialog box.
2. Select **Package** in the **O**bject Type list, and then select **OK**. The Object Packager window appears.
3. Pull down the **E**dit menu and select Co**m**mand Line. Object Packager displays the Command Line dialog box.
4. Enter the name of the file or program you want to launch and select **OK**. If the file isn't in the WINDOWS directory, be sure to include the appropriate drive and directory. For WIN.INI, you can just enter **WIN.INI**.
5. Select the Insert **I**con button, choose an icon from the Insert Icon dialog box, and then select **OK**. (Remember that you can get a better

choice of icons by typing **MORICONS.DLL** in the File Name text box and pressing **Enter**. For WIN.INI, you can use the Notepad icon by entering **NOTEPAD.EXE.**)

6. Select the **F**ile menu's Exit command and, when Object Packager asks if you want to update the Write document, select **Y**es. The icon appears inside the Write document.
7. Move the cursor below the icon and enter a description for the file. Since you're just typing text in Write, you have no practical limit on the length of the description. You can also format the description to your heart's content (something else you can't do easily in Program Manager).

> **E-Z**
>
> To have your fancy new program launcher available all the time, be sure to add an icon for it to Program Manager's Startup group.

8. Save the document, and repeat steps 1–7 to add other icons.

The picture below shows a Write document with several document icons. To start any of these documents, just double-click on the icon. Note, as well, that I've included an icon for another Write document (LETTERS.WRI). This file has its own icons, so it's easy to nest groups within groups. If you need to make changes to a package, select it, pull down the **E**dit menu, select Package **O**bject, and then select **E**dit Package.

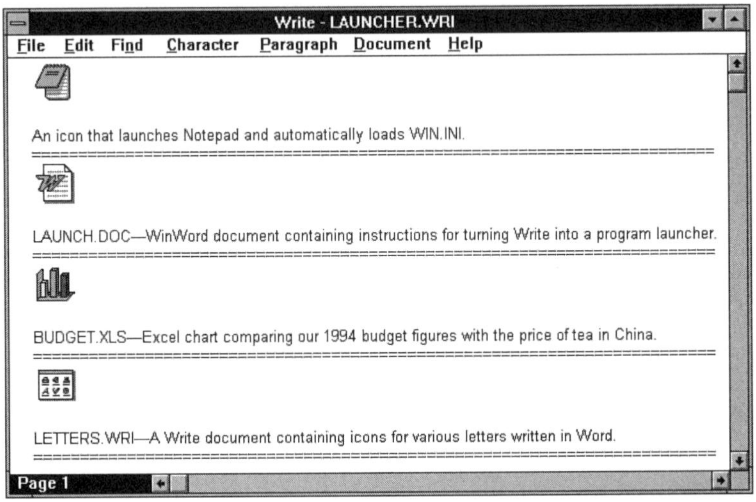

A Write file with icons that launch documents.

For the Adventurous: Using Write to Improve Notepad

For our final exercise, I'll show you one of Write's most amazing tricks: it can actually change the way other applications work! As an example, we'll use Write to fix one of Notepad's niggling little frustrations. As you may know, when you select Notepad's **O**pen command, the Open dialog box only shows files with the TXT extension. But there are all kinds of text files that don't have that extension: INI, BAT, DOC, etc. To open one of these files, you either have to type the correct file name, or you have to choose **All Files (*.*)** from the List Files of **T**ype box. In the following steps, we'll "fix" Notepad so it always shows every file in the Open dialog box. (Make sure Notepad isn't running before starting this procedure.)

1. In File Manager, highlight the file **NOTEPAD.EXE** in the WINDOWS directory, press **F8** to display the Copy dialog box, type **NOTEPAD.BAK**, and then select **OK**. This gives us a backup copy of NOTEPAD.EXE, just in case anything goes awry later in the steps.
2. In Write, select the **F**ile menu's **O**pen command, type **NOTEPAD.EXE**, and then select **OK**. Write asks whether you want to convert the file.
3. Select the **N**o Conversion button to open NOTEPAD.EXE in its native format. As you can see in the picture below, this is one weird-looking file.

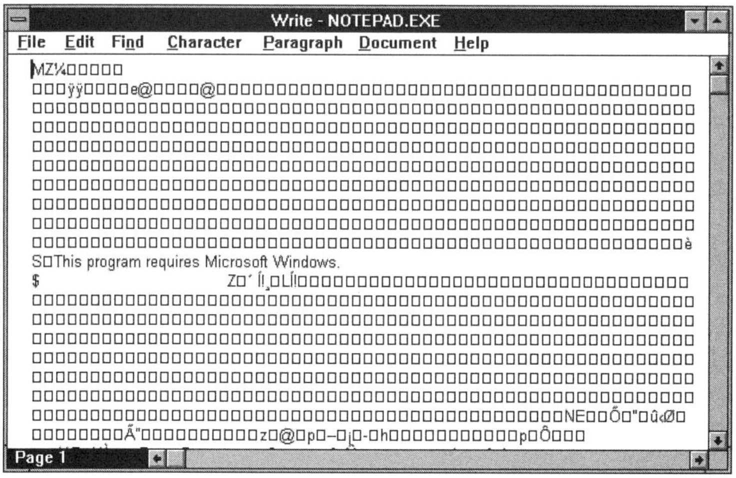

NOTEPAD.EXE appears to be written in some extraterrestrial language!

4. Pull down the **Find** menu and select the **Replace** command to display the Replace dialog box.
5. In the Find What text box, type ***.TXT**, and in the Replace With text box, type ***.*** *followed by two spaces*. When working in an EXE, it is absolutely crucial that you replace text with something that has exactly the same length.
6. Select the **Find Next** button *twice* to highlight the second occurrence of *.TXT.
7. Select the **Replace** button and select **Close**.
8. Exit Write and save your changes.
9. Start Notepad and select the **File** menu's **Open** command. Voilà! The Open dialog box now displays every file (see below).

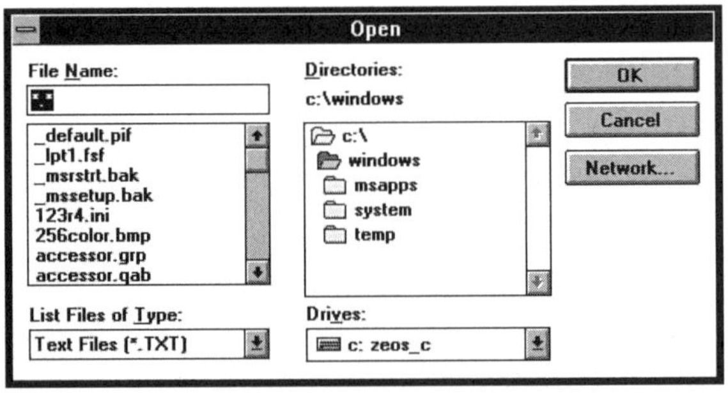

After you patch NOTEPAD.EXE, the Open dialog box displays every file.

The Least You Need to Know

This chapter showed you several tricks and techniques designed to improve your Write skills. Here's a rehash of the good bits:

- Use the Fi**n**d menu's **F**ind command to search for text in a Write document. If you want to search for and replace text, select the Fi**n**d menu's R**e**place command.
- You can use the Ruler to make your Write formatting chores a little less tiresome. To display it, pull down the **D**ocument menu and select **R**uler On.
- A header is text that appears at the top of each page, and a footer is text that appears at the bottom of each page. To add a header or footer to a Write document, pull down the **D**ocument menu and select either **H**eader or **F**ooter.
- Write's OLE capabilities make it easy to add pictures to your documents. Use the **E**dit menu's **S**ize Picture and **M**ove Picture commands to make changes to your pictures.

Chapter 15
A Master Class in Paintbrush

In This Chapter

- Zooming in for detail work
- Using the Pick and Scissors tools
- Working with Paintbrush's way-out special effects
- Controlling image attributes and editing colors
- A passel of Paintbrush perks that'll have your right brain singing for joy

For sheer, unadulterated, my-how-time-flies-when-you're-having-fun enjoyment, you can't beat Paintbrush. What's that? Drawing was never your strong suit. Don't worry about it. Even if you're no Michelangelo, there are still plenty of wild things Paintbrush can do to turn even the humblest drawing into a veritable masterpiece. In this chapter, we go beyond the basic shape-drawing skills we looked at in *The Complete Idiot's Guide to Windows* to cover Paintbrush's most powerful and most interesting features.

First, the 50¢ Paintbrush Tour

Just to make sure we're all painting on the same canvas, so to speak, let's begin with a quick trip around the Paintbrush screen. The picture below shows the basic Paintbrush window you get when you select the **Paintbrush** icon from Program Manager's **Accessories** group.

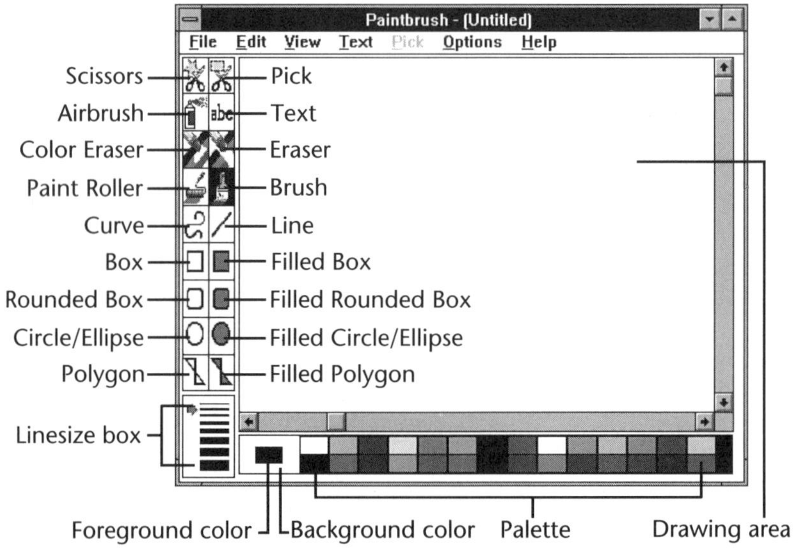

Yer basic Paintbrush window.

Here's a summary of the various features of the Paintbrush landscape:

Tools Paintbrush is full to bursting with no less than 18 tools you can use to create or work with your pictures. I'm going to assume you're familiar with each of these tools except the Scissors and Pick tools, which we'll get to later in this chapter.

Linesize box The line thickness you select from this box applies to the Brush, both erasers, the Airbrush spray, and the borders of the various lines and shapes.

Palette The boxes in the Palette represent the available colors you can use for your picture. In most cases, Paintbrush applies the foreground color to the borders of your shapes. If you're using one of the "filled" tools, however, the shape's border uses the background color, and the inside of the shape uses the foreground color. To select a new foreground color, click on one of the color rectangles in the Palette; to select a new background color, right-click on a color.

Drawing area This is where you draw and work with your objects.

Using Zoom In to Get the Small Picture

The biggest complaint most people have with Paintbrush is that it's just too hard to draw proper freehand lines using the Brush tool. The problem, of course, is that as a brush, the mouse makes a great sledgehammer. If you're having trouble getting any kind of fine control over your lines, join the club. Even expert mouse users have a difficult time making the pointer behave itself.

The usual result of all this mouse monkeying around is that your Paintbrush drawings end up with wayward lines sticking out all over the place. To help get rid of these strays and to whip your good lines into shape, Paintbrush has a Zoom In feature that can magnify a section of your drawing. This enlarged area makes it a breeze to do fine detail work. Here's how to use the Zoom In feature:

1. With your Paintbrush picture open, pull down the **V**iew menu and select the Zoom **I**n command (or press **Ctrl+N**). The mouse pointer changes to a rectangle, as shown in the picture below.

The Zoom In rectangle

After you select the Zoom In command, position the rectangle over the area you want to magnify.

2. Position the rectangle over the area you want to enlarge. If you're using a mouse, just drag the rectangle to the appropriate location; from the keyboard, use the arrow keys.

3. Click the mouse or press **Insert**. As shown below, Paintbrush magnifies the area inside the rectangle and displays the normal view of the enlarged area in the upper left corner. Each square you see represents a single pixel from the drawing.

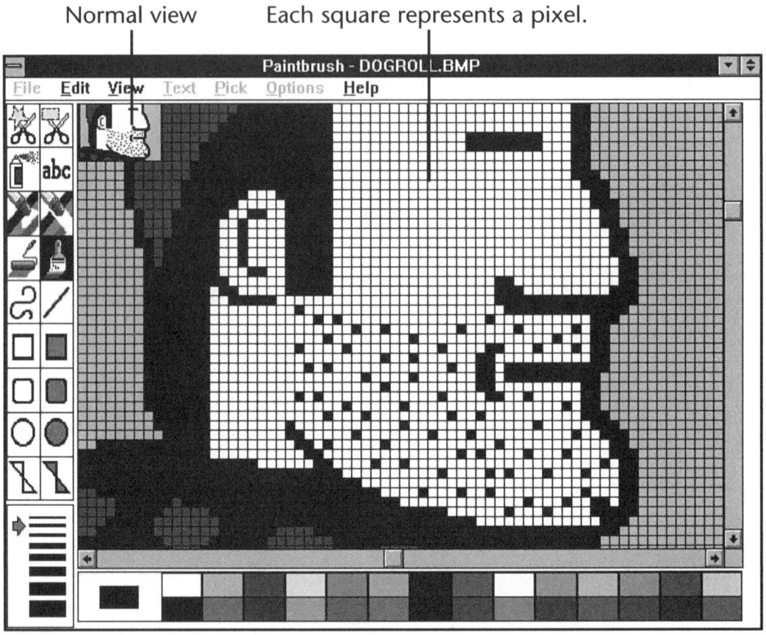

4. Use the Brush or Paint Roller to edit the individual pixels. With the Brush, you can use any of the following three techniques:

   - If you click on a pixel, Paintbrush applies the current foreground color.
   - If you right-click on a pixel, Paintbrush applies the current background color.
   - If you hold the left button (for the foreground color) or the right button (for the background color) and drag the mouse across the pixels, Paintbrush applies the appropriate color to all affected pixels.

5. When you're done, select the **V**iew menu's Zoom **O**ut command (or press **Ctrl+O**) to return to the regular view.

Selecting with the Scissors and Pick Tools

Paintbrush lets you select, or *cut out*, chunks of your pictures using the Scissors or Pick tools. (These chunks are called *cutouts*.) Why would you want to do such a thing? There are a few good reasons. For example, you can rearrange parts of your drawing. If something's not quite in the right place, it's a waste to erase it and start over. Instead, just cut it out and move it to the correct spot.

You can also use cutouts to make copies of existing objects in the drawing. Instead of reinventing the wheel each time you need a similar object, you can simply create one and make copies of it. And you can copy cutouts to the Clipboard and paste, link, or embed them into other documents.

In addition, you can apply some really far-out special effects to a cutout. For example, you can flip it, tilt it, shrink it, and more. And you can even save cutouts in their own file. Here are the steps to follow to cut out a piece of a picture:

> E-Z
>
> Paintbrush only lets you cut out what you can see in the drawing area. To cut out a larger area, first select the **V**iew menu's Zoom **O**ut command (or press **Ctrl+O**). This displays the entire picture in the drawing area.

1. If you want to cut out a rectangular area, select the Pick tool. If you want to cut out a freeform area, select the Scissors tool.
2. Move the mouse pointer into the drawing area (the pointer changes into a cross hair), and position it where you want your cutout to begin.
3. Hold down the left mouse button, drag the mouse until the cutout is the size and shape you want, and then release the button. (If you're using the Pick tool, you can make your cutout a square by holding down the **Shift** key while you drag the mouse.) Paintbrush displays a dashed line to show the boundaries of the cutout.

Amazing Things You Can Do with Cutouts

Now that you know how to produce cutouts, let's have some fun looking at the wide variety of ways you can play with them. Here's a review of the various cutout tricks you can use to impress your friends at parties:

Dragging-and-dropping a cutout. If you need to move a cutout or make one or more copies of a cutout, don't bother with the Cut, Copy, and Paste commands. You can move a cutout just by dragging it with your mouse and dropping it in the new location. To copy the cutout, hold down the **Ctrl** key while you drag it.

Creating sweeps. This one's a real crowd-pleaser! Hold down the **Shift** key, and then drag the cutout around the drawing area. Whoa! As you drag the mouse, Paintbrush leaves multiple copies of the cutout in its wake. For a slightly different effect, hold down **Shift** and try dragging the cutout by holding down the *right* mouse button. In this case, the copies Paintbrush makes are opaque (see the picture, below).

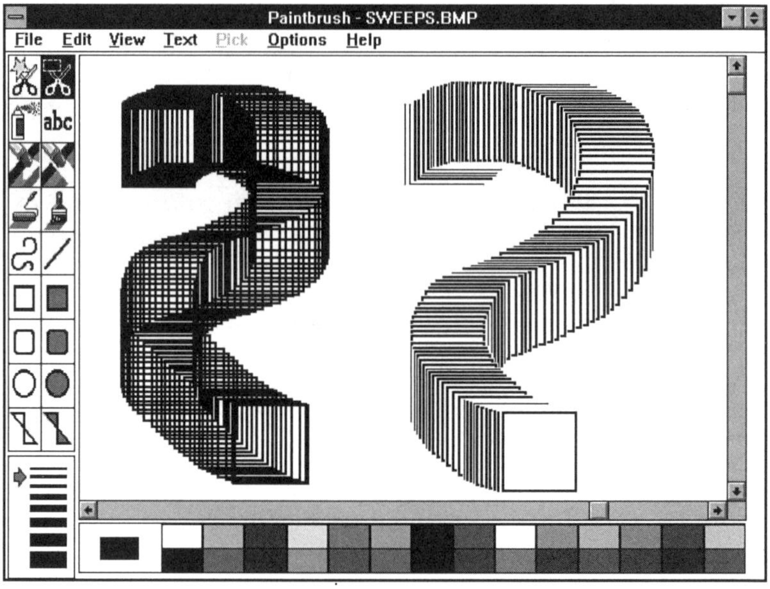

Sweeps created by holding down Shift and dragging a cutout with the left button (the left image) and the right button (the right image).

Saving a cutout to its own file. If you think you might need to use a cutout in other pictures, you can save it to its own file and then retrieve it when you need it. Pull down the Edit menu, select Copy To, enter a file name in the Copy To dialog box, and select **OK**. When you want to use the cutout, select the Edit menu's Paste From command, highlight the cutout file in the Paste From dialog box, and then select **OK**.

Flipping a cutout. You can flip a cutout either horizontally (so that left becomes right and vice-versa) or vertically (so that up becomes down and vice versa). All you do is pull down the Pick menu and select either the Flip Horizontal or Flip Vertical command.

Inverting a cutout's colors. *Inverting* colors means that black changes to white, white changes to black, and the other colors change to their complementary colors. To invert the colors in a cutout, select the Pick menu's Inverse command.

Shrinking and growing a cutout. If you need to scale a cutout to either a smaller or larger size, the Shrink + Grow command can do the job. Here's how it works:

1. Select the cutout.
2. You can either create the scaled version of the cutout and leave the original intact, or replace the original with the scaled version. To leave the original intact, make sure the Pick menu's Clear command is deactivated (it doesn't have a check mark beside it). If you prefer to replace the original, activate the Clear command.
3. Select the Pick menu's Shrink + Grow command.
4. Move the pointer to where you want the scaled version of the cutout to appear, hold down the left mouse button, and then drag the mouse. Paintbrush displays a dashed line that shows you what the cutout's new dimensions will be.
5. When the cutout is the size and shape you want, release the mouse button. Paintbrush redraws the cutout.
6. Select the Pick menu's Shrink + Grow command again to turn it off.

> **OOPS!**
>
> If you activate the Clear command, make sure the current background color is the same as the background color of the cutout. Why? Because Paintbrush fills in the original cutout area with the current background color.

Tilting a cutout. To display your cutouts at jaunty angles, Paintbrush provides a Tilt command. The following steps show you how to use it:

1. Select the cutout.
2. As with Shrink + Grow, either activate the Clear command to replace the original cutout, or deactivate Clear to keep the original as is.
3. Select Tilt from the Pick menu.
4. Move the pointer to where you want the tilted version of the cutout to appear, hold down the left mouse button, and then drag the mouse. Paintbrush displays a dashed line that shows you what the cutout's new angle will be.
5. When the cutout is the angle you want, release the mouse button. Paintbrush redraws the cutout.
6. Select the Tilt command again to turn it off.

The picture below shows examples of each of these effects.

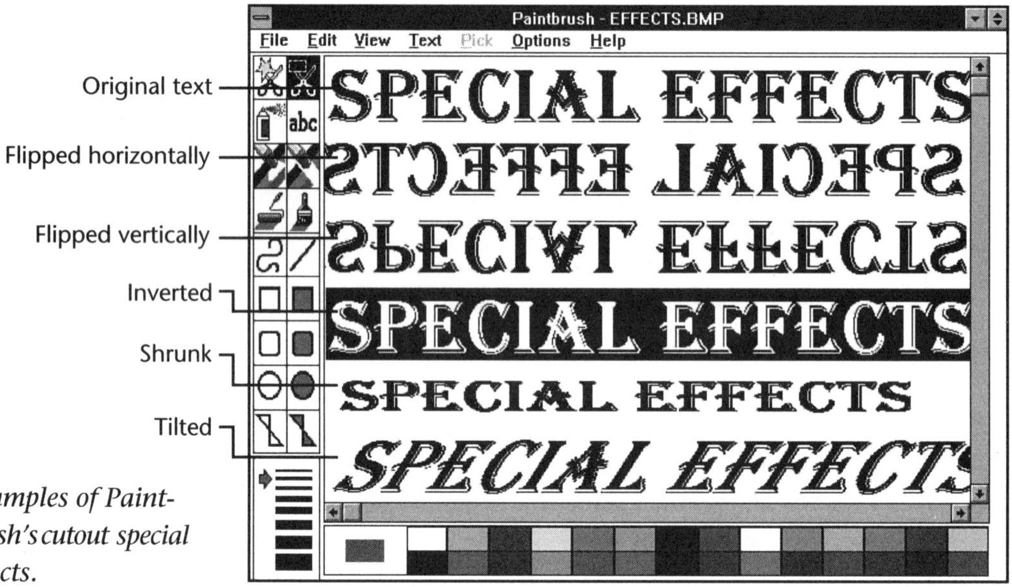

Examples of Paintbrush's cutout special effects.

Checking Out Paintbrush's Options

Paintbrush's Options menu features several commands that may come in handy for some of your work. Let's take a brief look at each of these commands to see what they can do:

Image Attributes   This command displays the Image Attributes dialog box (see below), which controls the size of your new pictures and whether or not they display colors. (You can't use this dialog box to change an existing picture.) The numbers displayed in the **Width** and **Height** text boxes use the measurement units selected in the Units group. (In this group, "pels" means "pixels.")

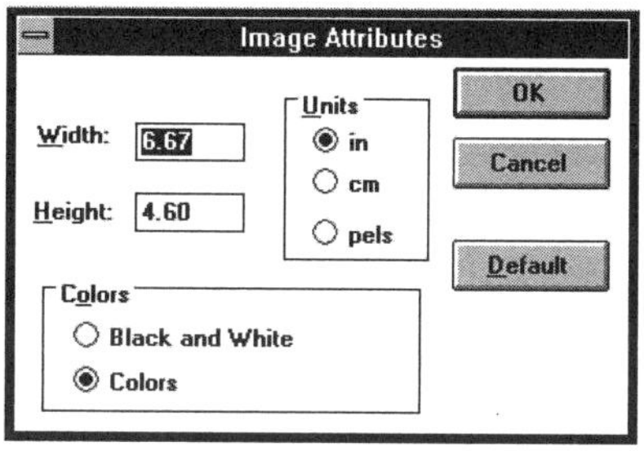

Use the Image Attributes dialog box to change the size of a picture and toggle colors on and off.

Brush Shapes   This command displays the Brush Shapes dialog box, which contains several different shapes you can use with the Brush tool for some interesting effects.

Edit Colors   If the Palette doesn't have a color you need, you can create the color yourself using this command. First, select the Palette color you want to replace. Then select this command and, in the Edit Colors dialog box that appears, use the **R**ed, **G**reen, and **B**lue scroll bars to mix the color you want.

Save Colors   If you've created some custom colors, use this command to save them to a Color Palette file. In the Save Colors As dialog box that appears, enter a file name (don't bother with an extension; Paintbrush will add .PAL automatically), and then select **OK**.

Get Colors   Once you've saved a Color Palette file, you can retrieve it using this command. When Paintbrush displays the Get Colors dialog box, choose a PAL file and select **OK**.

Omit Picture Format   After copying a Paintbrush image to the Clipboard, you may have trouble pasting it into some other applications. If so, select this command to force Paintbrush to copy a less complex image to the Clipboard.

Exercises for the Anxious, Eager, and Adventurous

Okay, it's time to put some of your newfound Paintbrush knowledge to work. The next few sections present some exercises that put Paintbrush through its paces.

For the Anxious: Easy Wallpaper

Way back in Chapter 2, "Dressing Windows for Success: Customization Fun," I told you that you could create your own Windows wallpapers by creating BMP files in Paintbrush and saving them in your WINDOWS directory. However, creating a picture large enough to cover the desktop is a daunting task even for the artists among us. If you like seeing different wallpapers, but you don't want to expend much energy to create them, there's an easy way to do it. The idea is that you'll cut out a piece of a Windows screen, save it to a BMP file, use this file as your wallpaper, and tile it to cover the entire desktop. Here are the steps to follow:

1. Arrange your screen so it contains some image you'd like to use for your wallpaper. For example, you might want to use one of Program Manager's icons.
2. Press the **Print Screen** key to save the screen to the Clipboard.
3. In Paintbrush, start a new file, pull down the **E**dit menu, and select the **P**aste command. Paintbrush pastes the screen shot.
4. Use the Pick tool to create a cutout of the image you want to use.
5. Select the **E**dit menu's C**o**py To command, enter a name in the Copy To dialog box (make sure the WINDOWS directory is selected, as well), and then select **OK**.
6. Now start Control Panel and select the **Desktop** icon.
7. In the Wallpaper group, use the **F**ile drop-down list to select the BMP file you just created, and then activate the **T**ile option.
8. Select **OK** and exit Control Panel. The cutout you stored in the BMP file appears tiled as the wallpaper. The following picture shows a wallpaper that uses the Character Map icon.

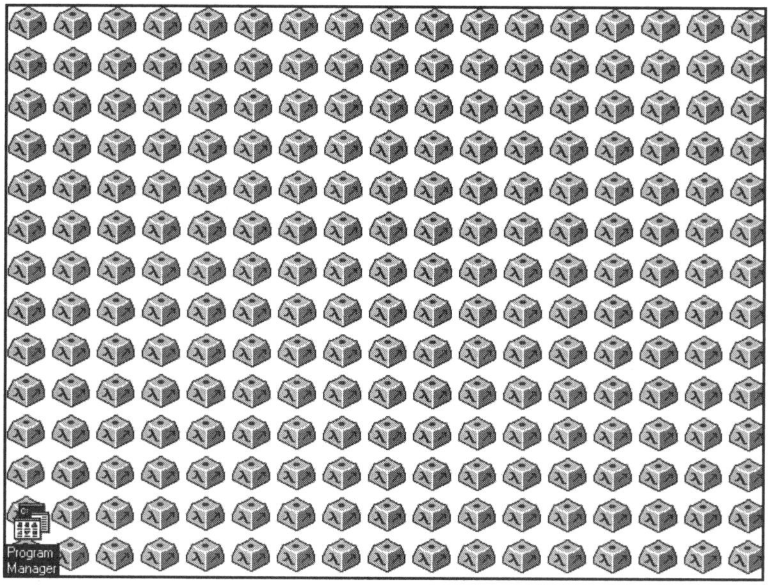

A wallpaper created from a cutout of the Character Map icon.

For the Eager: Adding Your Signature to Faxes

If you have a fax/modem, you know how convenient it is to just create a document and then fax it off to all and sundry without having to print out a hard copy. The only downside to this is that you have no way to sign your fax—until now that is. The following procedure shows you a way to grab your moniker electronically and include it at the bottom of all your faxes.

Note that the following steps assume you don't have access to a scanner. If you do have a scanner nearby, scan a document that contains your signature, and then skip to step 3.

1. First, scribble your signature on a piece of paper. Make sure you use a pen with good dark ink, or a felt marker. Pencil won't work.
2. Head to another fax machine and send the document to your computer. (You should, of course, have your fax software set up and ready to receive.)

3. Save the fax as a .PCX file, and then open the file in Paintbrush.
4. Make a cutout of your signature and use the Edit menu's Copy To command to save the cutout to its own .PCX file.

Now it's easy to add your signature into your word processor each time you want to send a document by fax. Just open the signature's .PCX file in Paintbrush, select the signature with the Pick tool, copy it to the Clipboard, and then paste it into the document.

For the Adventurous: Forcing Paintbrush to Save PCX Files

Paintbrush can view files from four different formats: BMP, PCX, DIB, and MSP. Of these four, however, it can only save images in PCX and BMP. Paintbrush defaults to the BMP format, but does it matter which of the two we use to save our files? It sure does. PCX files, you see, are much more efficient than their bloated BMP counterparts. For example, the DOGROLL.BMP file I was using earlier takes up a whopping 308,278 bytes. When I converted it to PCX format, it shrunk down to a tidy 42,406 bytes. That's a big savings! For other, more complex pictures, the reduction may only be 10% or 20%, but you probably save around 50% on average. The moral of this story: always save your work in PCX format. (The exception, of course, is when you're creating wallpaper, because Windows only looks for BMP files.)

If you're going to be working with lots of PCX files, it's a pain that Paintbrush's Open dialog box only shows BMP files by default. Chapter 14, "Improving Your Write Skills," included an "Exercise for the Adventurous" that showed you how to use Write to modify NOTEPAD.EXE. In this exercise, we'll use the same technique to make changes to PBRUSH.EXE, Paintbrush's executable file. In this case, we'll change Paintbrush so it always displays both BMP and PCX files in its Open dialog box.

1. First use File Manager to make the all-important backup copy of Paintbrush (in case things get messed up later) by copying PBRUSH.EXE (it's in your WINDOWS directory) to PBRUSH.BAK.

2. Start Write, select the File menu's Open command, type **PBRUSH.EXE**, and then select **OK**. A dialog box appears asking if you want to convert the file.
3. Select the No Conversion button. When PBRUSH.EXE opens, it'll look a lot like NOTEPAD.EXE.
4. Select Replace from the Find menu, type ***.DIB** in the Find What text box, type ***.PCX** in the Replace With text box, and then select the Replace All button.
5. Select Close, and then exit Write and save your changes.

When you start Paintbrush and select the File menu's Open command, you'll see both BMP and PCX files gracing the Open dialog box.

The Least You Need to Know

This chapter took you through various Paintbrush features that are practically guaranteed to bring out the artist in you. Here's a retrospective of what we dabbled with:

- For fine detail work, use the Zoom In command to magnify a section of your drawing.
- To create cutouts, use either the Scissors tool (for a freehand shape) or the Pick tool (for a rectangular shape).
- Once you've created a cutout, you can move or copy it, create sweeps, or perform special effects such as flipping, tilting, shrinking, and growing.
- With the commands in Paintbrush's Options menu, you can control things like the image attributes, the shape used for the Brush, the colors, and more.

Chapter 16
Working with a Net: Using Microsoft Backup

In This Chapter

- Starting and configuring Backup
- Selecting the files to back up
- Working with setup files
- Restoring backed up files
- Real world backup tips and strategies designed to help you sleep better at night

These days there's no shortage of books and magazine articles that list all the possible ways your hard disk can crash. Computer veterans seem to delight in telling war stories about hard disks giving up the ghost, rogue programs running amok, lightning storm meltdowns, and—more and more often—vicious, disk-trashing viruses that give no quarter to your valuable data.

All these stories lead us to one inescapable conclusion: protecting our data by making backup copies is definitely a good thing. Happily, DOS 6's Backup utility makes backing up a relatively painless procedure. You just select the files you want to back up, and the program copies them to floppy disks. If any disaster should occur, you can use Backup to restore your data from the disks. This chapter takes you through the basics.

Up an' at 'Em: Starting Backup

To start Backup, first open Program Manager's **Microsoft Tools** program group. Then double-click on the **Backup** icon (or highlight the icon and press **Enter**). You can also use File Manager to start Backup. Just pull down the Tools menu and select the **B**ackup command.

If you're starting Backup for the first time, a dialog box appears on-screen to ask whether you want to "automatically configure" the program. Select **Y**es to perform the configuration (see the next section).

The Configuration Rigmarole

To make sure your backups are reliable, the Backup program configures itself to your system. This process is a bit of a pain, but it's worth the extra peace of mind. (If you selected **N**o when you were asked about performing the configuration, you can still change your mind. In the Backup window, select the Co**n**figure button and then select the A**u**to Floppy Configure button.)

Backup first asks you to remove any disks you may have in your computer's disk drives. When you're ready, select **OK**, and the program displays the Compatibility Test dialog box. (If you don't see this dialog box, select the Com**p**atibility Test button in the Configure screen.)

This test is just a practice backup that will be used to make sure your data can be backed up and restored without mishap. Use the **D**rive To Test drop-down list to select the disk drive you'll be using to make backup disks. It's best to select the disk drive with the highest capacity because you can fit more data on disks that use that drive—which means the backup process will use fewer disks, and the whole ordeal will be over faster. Select the **Start** button to perform the test.

Backup then displays a long-winded message telling you not to use the disk drive while the backup and restore operations are in progress. Duh. Grab a couple of floppy disks that contain no useful data (Backup will overwrite any existing files, so be sure the disks contain only expendable data), and insert one of them in the disk drive you selected earlier. When you're ready to go, select **OK**.

If the disk contains data, Backup displays a partial list of the files. If you want to overwrite the files, select the **O**verwrite button. If you don't want to use this disk after all, swap another disk into the drive and select the **R**etry button.

Backup then starts copying files to the floppy disk. When the disk is full, you'll be prompted to insert the second disk. Remove the first disk, place the second disk in the drive, and then select **OK** if necessary. (If Backup detects files on the new disk, you'll have to go through the same overwrite/retry hassle.)

When the second disk is done, Backup lets you know and asks you to reinsert the first disk. The program then attempts to restore the files it backed up. Insert the first disk and select **OK**. As you've probably guessed, when the first disk is done, you'll be asked to reinsert the second disk. (Don't worry, we're almost done.) Insert the disk and select **OK** if necessary.

After a few seconds, Backup reports that the "Compare phase" of the compatibility test is done. Select **OK**. Yet another dialog box appears (yes, this *is* getting ridiculous!) to tell you that you can now safely perform your backups. Hallelujah! (Didn't someone say this was supposed to be an "automatic" configuration? Sheesh!) For the last time, select **OK** to return to the Backup window. Select the **B**ackup button to display the Backup screen (see below).

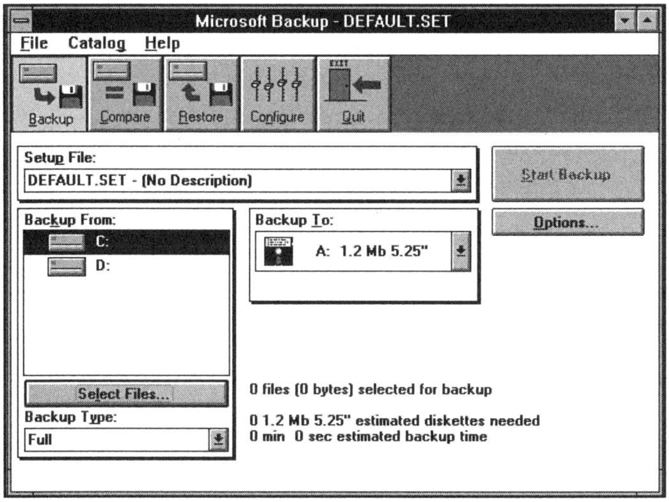

Use the Backup screen to select the files to back up and the floppy disk to use for the backup.

Preparing to Back Up

Before you can perform a backup, you need to follow these steps to get things ready:

1. Highlight your hard disk in the Backup From list (you don't have to do anything if the list only displays one drive).
2. Choose the Select Files button and select the files you want to back up from the Select Backup Files window (this is explained in the section called "Selecting the Files to Back Up").
3. In the Backup To drop-down list, select the drive you'll be using for the backup (you should select the same drive you used earlier in the configuration). If you want to back up to another hard drive or to a directory on the current hard drive, select **MS-DOS Path** and enter the drive and directory in the text box that appears below the Backup To list.
4. In the Backup Type drop-down list, choose a backup type. Select Full to back up all the files you selected in step 2. Select Incremental to back up only those files that have changed since the last time you did a full or differential backup. Or select Differential to back up only those files that have changed since the last full backup.

Backing Up Is Hard to Do

Before you get down to business, you need to ask yourself which files you want to include in the backup. Your first inclination might be to include every file just to be safe. The problem with this approach is that even a small hard disk contains enough data to fill a couple of dozen floppies. Believe me, shuffling that many disks in and out of your machine every time you do a backup will get old *really* fast. Instead, you need to take a "real-world" approach to backups, as explained in the following paragraphs.

The problem with a full backup is that it includes all your program files (the ones that run your applications). Presumably, however, you have these files on disk somewhere, so why include them in a backup? If worst comes to worst, you can always re-install your programs. If you're going to leave out your program files, however, make backup copies of your program disks. You only have to do it once and you probably only have to do it for your most important programs.

All of the energy you put into backing up should go toward protecting your data files because, unlike your programs, these are usually irreplaceable. To make life easier, create separate subdirectories to hold only your data. For example, if you use Word for Windows, create a subdirectory of your main WINWORD directory called DOCS to hold your documents.

Take advantage of the Incremental backup type to do incremental backups. Remember, an incremental backup only looks for those files that you've modified since the last full or differential backup, so this can really cut down on the number of files involved.

Your overall backup strategy might look something like this:

1. Perform a full backup of all your data once a month or so.
2. If you do most of your work in one or two programs, do a full backup of these programs' data directories every week or two.
3. Do an incremental backup of modified files every couple of days (although you might consider backing up really important stuff every day).

If, after all this weeding out process, you still have a few dozen megabytes or more to back up, forget floppies altogether and invest in a tape drive. They're a little pricey, but they can hold hundreds of megabytes, and they do it all while you're doing lunch.

Selecting the Files to Back Up

When you click on the Select Files button, Backup displays the Select Backup Files window, as shown in the following figure. You use this window to include and exclude files from the selection. You can select files individually or in a group.

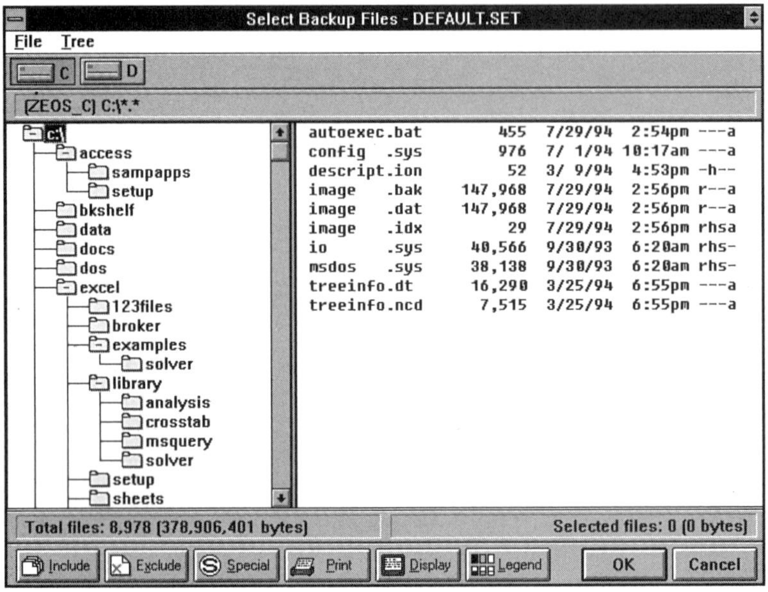

Use the Select Backup Files screen to select the files you want to include in your backup.

To include an individual file, first use the left side of the window to select a directory. (You can either click on the directory or use the up and down arrow keys.) Then, on the right side of the window, double-click on the file you want to include. (From the keyboard, press **Tab** to move to the right side, use the up and down arrows to highlight the file, and then press the **Spacebar**.)

To select a group of files, highlight the directory containing the files, and then select the Include button. This displays the Include/Exclude Files dialog box. If you want to include every file in the directory, select the Add button and select **OK**. More likely, you'll only want to include files with certain extensions (i.e., your data files). For example, if you're in your word processor directory and all your documents use the DOC extension, you'd enter ***.doc** in the File text box. Similarly, you might use ***.xls** or ***.wks** for your spreadsheet files, ***.wri** for your Write files, ***.bmp** for your Paintbrush files, and so on. Select Add and select **OK** to return to the Select Backup Files window.

Once you've selected all your data files, select **OK** to return to the Backup window.

Doing the Backup Thing

Well, at long last we're just about ready to roll. Here are the steps to follow to back up your data:

1. Gather the appropriate number of floppy disks for the backup (the Backup screen tells you approximately how many you'll need), and place one of the disks in the drive. Again, Backup will overwrite any files on the disk so make sure it contains no valuable info.
2. Select the **S**tart Backup button. Backup displays a message about not accessing the drive during the backup. (I'd recommend activating the **D**isable this message check box so you won't have to read this missive again.) Select **OK** to continue.
3. If the disk contains data, Backup displays a warning. Select **O**verwrite or **R**etry, as appropriate. The Backup Progress window that appears lets you keep track of the backup.
4. Depending on the number and size of the files you selected, Backup will occasionally prompt you to enter more disks. Wait until the drive light goes out, insert the new disk, and select **OK** if necessary. When you're done with a disk, you should label it for future reference (for example, Backup Disk #1).

Using Backup's Setup Files

Setup files are one of the most powerful features of Microsoft Backup. Setup files "remember" things like the files you selected, the backup type, the floppy drive used for the backup, and whatever other options you've chosen. In the future, then, all you have to do is select the appropriate setup file, and Backup configures everything automatically.

To create a setup file, first get Microsoft Backup set up the way you want (file selections, backup type, and so on), and then select the Save Setup **A**s option from the **F**ile menu. In the dialog box that appears, use the File **N**ame box to enter an eight-character file name. If you also want to enter a description of the setup (it's probably a good idea), use the Description box. Now just select the **OK** button, and you're done.

Anytime you need to use a setup file, use the Setu**p** File list to select the one you want.

Fine-Tuning Microsoft Backup

If you select the Options button in the Backup window, you'll see the Backup Options dialog box, shown below. Most of these options have some effect on either the speed of the program or the security of the backed-up data. By turning on some options and turning off others, you can fine-tune Backup to work the way you're most comfortable.

When choosing your options, you need to keep in mind that you're dealing with a zero-sum game. You can make Backup perform faster, but usually at the cost of some security. Conversely, the more secure you make your data, the slower the program becomes. Which route you choose depends on how much patience you have and how good your nerves are.

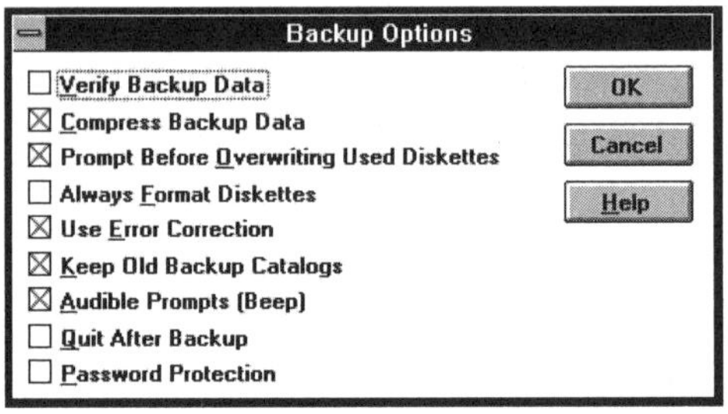

Use the Backup Options dialog box to control how Backup backs up your data.

Going for Speed

For the Type-A personalities in the crowd, here are some tips to make Microsoft Backup faster:

- Turn off the Verify Backup Data option. Data verification rereads the data written to the disk and compares it to the original files, which can really slow things down. Turning off Verify Backup Data is less of a risk if you keep it on the first time you use a disk (or if you're using really old disks, which is never a good idea). The program alerts you if the disk contains any bad sectors.
- Activate the Compress Backup Data check box. This saves time not only by speeding up the program, but by shrinking the data so that it can fit on fewer disks.

TECHNO NERD TEACHES...

Activating Compress Backup Data also speeds up Backup by switching to a sophisticated algorithm that tries to steal processor time between the moments it's reading data from the hard disk and writing it to the floppy. (You can tell this is going on when you see both the hard disk light and the floppy drive light on at the same time.)

- Turn off the Prompt Before Overwriting Used Diskettes check box. If the disk you insert contains any data, Backup warns you that it will destroy any information on the previously used disk. You don't need this convenience if you're recycling your backup disks.
- Be sure the Always Format Diskettes option is deactivated. If you're backing up to used disks, this option really slows you down because it formats every disk you use.
- Turn off the Use Error Correction feature. Error Correction writes information to a disk that lets you restore files from the disk if it becomes damaged. These disk writes themselves take only a marginal amount of time, but they use up valuable disk space (13% of a 1.2MB disk; 11% of a 1.44MB disk).
- Use high-density disks (especially 1.44MB, if possible). Not only do these disks hold more data (which means you need fewer disks), but files can be written to high-density disks faster than they can to the low-density variety.

Going for Safety

For paranoid types, here are a few suggestions for maximizing the security of your data:

- Turn on the Verify Backup Data option. This is an option that leaves nothing to chance. Each hunk of data written to the floppy disk is reread and carefully compared to the original. This lets Backup detect defective floppies and data transfer errors, but it basically doubles the backup time.

- Turn on the Always Format Diskettes option. For the truly paranoid, this option is a safeguard against writing data to a disk that was formatted on a drive with its heads out of alignment.
- Select the Use Error Correction option. This option saves information on each backup disk that can be used to restore your files should the disk become damaged.

Backup Dos and Don'ts

Here are a few more hints and suggestions to make backing up easier and safer:

- Do run ScanDisk before a major backup to look for any problems. (See Chapter 20, "An Ounce of Prevention: Avoiding Trouble," for the lowdown on using ScanDisk.)
- Do set up a backup strategy and stick to it. Otherwise, you'll fall victim to one of computerdom's strictest laws: hard disks only crash when they have priceless, irreplaceable data that isn't backed up.
- Do use setup files to configure the program quickly.
- Do have your pet spayed or neutered.
- Don't use 5.25-inch disks unless you have to. With high-density 3.5-inch disks, you not only get a little more data on each disk, you also get the added safety of a sturdy case.
- Don't keep all your backup disks in one place. If a thief happens upon them, you'll be out of luck. Some folks go as far as keeping a copy in an offsite location, such as a safety deposit box.
- Don't use low-priced, no-name disks for your backups. Stick with high-quality disks, and you'll sleep better at night.
- Don't be lazy. Back up your files now!

Restoring Your Data

If disaster should occur, you'll need to restore your data from the backups. Here are the steps to follow:

1. Select the Restore button to display the Restore screen shown in the following figure.

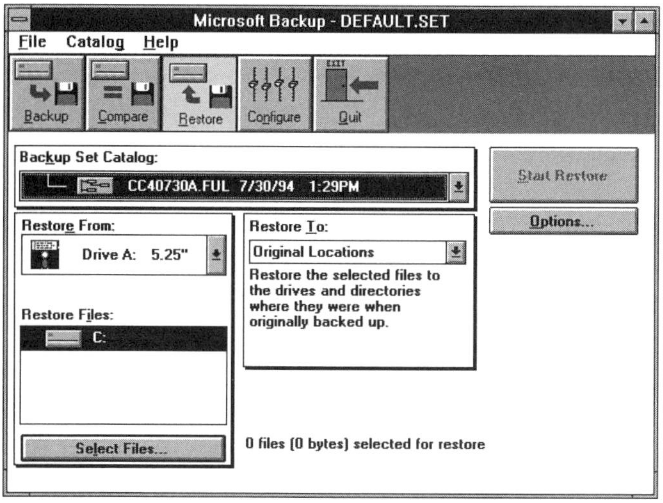

Use the Restore screen to select the files you want to restore.

2. Use the Backup Set Catalog drop-down list to select the appropriate backup catalog. A catalog is just a list of the files you included in your backup. How do you know which catalog is the "appropriate" one? Backup gives you three clues: the catalog's extension tells you what kind of backup was performed (.FUL for Full, .INC for Incremental, and .DIF for Differential); the date tells you what date the backup was performed; the time tells you when the backup was performed.

3. Choose the Select Files button and select the files you want to restore (this is the same as selecting files for a backup).

4. If necessary, use the Restore From list to select the drive containing the backup disk. Also, use the Restore To list to select where you want Backup to restore the files. You'll normally select **Original Locations**, but you can also choose **Alternate Drives** or **Alternate Directories**. For the latter two, Backup will ask you where you want the files restored once you start the restoration process.

5. Select the Start Restore button. If a message appears warning you about accessing the floppy drive during the restore, select **OK** to continue. After a few seconds, Backup prompts you to enter one of the disks from your backup (this is why you need to label your disks).

6. Insert the disk and select **OK**. Backup starts the restoration. You may be prompted to insert one or more other disks from the backup set.

Exiting Backup

When you're done with Backup, you can use either of the following methods to exit the program and return to Program Manager:

- Pull down the **F**ile menu and select the E**x**it command.
- Select the **Q**uit button.

In the Exit Backup dialog box that appears, select **OK**.

The Least You Need to Know

This chapter showed you how to use Microsoft Backup to achieve the peace of mind that comes when you know your precious data is safe and sound. Here's a condensed version of the important stuff:

- To start Microsoft Backup, open Program Manager's **Microsoft Tools** group and select the **Microsoft Backup** icon.
- If you're starting Backup for the first time, be sure to perform the configuration so you know your backups will be reliable.
- To save time, back up only your data, use the highest capacity disks you can find, and take advantage of the Incremental backup type.
- To select the files to back up, choose the Se**l**ect Files button, and then use the Select Backup Files window to highlight the files you want included.
- To run the backup, select the **S**tart backup button and follow the on-screen prompts.
- If you need to restore some backed up files, select the **R**estore button, select a catalog and the files, and then select **S**tart Restore.

Chapter 17
Getting Wired with Terminal

In This Chapter

- Making voice calls from Terminal
- Setting up your modem
- Dialing online services
- Transferring files to and from online services
- An example session with a real bulletin board
- Your personal on-ramp to the information superhighway

As you've no doubt figured out by now, computer nerds thrive on jargon and buzzwords. These terms range from the useful (such as *multimedia* and *drag-and-drop*) to the downright silly (*GUI* and *boot* come to mind). Fortunately, most jargon never makes it past the narrow confines of each nerd's subspecialty (which means the rest don't have to know about scary-sounding things like *TCP/IP* and *client-server*).

Occasionally, however, the odd buzzword makes it into the mainstream where, tragically, it's quickly trampled to death from media overkill. (I call it the "cachet-to-cliché" syndrome.) The most spectacular example of this was the phrase "user friendly" that appeared *ad nauseum* a few years back.

The current champ in the overused-phrase category is "information superhighway." Heck, the thing doesn't even exist yet, and we're already sick of hearing about it!

But just as "user friendly" was a good idea before it was knocked silly (after all, who'd want to use something that was "user hostile"?), so too is the information superhighway a good idea obscured by hype. In this chapter, we'll ignore the hype, and I'll show you how to use Windows' Terminal accessory to tap into the existing services (such as bulletin board systems and large-scale data marketplaces such as CompuServe) that are the precursors of the info autobahn.

TECHNO NERD TEACHES...

To use Terminal, you need to have a modem attached to one of your computer's serial ports, and you need a phone line attached to the modem. Confused already? Hey, it can happen. For fast relief, I'd suggest you pick up a copy of *The Complete Idiot's Guide to Modems and Online Services* by Sherry Kinkoph. It's coming to your local bookstore soon.

Starting Terminal

Starting Terminal is as easy as starting any other accessory: in Program Manager, open the **Accessories** group and double-click the **Terminal** icon. If Terminal asks you to select a default serial port, select the port your modem is attached to and then select **OK**. When Terminal loads, you'll see the window shown below. Not much to look at, is it? Well, that's in keeping with Terminal's spartan nature. This is a real bare-bones communications program that lacks most of the nice features you get in commercial applications (but, hey, whaddya want for nothing?).

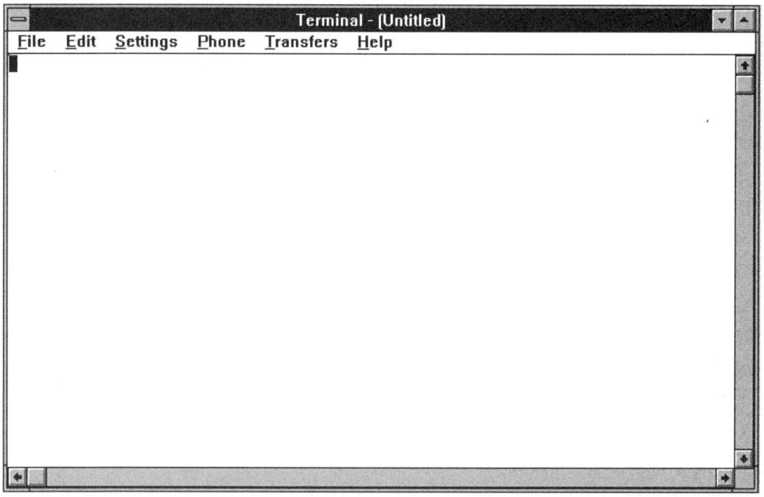

The Terminal window.

The Simplest Case: Dialing a Voice Call

Although you'll normally use Terminal to connect your modem to another modem in some far-flung corner of the world, you can also use it simply to dial your phone for a voice call. This section takes you through this simplest case before we move on to the more complex world of modem-to-modem communications. (For a more convenient way to dial voice calls, check out Cardfile's AutoDial feature.)

Entering a Phone Number

The first thing you need to do is tell Terminal which phone number you want to dial. You do this by pulling down the **S**ettings menu and selecting the Phone **N**umber command. You'll see the Phone Number dialog box, shown in the next figure. In the **D**ial text box, type the phone number, and then press **Enter** (you can ignore the other controls in this dialog box). Here are a few points to keep in mind when entering a phone number:

- If the number is long distance, be sure to enter both the country code and the area code.
- You can enter dashes and parentheses to make the number more readable, but Terminal ignores them.
- If you need to dial 9 to get an outside line, enter a 9 and a comma (,) before the phone number. The comma tells the modem to pause for two seconds before dialing the number, which should be enough time to get the outside line; if not, enter a second comma to pause for four seconds. For example, the following entry dials 9, pauses for two seconds, and then dials a long distance number:

  9,1-123-555-1234

Use the Phone Number dialog box to enter the phone number you want Terminal to dial.

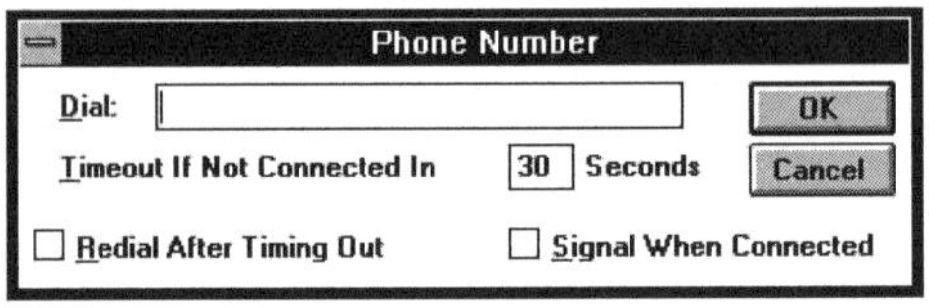

Dialing the Phone

Once you've entered the number, you're ready to dial. Before you proceed, you'll need to check a few things. Make sure that your modem is turned on and that the modem cable is attached to a serial port. Then verify that a phone line is attached to the modem, and see that you have a phone nearby that uses the same line.

To dial the phone, follow these steps:

1. Select the **Dial** command from the **Phone** menu. A dialog box appears showing you what phone number Terminal is dialing.
2. Immediately pick up the phone's receiver.
3. When the modem finishes dialing, press **Enter** or **Esc** to remove the dialog box (this hands control of the call over to the phone). At this point, the call becomes a regular voice call.

If you're getting busy signals, constant redialing can quickly become a pain. Why not let Terminal do the dirty work for you? Select the Phone

Number command from the **S**ettings menu and, in the Phone Number dialog box, activate the **R**edial After Timing Out check box. Now, when you dial, you'll have two choices. If you hear the other phone ringing, press **Enter** or **Esc** to remove the Terminal dialog box, as usual. If you hear a busy signal, hang up the receiver, but don't press **Enter** or **Esc**. Terminal will count down to 0 and then automatically redial.

> **TECHNO NERD TEACHES...**
>
> Whenever you dial in Terminal, you'll see some incomprehensible letters and numbers appear inside the Terminal window. These hieroglyphics are commands that Terminal sends to your modem. For example, when you dial, you usually see a command that begins with ATDT and ends with the phone number. The AT part is short for ATtention; it acts as a sort of "Ahem!" command. The DT stands for Dial Tone, and it tells the modem to get a dial tone before dialing the number. The line after each of these AT commands is the modem's response (such as "OK"). Happily, you can ignore all this stuff.

Modem-to-Modem Missives

Of course, you didn't spend your hard-earned money on a modem just so you could dial up your friends and family. For real computer communications kicks, you need to go "online" and connect to another modem. The rest of this chapter shows you how to do just that. You'll learn how to prepare Terminal for the ordeal to come, how to log on, how to receive and send files, and then how to hang up when you're done. As a hands-on example, I'll show you how to connect to the Microsoft Download Service BBS (bulletin-board service) and how to download a file to your computer.

Getting Terminal Ready for Action

We now turn to the "Tower of Babel" problem in modem communications. Modems, you see, have the darnedest time talking to each other. Even the simplest exchange requires jumping through a few bizarre and hopelessly technical hoops. The problem isn't that each modem speaks a

> **SPEAK LIKE A GEEK**
>
> In modem-speak, **downloading** means to transfer a file from another computer to your computer. **Uploading** is, not surprisingly, the opposite: it means to transfer a file from your computer to another computer. Terminal, in a rare moment of Windows clarity, uses the terms *receive* (instead of download) and *send* (instead of upload).

different "language," but that all modems can speak many different dialects of the same language. These dialects are called "communications settings," and they're critical if you hope to get anywhere with this stuff.

The basic idea is that the settings your modem uses must be identical to those used by the remote modem. If they're different, chaos reigns, and communication is usually impossible. How do you know which settings the other modem uses? That's a good question! Many BBS operators and information services have a voice line you can call to ask about the proper settings. Failing that, there are a couple of common settings you can try.

To set the communications settings, pull down the **S**ettings menu and select the **C**ommunications command. You'll see the Communications dialog box, shown next. My, doesn't that look like fun! Here's the bare minimum you need to know about this gobbledygook:

Baud Rate: This is the rate at which data will be transferred between the two modems (the higher the better). Most modems today operate at 2400 baud, but 9600 baud modems are becoming the standard.

Data Bits: In the vast majority of cases, you'll choose either 7 or 8 in this section.

Parity: Here, the usual settings are either **None** or **Even**. If you select 8 data bits, you must select **None** (Terminal does this for you automatically).

Stop Bits: This is almost always set to 1.

C**o**nnector: This is the serial port your modem is connected to.

Here are the two setups that will work 99% of the time:

- 2400 baud, 8 data bits, no parity, 1 stop bit (this is usually abbreviated as 2400,8,N,1). We'll be using this setup to dial in to the Microsoft Download Service.

- 2400 baud, 7 data bits, even parity, 1 stop bit (this is usually abbreviated as 2400,7,E,1).

Once you've entered your settings, select **OK** to return to the Terminal window.

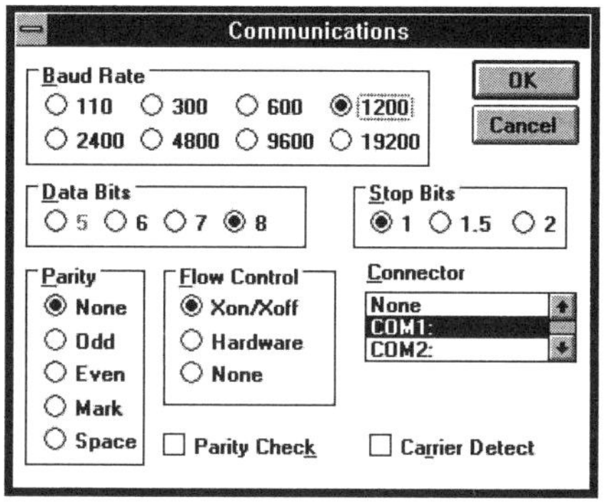

The Communications dialog box: a finalist for the Scariest-Looking Dialog Box Award.

The File Transfer Thing

Depending on which service you call, there are all kinds of fun things you can do online. For example, you can have "chats" with other people who have dialed in to the same service, send electronic mail, or look up information in one or more of the service's databases. Or you can send a file to the service, or receive a file from the service, just to name a few.

The steps you use to perform the first three example actions will vary from service to service. Most BBSs have an online help system you can use to find out what the heck you're supposed to do next. If you need to receive a file from the service (or, more rarely, send one of your own files to the service), you'll generally need to slog through the following steps:

1. Move to the appropriate file transfer area. All BBSs have different sections you can move in and out of. For example, there might be sections for browsing information, getting help, leaving messages, and so on. You'll usually get a menu of choices; look for a menu item such as Download (if you're receiving), Upload (if you're sending), or Files.

2. Tell the service you want to receive or send a file (how you do this will depend on the service). You'll be asked to enter the name of the file. If you're receiving a file and you're not sure of the name, most services allow you to browse through their files to find the one you want.
3. You'll also be asked which "transfer protocol" you want to use. This isn't as scary as it sounds because Terminal can only use two of these protocol things, and there's one you'll use almost all the time (I explain everything you need to know a little later).
4. Tell Terminal you want to perform a file transfer (I'll discuss this in detail in a sec).
5. When the transfer is complete, you'll usually have to press **Enter** or some other key to let the service know you're back.

The next couple of sections take a closer look at steps 2 and 3.

Following Protocol

In diplomacy, *protocol* defines the rules and formalities that smooth communications between nations. As we've seen, just to get two modems talking to each other requires perfect synchronization of communications settings. If we now want to actually exchange data—well, that just adds a whole new level of complexity.

The good news is that this complexity is something you and I can safely ignore because the world's modem nerds have worked out various solutions. These solutions are called *protocols* and, in the same way that diplomatic protocols make cultural exchanges easy, communications protocols are designed to make it easy for two modems to exchange data. The only thing we have to do is make sure both modems are using the same protocol. Otherwise, we'd end up like two diplomats trying to perform different ceremonies at the same time: things just wouldn't mesh properly.

Here's the way it works. When you let the online service know you want to receive or send a file, it will eventually display a list of the protocols it can use, and ask you to select the one you want to use during the transfer. Which one should you choose? Well, Terminal only supports two protocols: XModem/CRC and Kermit, so your choices are limited. However, I've yet to encounter a BBS that doesn't support at least XModem/CRC, so that's the one you'll use most of the time.

To tell Terminal which protocol to use, pull down the **S**ettings menu and select the **B**inary Transfers command. You'll see the Binary Transfers dialog box, shown below. Select the protocol you want, and then select **OK** or press **Enter**. You choose the protocol either before you dial up (if you know which one you'll need in advance) or while you're online. If you're not sure which one you need, wait until the service displays its list of available protocols.

Terminal gives you a choice of two protocols to use in your online diplomatic missions.

Receiving and Sending Files

Once you've told the online service the name of the file you want to receive or send and you've selected the protocol to use, the service will say something like **Ready to send/receive file. Please initiate file transfer.** At this point, pull down the Transfers menu and select one of the following commands:

Receive Binary **F**ile   Select this command when you want to receive a file from the service. The dialog box that appears is called Receive Binary File, and it lets you enter a name for the file and a location.

Send **B**inary File   Select this command when you want to send a file to the service. Terminal displays a dialog box named Send Binary File that lets you choose the file to send.

Both of these dialog boxes use the same layout as the Open dialog box you've probably seen *ad nauseum* by now. Once you've specified a file, select **OK** or press **Enter** to begin the file transfer. Terminal displays the progress of the transfer at the bottom of the window (see below). If for any reason you need to abort the transfer before it's complete, you can either select the Sto**p** command from the Transfers menu or click on the Stop button at the bottom in the progress bar.

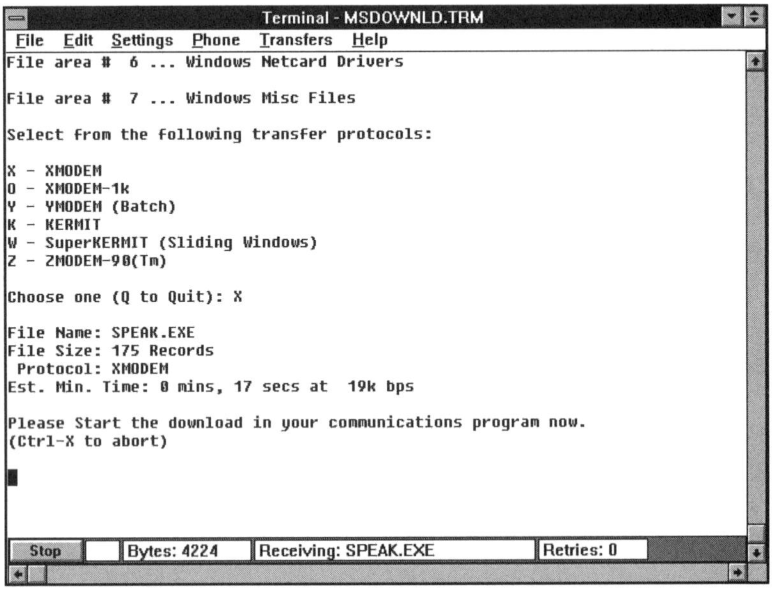

Once you start a file transfer, Terminal displays this progress bar at the bottom of the window.

When the transfer is complete, Terminal returns control to the service, and you can continue with other service options or log off.

Saving Your Settings

Terminal lets you save your settings (including the phone number and protocol) in a special file that you can open at any time. This allows you to create a separate file for each online service you'll be using. Once you've entered the data for a particular service, select the **Save** command from the **File** menu. In the Save dialog box that appears, enter an 8-character name for the file (Terminal will add its TRM extension automatically). Select **OK** or press **Enter** to save the file.

When you need to use one of the settings files, select the **File** menu's **Open** command, select the file you want to use from the Open dialog box, and then select **OK** or press **Enter**.

Do It Yourself: An Example Online Session

To get a feel for life online, let's go through an example session using the Microsoft Product Support Download Service bulletin board. This BBS contains mostly updated files that work with Microsoft products, and best of all, it's free (except for the long distance charges, of course; however, many BBSs also charge an access fee). We'll be downloading (receiving) a file named SPEAK.EXE. This file contains a device driver that lets your system play fancy-shmancy sounds even if you don't have a sound board (see Chapter 11, "Hopping on the Multimedia Bandwagon," for the complete sound scoop).

Here are the settings we'll need for this session:

Phone Number	1-206-936-6735
Baud Rate	1200, 2400, or 9600 (depending on the maximum baud rate of your modem)
Data Bits	8
Parity	None
Stop Bits	1
Connector	Select the appropriate serial port for your computer
Protocol	XModem/CRC

Be sure to save these settings before you continue (I named my settings file MSDOWNLD.TRM).

> **TECHNO NERD TEACHES...**
>
> I often get busy signals with the Microsoft BBS, so you'll probably want to activate the **R**edial After Timing Out check box in the Phone Number dialog box.

Practicing Safe Downloading

Although many bulletin boards test their software for viruses, you shouldn't take this for granted. Always download files into an empty directory (or even onto an empty floppy disk) where you can easily run a virus program to check for diseased files. (The Anti-Virus program you get with DOS 6 will do the job nicely. See Chapter 20, "An Ounce of Prevention: Avoiding Trouble," to find out more.)

Even if you don't have any anti-virus software, you should still place your downloads in an empty directory so you can check out all the files you end up with. This is, in fact, a must for downloading the PC Speaker driver file. If you don't have an empty directory, use File Manager to create a new directory called DOWNLOAD.

Logging On

With your settings entered and saved, you're ready to go. First, make sure your modem is turned on and the cables are attached properly. Now just select the Phone menu's Dial command to get the ball rolling. Note that you don't pick up the receiver in this case. In modem-to-modem communications, the two modems will do most of the talking; if your input is needed (say, to enter a password), you'll use your computer's keyboard to send messages to the other modem.

> **OOPS!**
>
> If you have call waiting on the phone line you'll be using, you should turn it off before starting an online session. Why? Well, because the call waiting beep can throw your modem for a loop and possibly disrupt communications. In most phone systems, you disable call waiting by pressing *70 (if you're not sure, check with your phone company). Call waiting resumes normal operation when you complete your online call.

When the other modem answers the call, you'll probably hear a cacophony of strange (and annoying) sounds. This is normal behavior as the two modems exchange pleasantries. If all goes well, the sounds will cease and the modems will continue their conversation in blissful silence. Terminal will also display a **CONNECT** message (e.g. CONNECT 9600) to let you know the modems are connected.

The Microsoft BBS (like most services) then asks you to enter your name. Just type in your full name and press **Enter**. You may also be asked other questions (such as where you're calling from). Enter the pertinent data and press **Enter** each time. If you're asked a yes or no question, press **Y** or **N** (as appropriate) without pressing **Enter**.

You'll then get several screenfuls of what's known as "read me" information. These notes give you updates about the service and other tidbits the operators think you may be interested in. Press **Enter** after each screen to move on. Eventually, you'll see the Microsoft Download Service Main Menu.

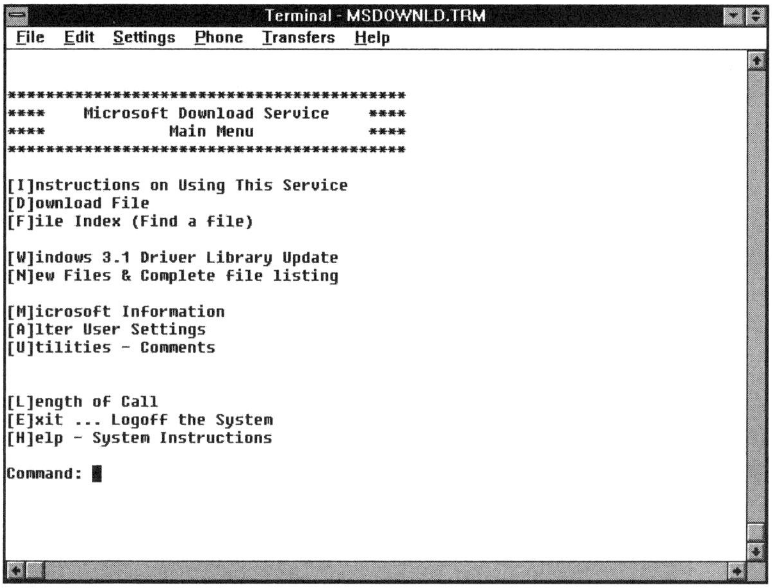

The Main Menu of the Microsoft BBS.

Notice that each menu item has one letter surrounded by square brackets ([ ]). These letters act just like the underlined letters in Windows' pull-down menus: you press the letter to select the menu option. For example, to enter the service's Help system, you'd press **H**.

In our case, we want to download a file, so you need to press **D**. The service then displays a list of options related to downloading. We want to get right to the file transfer, so press **D** again and press **Enter**. (Yes, it *is* a little confusing that sometimes you have to press **Enter** and sometimes you don't. Ah well, that's life in the fast lane of the information superhighway!)

The Microsoft BBS now asks you to enter the name of the file you want to receive. Type **SPEAK.EXE** and press **Enter**. The service takes a few seconds to search its file areas for the appropriate file and then displays a list of the protocols you can use. Hmmm, there's no option for XModem/

CRC. That's no problem because you're allowed to use plain XModem instead (don't use XModem-1K). To select this protocol, press **X**. The service displays the following message:

Please start the download in your communications program now.

That's our cue to tell Terminal to start the transfer. Select the Receive Binary **F**ile command from the **T**ransfers menu to display the Receive Binary File dialog box. You need to do two things:

- Change the directory to C:\DOWNLOAD (or whatever you named the empty directory you'll be using for downloads).
- In the File **N**ame text box, type **SPEAK.EXE**.

> **OOPS!**
>
> Always make sure you hang up when you've finished an online session. This will help you avoid running up a large tab in either long distance charges or online fees for services, such as CompuServe, where you pay by the minute.

When you're done, take a deep breath, and select **OK** or press **Enter**. Terminal displays the progress bar at the bottom of the window and starts receiving the file.

The transfer will take a minute or two depending on the speed of your modem. When it's done, you'll be returned to the Microsoft BBS screen. Press **Enter** to return to the Main menu. To exit the service, press **E**. Your last task is to hang up the phone. You do this by selecting the **H**angup command from the **P**hone menu.

Extracting the Speaker Driver

To make file transfers quicker, most BBSs store files in a compressed format. SPEAK.EXE is the compressed form of the device driver we need. To use this driver, you need to decompress the file. This is, fortunately, very easy in this case, as the following steps show:

1. Start File Manager.
2. Select the directory where you received SPEAK.EXE (i.e., your download directory).

3. In the file list, double-click on **SPEAK.EXE**, or highlight it and press **Enter**. A message appears on your screen warning you to use an empty directory (you're okay on this), and you're asked if you want to extract (decompress) the files.
4. Press **Y**. The files are decompressed, and you're returned to File Manager.
5. Press **F5** to refresh the screen and see all the files that were hiding in SPEAK.EXE (you'll probably now have six files in the directory).
6. Select all the files and move them to the C:\WINDOWS\SYSTEM directory.
7. Exit File Manager and follow the instructions from Chapter 11 for installing the PC Speaker driver.

TECHNO NERD TEACHES...

Many BBS files are compressed in what's called a ZIP format. These are files compressed using a program called PKZIP, and you can recognize them by looking for a .ZIP extension (e.g., SOMEFILE.ZIP). To decompress (or unzip, as the cognoscenti say) these files, you need another program called PKUNZIP. Most bulletin boards carry both programs. They're shareware, so if you use them regularly, you should send the small registration fee to the program's authors (the program provides all the details).

The Least You Need to Know

This chapter showed you how to get online with Windows' Terminal accessory. Here's a look back at some of the stuff you downloaded into your brain in this chapter:

- To start Terminal, select the **Terminal** icon in Program Manager's **Accessories** group.

continues

continued

- To enter a phone number, select the **S**ettings menu's Phone **N**umber command and enter the number in the dialog box that appears.
- To enter the communications settings for the service you'll be dialing, select the **C**ommunications command from the **S**ettings menu and enter the appropriate settings in the dialog box.
- If you need to select a file transfer protocol, select the **S**ettings menu's **B**inary Transfers command. In the dialog box, select either **X**Modem/CRC or **K**ermit.
- To dial the modem, pull down the **P**hone menu and select the **D**ial command.
- If you want to receive a file, wait until the BBS tells you to start the transfer and then select Receive Binary **F**ile from the **T**ransfers menu. To send a file, select the Send **B**inary File command from the **T**ransfers menu.

Chapter 18
Windows Robotics: Recording Recorder Macros

In This Chapter

- What in blue blazes is a macro?
- Using Recorder to record a macro
- How to get a macro off the ground
- Mucho macro examples

If there was such a thing as a Most Underrated Player award for Windows accessories, Recorder would win it hands down. Most Windows users barely even know the program exists, and the rest shudder at the very thought of actually using the darn thing. But ignorance isn't bliss in this case, because Recorder is actually one of the most useful of Windows' programs. And, as an added bonus, it's quite easy to use, too. Why, in just a few minutes you'll have learned enough to have Recorder performing tasks that duplicate some fancy utilities from third-party vendors (programs that other suckers are shelling out big bucks for). This chapter gives you the Recorder rundown by showing you how to create and run your own macros, and by giving you lots of examples that put your new knowledge to good use.

I, Macro: About Recorder's Robots

Besides the proverbial paperless office, the other thing we were supposed to have by now (at least according to the so-called "futurists" of 40 years ago) was an automated home where little Robbie-the-Robot types would whisk around taking care of all our dirty work.

Well, we're clearly a long way from that pipe dream, but you can get a step closer by automating your Windows house. How? By creating *macros* that whittle long-winded, repetitive tasks down to a single keystroke or mouse click. For example, suppose you like to change your wallpaper regularly. Well, the bare minimum number of mouse clicks required is 9, and a more realistic number is probably more like 15 (depending on which application you were in originally, which program groups are open, which wallpaper you choose, and so on). With a macro, however, you can bundle all those clicks into a single file and run the whole shebang at once.

The secret to creating these Windows robots is the Recorder accessory. The idea is that Recorder can "remember" any sequence of mouse clicks or keystrokes, and store them in a special format called a *macro*. You can then "play back" the macro by running it directly from the Recorder window or by assigning the macro a shortcut key combination.

SPEAK LIKE A GEEK

Any recorded sequence of mouse clicks or keystrokes is called a **macro**.

Building the Robot: How to Record a Macro

As you can imagine, creating a macro isn't all that difficult. It's really just a matter of starting Recorder, putting it in "record" mode, and then performing the actions you want to automate. However, Recorder has quite a few bells and whistles just to keep us on our toes. We'll look at many of these options and a few other recording particulars in the next few sections. To begin, start Recorder by selecting the **Recorder** icon from Program Manager's **Accessories** group.

The Recording Process

There's no time like the present, as they say, so let's start recording a macro. To give you something concrete to get your hands on, we'll go through an example: recording a long section of text that you use regularly. This could be your company name, a report title, a bit of boilerplate text, or a good joke you like to use a lot. For starters, open your word processor and position the cursor where you want to type your text. Now switch back to Recorder and follow these steps:

> **OOPS!**
>
> The biggest problem you'll face with Recorder is that if you botch the recording, you have to start the whole thing from scratch. (Sadly, Recorder doesn't let you edit an existing macro.) For complex recordings, you might consider a practice run or two to make sure you're comfortable with the keystrokes you need to perform.

1. Pull down Recorder's **M**acro menu and select the Record command. The Record Macro dialog box appears, as shown here.

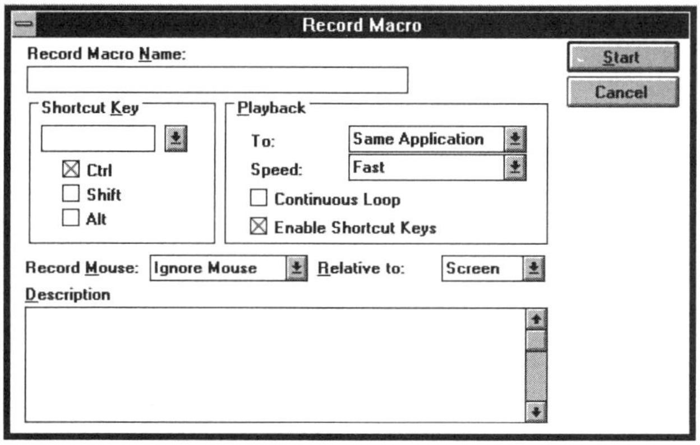

You use the Record Macro dialog box to enter the particulars for your macro.

2. In the Record Macro **N**ame text box, enter a name for the macro. (The name can be as long as 40 characters.)
3. Use the controls in the Shortcut **K**ey group to assign a shortcut key for the macro. You build the key combination by selecting one or more of the **Ctrl**, **Shift**, and **Alt** check boxes, and then

either entering a letter or number in the text box or selecting a key from the drop-down list. For example, If you activate **Ctrl** and **Shift** and enter **T** in the text box, your shortcut key will be **Ctrl+Shift+T**.

4. Use the Playback group to determine how Recorder should play the macro. You have the following options:

   To The options in this drop-down list determine where Recorder plays back the macro. If you select Same Application, the macro only runs in the application you used for the original recording. Any Application tells Recorder to play back the macro in any application. For our example, select **Same Application**.

   Speed This drop-down list's options determine how fast Recorder plays back the macro. Fast plays the macro at top speed, while Recorded Speed runs the macro at the same tempo you used during the recording. Only choose Recorded Speed when your macro has to wait for an operation (such as a file search in File Manager) to finish before moving on. For the example, select **Fast**.

   Continuous Loop You only activate this check box when you want Recorder to play back the macro continuously. Leave this option unchecked for the example.

   Enable Shortcut Keys When this check box is activated, Recorder allows you to run other macros you've recorded by pressing their shortcut keys while recording a new macro. Although we don't need this feature for the example, it doesn't hurt to leave this option turned on.

5. Use the Record Mouse drop-down list to tell Recorder whether you want to record just keystrokes (Ignore Mouse), just mouse actions—including mouse actions performed while holding down a key—(Clicks + Drags), or both (Everything). Recorder is at its most reliable when you use only keystrokes for your macros, so you should always select **Ignore Mouse** for this option.

TECHNO NERD TEACHES...

Why is Recorder unreliable when you use mouse clicks? The problem is that when you click, Recorder memorizes the position of the mouse relative to either the screen or the active window (as given by the setting in the **R**elative to drop-down list). But this position may be way off if, when you run the macro, the window has changed size or position, or you're using a different screen resolution.

6. If you like, you can also use the **D**escription box to enter a detailed explanation of what the macro does. In our example, for instance, you might want to mention that you need to have your word processor up and running before playing this macro.
7. Select the **S**tart button. Recorder minimizes itself to an icon. The icon flashes on and off to let you know that a recording is in progress.
8. Enter the keystrokes necessary to perform the operation you want to automate. In our example, you'd first switch to your word processor (using **Alt+Tab**), and then type in the text.
9. When you're done, pause Recorder either by pressing **Ctrl+Break** or by clicking on the flashing Recorder icon. The Recorder dialog box appears, as shown below.

This dialog box appears when you press Ctrl+Break or click the Recorder icon.

10. Activate the **S**ave Macro option and select **OK**. If you prefer to continue the recording (say, after making some adjustments), activate **R**esume Recording, instead. If the recording is a total fiasco, choose **C**ancel Recording to forget the whole thing.

Saving the Recorder File

When you've finished a recording, you're returned to the Recorder window, and your macro's name and shortcut key are displayed, as shown in the next figure. You're free to add as many macros as you like to a Recorder file. However, you should save your macros for posterity after each recording. To do this, select the **F**ile menu's **S**ave command, enter a name for the file (don't bother with an extension; Recorder adds its .REC extension automatically), and then select **OK**.

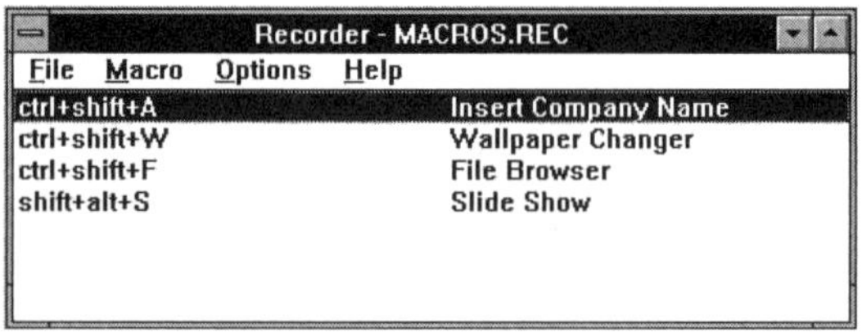

The Recorder window shows the name and shortcut key for each macro you've recorded.

Working with Your Macros

Once you've recorded a macro or two, Recorder's **M**acro menu gives you a couple of commands for working with them. You can select **D**elete to delete the currently highlighted macro. Recorder displays a dialog box asking if you're sure you want to delete the macro. Select **OK**. Or, you can highlight a macro and select **P**roperties to display the Macro Properties dialog box. This dialog box shows the properties (name, shortcut key, and so on) for the macro. Make your changes, if necessary, and then select **OK**.

Activating the Robot: How to Run a Macro

The whole purpose of Recorder macros, of course, is to play back their contents at will. To do this, first start Recorder and open the Recorder file that contains the macro you want to run (by using the **F**ile menu's **O**pen command). You can now run the macro using either of the following techniques:

- If the macro has a shortcut key, switch to the application in which you want to play the macro back, position the cursor (if necessary), and then press the shortcut key combination.
- In the Recorder window, highlight the macro you want to run and select the **M**acro menu's **R**un command. You can also simply double-click on the macro.

If you need to stop a macro in progress, press **Ctrl+Break**, and then select **OK** in the dialog box that appears.

Do-It-Yourself: Creating an Icon for a Macro

There's a third, undocumented method for starting a Recorder macro: you can create an icon for the macro in Program Manager. Open the group you want to use for the icon, select the File menu's New command, and then select **OK** in the dialog box that appears. In the Program Item Properties dialog box, use the Command Line box to enter a command of the following general form:

RECORDER -H*ShortcutKeySymbols RecorderFilename*

Here, *ShortcutKeySymbols* are characters that represent the shortcut you assigned to the macro. (You can't use this technique if you didn't assign a shortcut key to the macro.) For Ctrl, Shift, and Alt, use the following characters:

Use	To represent
^	Ctrl
+	Shift
%	Alt

For example, you'd enter **^+T** to represent the shortcut key Ctrl+Shift+T. Similarly, **^%INSERT** would represent Ctrl+Alt+Insert.

The *RecorderFilename* part is just the name of the recorder file that contains the macro. For example, suppose your macro is in the file MACROS.REC and uses the shortcut key Ctrl+Shift+Alt+F5. Your Command Line would look like this:

RECORDER -H^+%F5 MACROS.REC

Keep in mind that your macro icon won't work properly if Recorder is already running.

Recorder Exercises for the Anxious, Eager, and Adventurous

Once you get the hang of the Recorder, you'll probably think of a thousand-and-one ways that macros will reduce your day-to-day Windows drudgery. To get you started, though, the next few sections offer up some of my personal favorites.

For the Anxious: Changing Wallpaper in Each Windows Session

I like to use Windows' wallpaper, but I tend to get sick of a particular pattern after a while. To prevent this wallpaper burnout, it would be nice if I could have a different wallpaper every time I started Windows. There are programs you can buy that'll do this, but why bother when a Recorder macro can do the job? Here's how:

1. Start Recorder, select the **M**acro menu's Re**c**ord command, and then enter the following in the Record Macro dialog box:

Record Macro Name	**Wallpaper Changer**
Shortcut **K**ey	Alt+Shift+W
Playback To	Same Application
Playback Speed	Fast
Record **M**ouse	Ignore Mouse

2. Select **S**tart to begin recording.
3. Press **Alt+Tab** until you're back in Program Manager.
4. Press **Alt+F** and then **R** to display the Run dialog box, and then type **CONTROL** and press **Enter** to display Control Panel.
5. Press **Alt+S** and press **D** to display the Desktop dialog box.
6. Press **Alt+F** to select the **F**ile drop-down list, press down arrow to display the next wallpaper, press **Alt+T** to select the **T**ile option, and then press **Enter**.
7. Press **Alt+F4** to exit Control Panel.

8. Press **Ctrl+Break** to interrupt the recording, choose Save Macro, and then select **OK**. Make sure you save the Recorder file when you get back to the Recorder Window.

Now you can get a different wallpaper just by pressing **Alt+Shift+W**. If you'd like a different wallpaper each time you start Windows, create an icon in the Startup group that uses the following Command Line (assuming the macro is stored in MACROS.REC):

RECORDER -H^+W MACROS.REC

Note that this macro will fall down on the job once it hits the bottom of your wallpaper list (probably ZIGZAG.BMP). When this happens, you'll need to display the Desktop dialog box and return the File drop-down list back to the top.

For the Eager: A File Manager File Browser

One of File Manager's most glaring weaknesses is that it has no way of showing you the contents of a file. This is a problem because DOS's dumb 8-character limit on file names means you can't always tell what's in a file just by its name. To overcome this, let's take advantage of the fact that Write can display the contents of any file. The following steps show you how to create a macro that turns Write into a true "file browser" that shows the contents of the currently selected File Manager file.

1. Start File Manager and select the file you want to view.
2. Start Recorder, select Record from the Macro menu, and then enter the following in the Record Macro dialog box:

Record Macro	Name File Browser
Shortcut Key	Alt+Shift+F
Playback Speed	Fast
Playback To	Same Application
Record Mouse	Ignore Mouse

3. Select **Start** to begin recording.
4. Press **Alt+Tab** until you're back in File Manager.

5. Press **Alt+F** and then **R** to display the Run dialog box. The name of the file appears in the Command Line text box.
6. Press **Ctrl+X** to cut the file name to the Clipboard, and then type **WRITE** and press **Enter** to start Write.
7. Press **Alt+F** to pull down the **F**ile menu, and then press **O** to display the Open dialog box.
8. Press **Ctrl+V** to paste the file name, and then press **Enter**. When Write asks if you want to convert the file, press **N**. Write then opens the file in all its glory. (Depending on the type of file you're viewing, you may see what looks like a bunch of junk in the Write window; this is perfectly normal for some files. Make sure, though, that you don't make any changes to these files.)

> **TECHNO NERD TEACHES...**
>
> If you're viewing a Write file (extension WRI), of course, the program won't ask if you want to convert the file. So this macro will actually generate an error if you run it on a Write file. You might consider creating a second macro that works just for Write files.

9. Press **Ctrl+Break**, choose **S**ave Macro, and then select **OK**. Again, make sure you save the Recorder file.

To use this macro, highlight a file in File Manager, and then press **Alt+Shift+F**. The Write window appears, and the file's contents show up a second or two later. When you've finished looking at the file, exit Write to return to File Manager.

For the Adventurous: A Paintbrush Slide Show

What do you do if you want to display a series of pictures on your monitor, but you don't want to spring for a dedicated presentation graphics program? Easy: you create a Recorder macro that uses Paintbrush to display a sequence of graphics files with a simple key combination. To prepare for this exercise, you need to do the following:

- Use File Manager to create a new directory to hold the graphics files. This directory should contain no other files.
- Make sure all the files you need for the presentation use the same format (either BMP or PCX). The macro won't work properly if you mix formats.
- When you create your graphics files (they could be your own drawings, screen shots, scanned images, clip art, or whatever), make sure you name them so that, when they're arranged alphabetically, they appear in the order you want to show them. (e.g., SLIDE001.PCX, SLIDE002.PCX, and so on). Make sure you store them in the new directory.
- Here's where things get strange: Now you need to add eight dummy files to your slide show directory (I'll explain why a little later). These files need to be in the same format as the other files, and they must be named to ensure they appear at the top of the list (something like 001.PCX, 002.PCX, and so on, should do). Now you don't want these dummy files to take up all kinds of room, so you should make them as small as possible. In Paintbrush, select Image Attributes from the Options menu, select **pels**, enter **1** in both the Width and Height text boxes, select **Black and White**, and then select **OK**. Save the file (it's a mere 66 bytes in size), and then create the other seven (it's probably easier to use File Manager's Copy command to do this).

With all that rigmarole out of the way, you're ready to begin:

1. Start Paintbrush and open the first file in your slide show.
2. Start Recorder, select the Macro menu's Record command, and then enter the following in the Record Macro dialog box:

Record Macro Name	Slide Show
Shortcut Key	Alt+Shift+S (don't use Ctrl for this macro)
Playback Speed	Fast
Playback To	Same Application
Record Mouse	Ignore Mouse

3. Select **S**tart to begin recording.
4. Press **Alt+Tab** until you're back in Paintbrush.
5. Press **Alt+F** and then press **O** to display the Open dialog box. The name of the first slide appears in the File **N**ame text box.
6. Press **Tab** to move into the file list and press down arrow twice to highlight the next slide.

> **TECHNO NERD TEACHES...**
>
> Now you see why you had to add the eight dummy files. Without them, pressing **Tab** and then the down arrow twice would just highlight the second file in the list every time.

7. Press **Enter** to open the file, and then press **Ctrl+P** to display the file full-screen.
8. Press **Ctrl+Break** to interrupt the recording, choose **S**ave Macro, and then select **OK**. Make sure you save the Recorder file when you get back to the Recorder Window.

To use this macro, start Paintbrush, open the first file in your slide show, press **Ctrl+P** to display it full-screen, and then press **Alt+Shift+S** when you need to display the next slide. When you're done, click the screen a few times to get back to Paintbrush.

> ## The Least You Need to Know
>
> This chapter showed you how to wield one of Windows' most versatile tools: the Recorder. Here's the highlight film:
>
> - Macros are a recorded sequence of keystrokes or mouse clicks.
> - To record a macro, select the **M**acro menu's **R**ecord command, enter the macro details, select **S**tart, and then enter your keystrokes.

- ☛ For best results, use only keystrokes in a macro.
- ☛ Don't forget to save your Recorder files by selecting the **F**ile menu's **S**ave command.
- ☛ To run a macro, either press the shortcut key, or highlight the macro and select the **M**acro menu's **R**un command.

Chapter 19

How to Uninstall a Windows Application

In This Chapter

- Expunging the application's files
- Cleaning out Program Manager
- Editing your configuration files to remove any references to the application
- Your step-by-step guide to getting pesky applications the heck out of your life

Windows applications, like the people we meet, fall into three categories: friends for life, acquaintances we deal with occasionally, and those we hope we never have to speak to again. Avoiding people we dislike is usually just a matter of staying away from them, and they get the hint after a while. Unlikable Windows applications, however, just don't seem to get it. They keep hanging around like the proverbial party guests that won't leave. If you have a Windows application that's worn out its welcome, this chapter shows you the proper way to uninstall the darn thing so it's out of your life forever.

What's the Big Deal About Uninstalling?

You may be wondering why the heck I'd need to devote an entire chapter to something so simple as blowing away an application. After all, isn't it just a matter of getting rid of a Program Manager icon, and maybe deleting a file or two? Hah, you wish! First of all, Windows applications seem to enjoy scattering files left, right, and center over your hard disk. Secondly, most Windows programs make at least a few changes to WIN.INI, SYSTEM.INI, AUTOEXEC.BAT, and various and sundry other files. (To learn more about INI files, you need to read Chapter 9, "Learning to Love Those Strange INI Files.") To make sure no piece of an old application ever rears its ugly head (usually as some kind of impenetrable error message), you need to disinfect these files by editing out lines you no longer need.

If it all sounds like a lot of work, well yes, I suppose it is. To prove to you that it's worth the hassle, here are just a few of the benefits you'll reap:

Extra hard disk space Some of today's behemoth Windows applications can chew up 10, 20, or even 30 megabytes of precious hard disk property. With hard disk space at a premium these days, you can't afford to waste even half a megabyte on some dog of a program (much less 20 or 30).

Easier navigation Getting rid of groups and icons in Program Manager, and directories and files in File Manager, makes it easier to get around in these programs.

Faster performance Sending an application packing can sometimes improve your computer's performance. Depending on the type of program, you could end up with more memory, a faster loading time for Windows, and faster execution of your other programs.

The sheer thrill of nuking stuff We spend most of our File Manager time being careful not to accidentally delete important files. What a guilty pleasure it is, then, to blow away entire directories stuffed with formerly important files and subdirectories.

Whatever the reason, there's no doubt uninstalling is worthwhile. To make the whole chore easier, I've divided it up into five steps that cover everything from deleting files and icons to editing the appropriate initialization files. The next few sections take you through step by step. Just so we have an example to work with, I'll delete an old beta copy of

WordPerfect for Windows 6 from my computer. (A *beta* copy, in case you're wondering, is a pre-release—and usually bug-riddled—version of a program. The developers send these out to suckers like me so we'll try them and report back how terrible things are.)

TECHNO NERD TEACHES...

Some enlightened Windows applications actually come with an "Uninstall" feature built right in. In some cases, you'll see an **Uninstall** icon in the application's program group. Other applications' Setup programs do the uninstall dirty work. (They usually operate something like the Windows Setup program we looked at back in Chapter 3, "Tweaking Windows with Setup.")

Step 1: Deleting the Application's Files

The first stage of our uninstalling tour involves obliterating any files and directories created by the application's installation program. To do this, you'll need to know the name of the program's main directory. If you can't remember, here are three ways to find out:

- In Program Manager, highlight the application's icon and then display the Program Item Properties dialog box (either by holding down **Alt** and double-clicking on the icon or by pressing **Alt+Enter**). Check out the **C**ommand Line text box (or, less accurately, the **W**orking Directory text box) to see if it contains a directory name. For example, WordPerfect for Windows 6 displays C:\WPWIN60\WPWIN.EXE, so I know its main directory is C:\WPWIN60.
- In File Manager, look for a directory name that closely resembles the name of the application. For example, Excel's main directory is EXCEL, and Word for Windows' main directory is WINWORD.
- Load the application, pull down its **F**ile menu, and select the **O**pen command. In the Open dialog box that appears, the **D**irectories box may display the program's main directory.

Deleting the Application's Main Directory

Now that you know where the application's files are hiding, start File Manager and highlight the directory. Before pounding the Delete key, though, take a quick look at the displayed files. Can you see a date and time common to most of them? (You may need to activate the View menu's All File Details and Sort by Date commands to get a true picture.) If so, make a note of both the date and time; we'll need them later on when we hunt down the application's other files. For example, the picture below shows my WPWIN60 directory; notice how all the files were created on April 9, 1994 at 6:01:00AM.

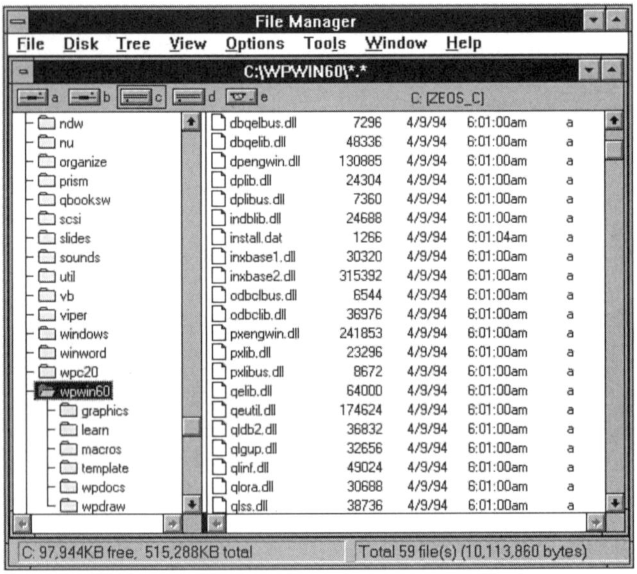

Most applications give their files the same date and time.

Next, you should check to see if the directory contains any data files you want to preserve. If you've spent any time at all creating documents (or whatever) in the application, it's a wise precaution to save them for posterity. For one thing, you may be able to use them in another application; for another, you may change your mind six months from now and decide to reinstall the application. If you want to save your data, highlight those files and then move (not copy) them to another directory or to a floppy disk.

TECHNO NERD TEACHES...

This is another good reason why you should store all the documents you create with an application in a separate directory. If you need to move the documents elsewhere, it's simply a matter of moving the entire data directory. (Otherwise, you would have to waste time picking out the data files from amongst the other chaff.)

Your last bit of business is to decide how cautious you want File Manager to be. If you're even the least bit scared of wiping out something by accident, pull down the Options menu, select Confirmation, and then make sure the File Delete and Directory Delete check boxes are activated. Select **OK** to put the settings into effect.

With all that out of the way, you're ready for the fun to begin. With the application's main directory highlighted, take a deep breath and press **Delete** (or select the File menu's Delete command). File Manager displays the Delete dialog box showing the directory name. Make sure it's the right directory, and then select **OK**.

If you have File Manager's Directory Delete confirmation turned on, you'll see the Confirm Directory Delete dialog box. Select Yes to delete the displayed directory. If you're also deleting subdirectories, you can select the Yes to All button to prevent this dialog box from showing up for each directory.

If you have File Manager's File Delete confirmation turned on, you'll then see the Confirm File Delete dialog box. Again, you can select Yes to delete the displayed file or, more likely, you can select Yes to All to let File Manager go crazy.

Deleting Other Files Installed by the Application

Your file deletion chores aren't quite done yet. As I mentioned earlier, many applications scatter a few of their files in various places. To give your hard disk a thorough cleaning, you'll need to seek out these rogue elements. Rather than trek through every single directory, though, you can narrow your search somewhat. In the vast majority of cases, you'll find any extraneous files lurking in your main Windows directory (usually WINDOWS), Windows' SYSTEM subdirectory, and your hard drive's root directory (usually C:\).

The bad news is that the WINDOWS and SYSTEM directories often contain hundreds of files. How can you tell which files belonged to the application? There's no foolproof method, but there are some clues you can keep an eye out for:

- Look for file names that suggest the original application. For example, I can be reasonably confident that a file name beginning with WP is probably a WordPerfect file.
- Look for files with dates and times that match the common date and time you observed earlier in the application's main directory.
- Look for specific file names in the WIN.INI and SYSTEM.INI files. As you'll see later, many applications modify these files, and these modifications often give hints about where certain files were stored.

The only exception to all this concerns font files (ones ending in FON, FOT, or TTF). You're better off deleting these files through the Control Panel (as described back in Chapter 7, "Flexing Your Font Muscles").

When your detective work is done, go ahead and delete the files. When the carnage is complete and the dust has settled, select the File menu's Exit command to return to Program Manager.

OOPS!

If you're just not sure about a particular file, especially one in your WINDOWS or SYSTEM directory, try moving it to another directory or to a floppy disk instead of deleting it outright. This way, if Windows or some application displays an error message complaining about the missing file, you can easily restore it.

Step 2: Deleting Program Manager Groups and Icons

This is the easy part. Go through your Program Manager groups and delete any icons that used to start either the application itself or one of its components. (You delete a highlighted icon by pressing **Delete** or by selecting the File menu's Delete command. When Program Manager asks if you're sure, select Yes.)

If the application installed its own program group, don't bother deleting the icons one-by-one. Instead, minimize the group and highlight it using either of the following techniques:

- Click on the icon, and then click on an empty part of the Program Manager window.
- Hold down **Ctrl** and tap **F6** until you get to the group.

Now just press **Delete**, and select Yes in the dialog box that appears (see below). Program Manager removes both the group and all its icons.

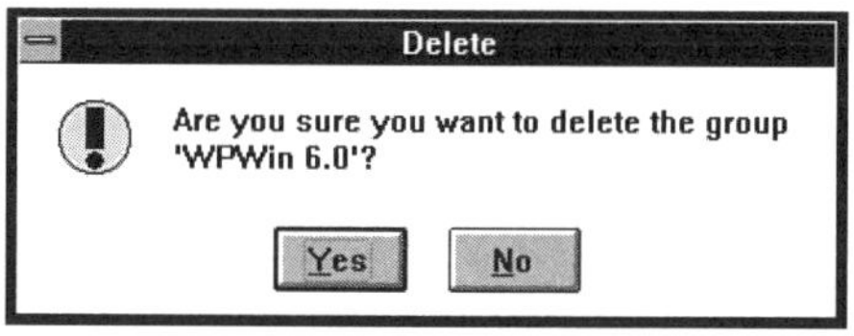

This dialog box appears when you try to fry a program group.

Step 3: Disinfecting WIN.INI

Okay, we're getting there. Your next task is to poke around in WIN.INI and look for any droppings the application may have deposited there. This is usually pretty easy, because most applications that add stuff to WIN.INI do it by creating one or more of their own sections. For example, the following picture shows a couple of sections that WordPerfect for Windows added to my WIN.INI file.

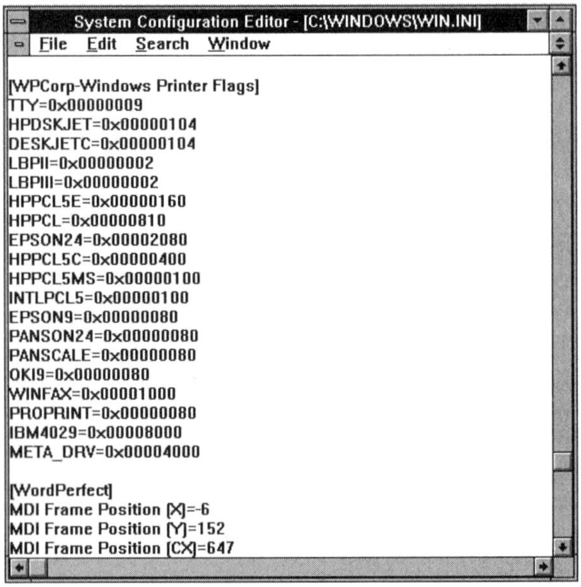
System Configuration Editor - [C:\WINDOWS\WIN.INI]
File Edit Search Window

[WPCorp-Windows Printer Flags]
TTY=0x00000009
HPDSKJET=0x00000104
DESKJETC=0x00000104
LBPII=0x00000002
LBPIII=0x00000002
HPPCL5E=0x00000160
HPPCL=0x00000810
EPSON24=0x00002080
HPPCL5C=0x00000400
HPPCL5MS=0x00000100
INTLPCL5=0x00000100
EPSON9=0x00000080
PANSON24=0x00000080
PANSCALE=0x00000080
OKI9=0x00000080
WINFAX=0x00001000
PROPRINT=0x00000080
IBM4029=0x00008000
META_DRV=0x00004000

[WordPerfect]
MDI Frame Position [X]=-6
MDI Frame Position [Y]=152
MDI Frame Position [CX]=647

A couple of the sections that WordPerfect for Windows added to my WIN.INI file.

OOPS!

Again, if you're not sure about whether or not to remove a line, err on the side of caution. In WIN.INI and SYSTEM.INI, you can disable a line without deleting it by adding a semi-colon (;) to the beginning of the line. In AUTOEXEC.BAT and CONFIG.SYS, you disable a line by typing **REM** and then a space at the beginning of the line.

I'd suggest opening WIN.INI using the System Registration Editor (select the File menu's **R**un command, type **SYSEDIT**, and then select **OK**). You'll be rustling around in SYSTEM.INI, AUTOEXEC.BAT, and CONFIG.SYS in the next section, so you may as well have everything open and ready to go. Once you're in, all you have to do is find one of the application's sections, and then delete the entire section (the section name and all the settings within the section).

Step 4: Decontaminating Other Important Files

Some installation programs, busy devils that they are, also like to modify your three other main configuration files: SYSTEM.INI, AUTOEXEC.BAT, and CONFIG.SYS. Unfortunately, you don't have any handy section names that refer directly to applications. Instead, you need to look for any lines that use the application directory you blew away earlier. In

AUTOEXEC.BAT, especially, look for a PATH statement that mentions the directory. For example, consider the following statement:

PATH=C:\DOS;C:\WINDOWS;C:\WPWIN60;C:\EXCEL

Since I've wiped out the C:\WPWIN60 directory, I can edit this line so it reads as follows:

PATH=C:\DOS;C:\WINDOWS;C:\EXCEL

Step 5: Sanitizing the Registration Database

We're in the home stretch now. The last thing you need to do is deal with any entries the application might have thrown into the registration database. (I talked briefly about this database in Chapter 12, "Let's Do Launch: Interesting Ways to Start Applications.") Pull down Program Manager's File menu, select Run, type **REGEDIT**, and then select **OK**.

In the Registration Info Editor window, look through the list of Registered File Types for anything related to the application. The picture below shows that WordPerfect for Windows has a few entries. For each entry, highlight it, pull down the Edit menu, and select Delete File Type. When the program asks if you're sure you want to delete the file type, select Yes. When you're done, select the File menu's Exit command to return to Program Manager.

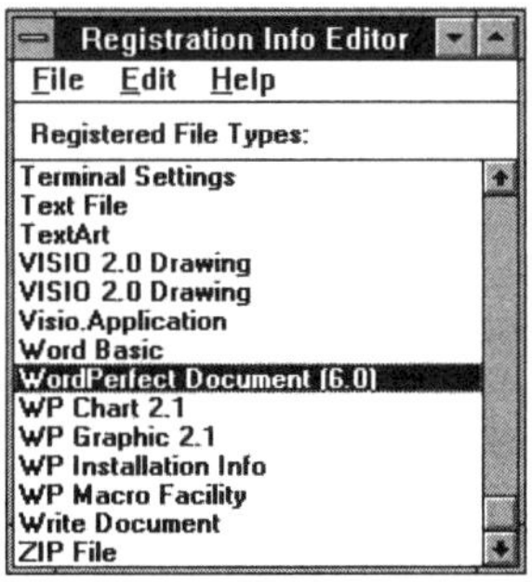

Scour the list of Registered File Types for anything related to the application you're uninstalling.

That's all she wrote. The only thing left to do is exit and then restart Windows. However, if you made changes to AUTOEXEC.BAT or CONFIG.SYS, you'll need to exit Windows and then reboot your computer.

The Least You Need to Know

This chapter showed you how to rid your life of unwelcome software guests. Here's a review of the steps you went through:

- In File Manager, highlight the directory containing the application's files, and then delete it (after first moving your data files to a safe location).
- In Program Manager, delete any icons or groups used by the application.
- Open WIN.INI, look for any sections created by the application, and then delete them.
- Open SYSTEM.INI, AUTOEXEC.BAT, and CONFIG.SYS and remove any references to the application's directory or files.
- In the Registration Info Editor, delete any file types associated with the application.

Part III

When Windows Won't Work: A Troubleshooting Guide

From time to time, I find myself actually enjoying working in Windows. I like the interface, the applications are great, and there are plenty of things you can do that DOS users can only dream about. But then I get an ***Out of memory*** *message, or the dreaded* ***General Application Fault*** *error rears its ugly head, and my good mood is gone for the day.*

Yes, Windows is nice, but it's so darned temperamental. Some days it seems you only have to cough a little too loudly, and Windows gives up the ghost. When faced with such flakiness, one of the keys to remaining a productive member of society is to minimize the amount of time you spend hunting down and fixing problems. The chapters here in Part III are designed to help you do just that. I've broken down Windows' woes into five easy-to-find and easy-to-digest chunks (installation and startup, memory, speed, applications, and hardware). And to help you avoid trouble in the first place, there's also a chapter that shows you how to perform some Windows preventive maintenance.

Chapter 20

An Ounce of Prevention: Avoiding Trouble

In This Chapter

- Recovering accidentally deleted files
- Foiling viruses with Microsoft Anti-Virus
- Guarding Windows with a password
- Using the ScanDisk utility that comes with DOS 6
- Avoiding the "pound of cure" thing with a little preventive maintenance

Computer problems seem to be, like the proverbial death and taxes, one of those constants in life. But that doesn't mean you just have to sit back and wait for trouble. Believe me, a few minutes of protection now can save you hours of grief down the road. And therein lies the good news: avoiding trouble really does take only a little extra work. Why, with just a few simple techniques and a quick tweak here and there, you can set up some powerful preventive measures in no time at all. This chapter tells you everything you need to know.

How Do You Spell Relief? U-N-D-E-L-E-T-E

It's an old saw that there are two types of computer users: those who've accidentally deleted files and those who will. If it's happened to you, you know only too well that sinking feeling you get in the pit of your stomach when you realize you've just consigned your life's work to nothingness.

When this happened to the world's programmers once too often, they decided to do something about it. The result was software that could actually undelete a trashed file. Now, with DOS 6, that power is available to us Windows users in the form of the Undelete application. To start Undelete, use either of the following methods:

- In Program Manager, open the **Microsoft Tools** group and select the **Undelete** icon.
- In File Manager, pull down the **F**ile menu and select the **U**ndelete command.

TECHNO NERD TEACHES...

If you don't have either a **Microsoft Tools** group, or an **U**ndelete command in File Manager's **F**ile menu, you'll need to return to your DOS 6 Setup disk and install the Undelete for Windows utility. In this case, start Setup using the command **SETUP /E** (this tells Setup you only want to install optional programs such as Undelete and Anti-Virus).

In either case, you'll see a Microsoft Undelete window similar to the one shown in the following figure. (Note: if you have a file you need to undelete, head immediately to the "Undeleting a File" section. The sooner you attempt to undelete the file, the better your chances of success.)

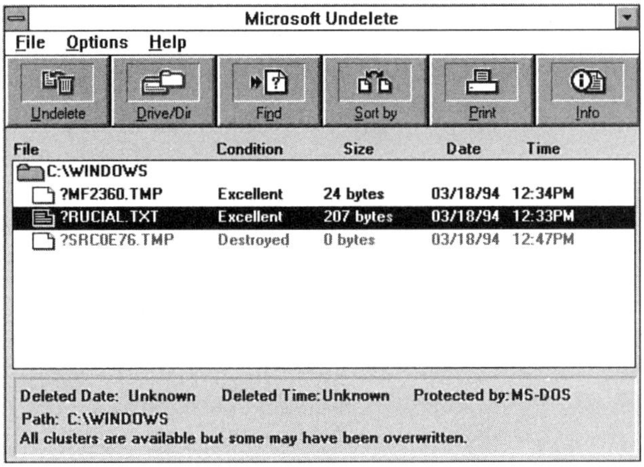

The Undelete window.

Protecting Your Files

Undelete can do a better job of recovering your files if you tell it you want them protected. In this case, "protection" just means that Undelete keeps track of certain types of information for every file you delete. When you need to recover a file you blew away by accident, Undelete uses this information to bring the file back from the dead. Follow these steps to set up deletion protection:

1. Pull down Undelete's **O**ptions menu and select the **C**onfigure Delete Protection command. Undelete displays the Configure Delete Protection dialog box.
2. Undelete gives you three protection options. Select the Delete **S**entry option (this is, by far, the safest and most reliable scheme), and then select **OK**. Undelete displays the Configure Delete Sentry dialog box, shown on the following page.

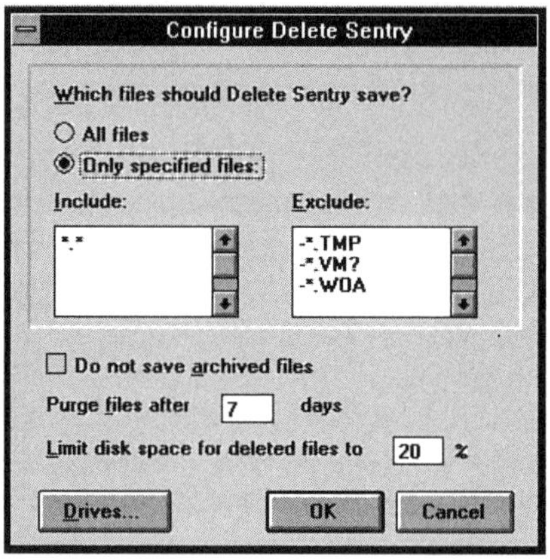

Undelete gives you all kinds of ways to configure the Delete Sentry.

3. You can ignore most of this stuff, but you'll probably want to change the value in the text box titled **Limit disk space for deleted files to**. The suggested value is 20%, which is absurdly high. I'd suggest changing this to a more reasonable 5%. If you're running out of room on your hard drive, you might want to go as low as 2% or 3%. (Keep in mind, though, that the lower the number, the fewer files Delete Sentry can protect.)

Delete Sentry works by creating a new directory called SENTRY on your hard drive. When you delete a file, Delete Sentry actually moves it to the SENTRY directory. Undeleting (as you'll see later in this chapter) is then a simple matter of restoring the file to its original directory.

4. Select the **Drives** button, select the drive or drives you want to protect (this will usually be your hard drive; you shouldn't bother with your floppy drives), and then select **OK** to return to the Configure Delete Sentry dialog box.
5. Select **OK**. Undelete lets you know if it needs to update your AUTOEXEC.BAT file. Select **OK** to let Undelete handle this chore for you.

6. Undelete next tells you to reboot your computer. Select **OK** and exit Undelete by pulling down the File menu and selecting Exit. Exit Windows, and then reboot (the easiest way to reboot is to press **Ctrl+Alt+Delete**).

Undeleting a File

The Undelete window shows a list of the recently deleted files for the selected directory. If you deleted the file from a directory other than the one shown (which is usually either WINDOWS or DOS), your first order of business is to display the proper directory. Begin by selecting Undelete's Drive/Dir button. In the Change Drive and Directory dialog box that appears, select the directory you want and then select **OK**.

In the list of deleted files, highlight the file you want to recover. If the file was deleted before you set up the Delete Sentry protection, you'll need to take into account the fact that the first letter of the file name has been changed to a question mark. For example, if you deleted a file named CRUCIAL.TXT, it will appear as ?RUCIAL.TXT.

TECHNO NERD TEACHES...

Why is there a question mark in front of files deleted without Delete Sentry? Well, when DOS deletes a file, it saves time by simply changing the file's first letter to a special character. This character signifies that the disk area used by the file is now available to other data. (This is why, if you're not using Delete Sentry, you should waste no time before trying to undelete the file: another file may overwrite your data, and then it will be lost for good.) To recover the file, all you have to do is restore the original first letter.

Now take a look at the file's condition (the second column of the file list). If it says Perfect or Excellent, you'll be able to recover the entire file; if it says Good, you can probably recover the file, but you may lose some data; if it says Poor or Destroyed, you're out of luck.

If the file is in Perfect, Excellent, or Good condition, select the **Undelete** button, and one of two things will happen. If the file was deleted after you set up Delete Sentry, Undelete recovers the file immediately. If the file name is missing its first letter, Undelete asks you to enter the original letter. Type the letter and select **OK**.

Guarding Against Viruses

Viruses are nasty little programs that live for the sheer thrill of trashing your valuable data. They're crafted in dank basements by repressed, pimple-faced, Jolt cola-fueled deviants—programming wizards who've succumbed to the dark side of the Force. These amoral hackers like to muddy the waters by describing their wicked offspring as "self-propagating, autonomous computer programs" and giving them innocent-sounding names such as Michelangelo and Christmas. But don't be fooled: these small slices of evil can do irreparable harm to your files. (Just so you know, many viruses have names that more directly reflect their intentions. These include Armageddon, Beast, Black Monday, Dark Avenger, and Darth Vader. I'll show you how to view a list of the known viruses a little later.)

Although virus infections are, fortunately, still relatively rare, they do happen. The fact that Microsoft decided to bundle an anti-virus program with its operating system is an indication that the problem is a real one and should be taken seriously.

Okay, now that I've scared the bejeebers out of everyone, it's time to get down to business. To start DOS 6's Anti-Virus program, open the **Microsoft Tools** group in Program Manager and select the **Anti-Virus** icon. You'll see the Microsoft Anti-Virus window, as shown in the following figure. (You can also start Anti-Virus from File Manager by pulling down the Tools menu and selecting the Antivirus command.)

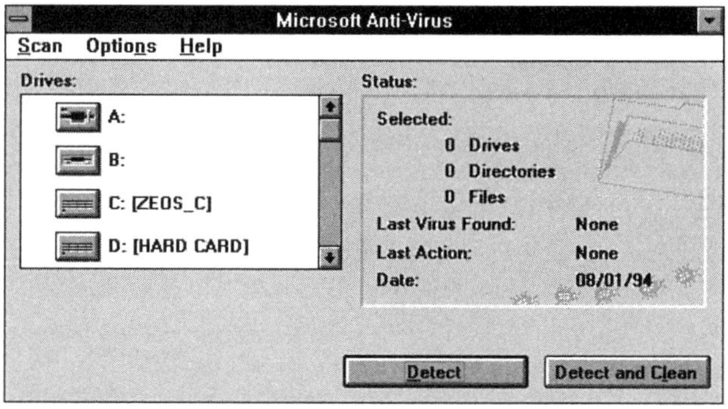

The Microsoft Anti-Virus window.

Detecting and Cleaning Viruses

To be safe, you should use Anti-Virus to perform a checkup on your system regularly. I'd recommend running the program at least once a month or anytime your computer seems to behave strangely. (I know, I know: computers *always* behave strangely!)

To get started, you first need to use the **Drives** box to select the drive (or drives) you want to scan. With your mouse, simply click on the drive. Or, with your keyboard, press **Tab** until one of the drives is highlighted, use the up and down arrow keys to highlight the drive you want to scan, and then press the **Spacebar**.

Anti-Virus takes a few seconds to read the disk's information. When it's done, select the Detect and Clean button. Anti-Virus first scans your system's memory (to check for viruses that may be skulking in the shadows), and then proceeds to check every file on the drive you selected. The scan takes a few minutes, so this would be a good time to go grab a cup of coffee or something. When its chores are complete, Anti-Virus displays a Statistics dialog box that tells you the number of files that were infected and cleaned.

TECHNO NERD TEACHES...

If you think there are only a few viruses out there, think again. There are, in fact, *hundreds*. To see for yourself, pull down the **S**can menu and select the **V**irus List command. This displays the Virus List dialog box that gives you information on all the known viruses. At the very bottom of the list you'll see the total number of viruses. In my case, the number is—brace yourself—1,234! (There are more viruses discovered every day, so your number may be different.)

Some Anti-Virus Tips

Besides using Anti-Virus regularly, here are a few other tips to help keep your system disease-free:

- Most viruses are transmitted from machine to machine via floppy disks, so you should always be careful about which used disks you trust in your computer. If you've inherited some old disks, you can make sure there are no viruses lurking in the weeds by formatting each one before you use it.
- Trust no one when it comes to loading programs on your machine. Whether they come from family, friends, or a BBS, use Anti-Virus to scan the files before you use them on your hard disk.
- Keep your virus list up to date. The DOS 6 manual has a coupon in the back that you can use to send away for virus updates. As you read this, there are probably dozens, maybe even hundreds, of amoral scumnerds designing even nastier viruses. Regular updates will help you keep up.

Protection Exercises for the Anxious, Eager, and Adventurous

I showed you how to use Windows' screen savers back in Chapter 2, "Dressing Windows for Success: Customization Fun." However, what I neglected to mention was that you can set up each screen saver to be *password protected*. This means that anyone who tries to interrupt the screen saver will first have to enter the magic password before he or she can get to Windows.

The next few sections provide you with three screen saver password exercises of increasing complexity. I'm sure you'll find one that's just right for you.

For the Anxious: Setting a Screen Saver Password

To enter a password, start Control Panel (by selecting the **Control Panel** icon in Program Manager's **Main** group), and then select the **Desktop** icon. Select the Set**u**p button and activate the **Password Protected** check box. Now select the **S**et Password button to display the Change Password dialog box shown below. Type your password in the **N**ew Password text box (it will be displayed as asterisks for extra security), and then confirm it by typing it again in the **R**etype New Password text box. Try to keep your passwords short and meaningful, so you can remember them easily. (Don't be too obvious though; using your first name isn't going to fool anyone.) Select **OK**, and then exit the remaining dialog boxes to set everything in motion.

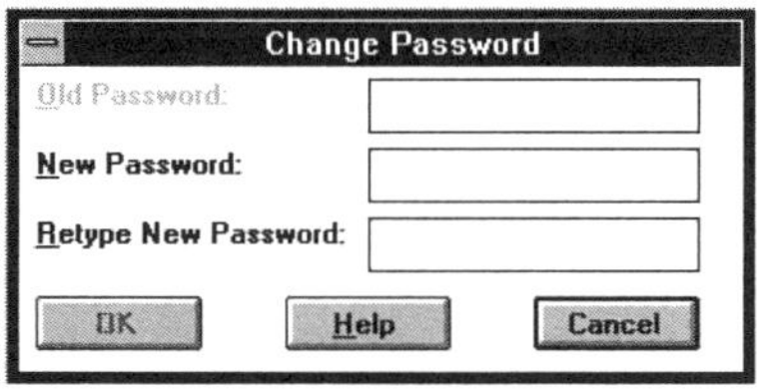

Use the Change Password dialog box to enter your password.

The next time you try to return from the screen saver to Windows, a dialog box will appear asking you to enter your password. Type it in the box provided and select **OK**.

For the Eager: What to Do If You Forget Your Password

The Achilles' heel of password protection schemes is that you have to remember your password. If you don't, you're usually just plain out of luck. (You might think you can get around the problem by rebooting, restarting Windows, and then changing the screen saver password. This doesn't work, though, because Windows asks you to enter the old password before it will assign a new one.)

There is a solution, however, if you don't mind editing an INI file (as described back in Chapter 9, "Learning to Love Those Strange INI Files"). Using a DOS-based text editor (such as the EDIT program that comes with DOS), load the CONTROL.INI file that you'll find in your Windows directory. Find the section for your screen saver (for example, [Screen Saver.Flying Windows], and look for the line that says **PWProtected=1**. Change this to read **PWProtected=0**. Now find the section titled [ScreenSaver], find the **Password=** line, and delete the entire line. Save the file, exit the text editor, and then start Windows. Your password protection is now disabled.

For the Adventurous: Full-Time Password Protection

There are two situations where the simple screen saver password protection we looked at earlier falls down on the job: when you leave your desk before the screen saver activates itself, and when you start Windows. Fortunately, it takes only a few extra steps to cover yourself in both scenarios.

The first thing you need to do is set up your screen saver so it kicks into gear with a simple key combination. Here are the steps to follow:

1. Load WIN.INI and look in the [Windows] section for the **Programs=** line. At the end of this line, type a space and then **scr**. The line should now look something like this:

    Programs=com exe bat pif scr

2. Exit and save WIN.INI, and then exit and restart Windows to put the new setting into effect.
3. In Program Manager, open the **Startup** group and create a new program item for your favorite screen saver. Be sure to include the following:

- In the Command Line text box, enter the name of the screen saver file (C:\WINDOWS\SSFLYWIN.SCR for Flying Windows, SSMARQUE.SCR for Marquee, SSMYST.SCR for Mystify, or SSSTARS.SCR for Starfield Simulation), a space, and then **/S** (for example, **SSFLYWIN.SCR /S**).
- In the Shortcut Key text box, set up a shortcut key. (For example, if you press **S**, Windows assigns a shortcut key of **Ctrl+Alt+S**.)

4. Select **OK** to return to Program Manager.
5. If haven't done so already, use Control Panel to add password protection to your screen saver, as described earlier.

With these simple steps, you've accomplished two important feats. First, your screen saver will load automatically each time you start Windows, and it will prompt you for your password when you try to exit the screen saver. In other words, nobody else can get into your copy of Windows unless he knows the proper password. Second, you can easily engage the screen saver at any time by switching to Program Manager and pressing the shortcut key.

Miscellaneous Protection

Just for the sake of dotting our protection i's and crossing our security t's, this section takes a quick peek at a few more features you can use to safeguard your system.

Use DOS 6.2's ScanDisk. If you've upgraded to DOS 6.2, you now own a little gem of a utility that you may not even know about: ScanDisk. ScanDisk is a hard disk diagnostic and repair utility that can sniff out hard drive problems and fix them on the spot. To try it out, exit Windows (or any other application, for that matter), type **scandisk /autofix /nosave /surface**, and press **Enter**. The program goes right to work looking for things that are messed up. (Note: the surface scan can take 15 minutes or even longer on large hard disks. If you don't have the time, leave off the **/surface** part of the ScanDisk command.)

Protect Program Manager. If you're worried about colleagues or the kids monkeying around with your precious Program Manager settings, you can easily add an extra level of protection. Edit the PROGMAN.INI file (you'll find it in your main Windows directory), find (or, more likely, create) the [Restrictions] section, and add the following lines:

NoFileMenu=1	This line removes Program Manager's File menu and disables its shortcut keys.
NoSaveSettings=1	This line prevents Windows from saving Program Manager's settings.
EditLevel=4	This lines prevents users from making any changes to the program items (including moving, copying, and deleting them).

Back up important Windows files. Chapter 16, "Working with a Net: Using Microsoft Backup," showed you how to back up files to a floppy disk. Even if you don't take advantage of the handy Backup program, you should at least make backups of your important Windows files. In File Manager, create a new directory called, say, BACKUPS. Display the WINDOWS directory, select all the .INI and .GRP files (the latter are the files that hold the info on your Program Manager groups), and then copy them to BACKUPS.

Keep File Manager confirmations turned on. File Manager can confirm potentially disastrous actions such as deleting a directory and replacing a file with another of the same name. To be safe, you should keep these confirmations turned on. Pull down the **O**ptions menu, select Confirmation, and then activate each check box in the Confirmation dialog box.

Avoid certain DOS commands. Some DOS commands are just plain dangerous and should be avoided at all costs in your Windows DOS sessions. These commands include CHKDSK /F, RECOVER, FASTOPEN, APPEND, DEBUG, and SUBST. Using any of these commands will cause Windows to choke, which can result in trashed data and extra ulcers.

The Least You Need to Know

This chapter got you started in this troubleshooting business by showing you some ways to avoid trouble in the first place. Here's a checklist to run through:

- Undelete can miraculously recover accidentally deleted files. For best results, use the Delete Sentry protection.
- To recover a deleted file, highlight it in the Undelete window and then select the **U**ndelete button.
- To check your hard drive for those nasty viruses, select **Anti-Virus** from the **Microsoft Tools** group, use the **Drives** box to select the drive to scan, and then select the Detect and C**l**ean button.
- To prevent unauthorized use of Windows, configure your favorite screen saver with password protection.
- If you have DOS 6.2, run ScanDisk once a day to check for errors on your hard drive.

Chapter 21
Ignition Trouble: Installation and Startup Woes

In This Chapter

- How to achieve something called a "clean boot"
- Some installation problems and their solutions
- Recovering from startup difficulties
- A ton of top-notch troubleshooting techniques

Perhaps the most frustrating of the many woes awaiting Windows users is when the program refuses to either install or start. You've spent all that money and now the evil beast won't even do anything! Before your blood pressure goes off the scale, take a look at this chapter. We'll examine the most common installation and startup problems, and I'll show you the easiest ways to fix 'em.

Cleaning Your Boots

In computer lingo, a *clean boot* has nothing to do with freshly shined shoes. Instead, it refers to the process of starting (or *booting*) your computer without loading any so-called *memory resident* programs (a.k.a. *terminate-and-stay-resident* programs or, simply, *TSRs*). This is one of the most common troubleshooting techniques, and it's one you'll be hearing *ad nauseum* throughout your computing career (at least until they start making reliable computers and software—hah!).

If you have DOS 6, getting a clean boot is as easy as pie. When you crank up your machine, wait until you see the message **Starting MS-DOS** on your screen. Then quickly press **F5** (you have about two seconds to do this). You'll immediately be taken to the DOS prompt.

If you have an earlier version of DOS, things aren't quite so simple. You first have to create a floppy disk that is "bootable" (this is also called a *system disk*) by following these steps:

1. Place an otherwise-expendable disk in drive A (it has to be drive A).
2. Start File Manager, pull down the **D**isk menu, and select the Format command. The Format Disk dialog box appears, as shown below.

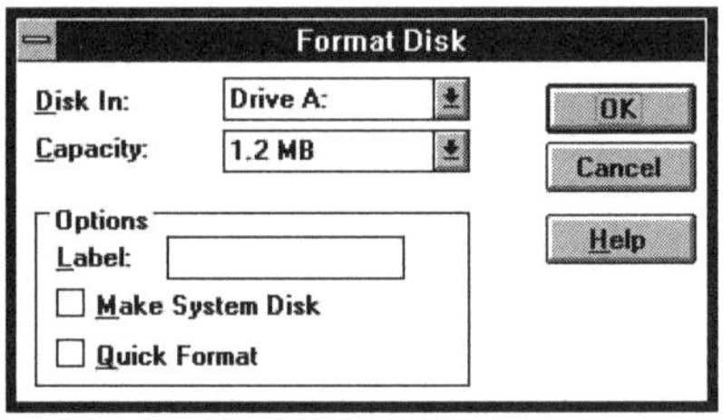

Use the Format Disk dialog box to create a disk for booting clean.

3. Make sure the **D**isk In box says **Drive A:**, and the **C**apacity box shows the appropriate capacity for the disk you're using.
4. Activate the **M**ake System Disk check box.
5. Select **OK**. File Manager asks you to confirm that you want to format the disk.
6. Select **Y**es. File Manager formats the disk. When the format is complete, the program asks you if you want to format another.
7. Select **N**o to return to File Manager.
8. Pull down the **F**ile menu and select the Exit command.

Now you need to create "clean" configuration files (i.e., files that DOS runs during the boot process that are stripped of any excess commands). Using Notepad or your favorite text editor, enter the following lines in a new file:

```
PATH=C:\DOS;C:\WINDOWS
PROMPT $P$G
SET TEMP=C:\WINDOWS\TEMP
```

Make sure your bootable disk is still in drive A, and then save this file with the name A:\AUTOEXEC.BAT. (Adding the A:\ at the beginning ensures that the file is saved to the bootable disk.) You also need to create another file called CONFIG.SYS for the bootable disk. Here are the lines to add to this file:

```
DEVICE=C:\WINDOWS\HIMEM.SYS
FILES=30
BUFFERS=20
SHELL=C:\DOS\COMMAND.COM C:\DOS /P /E:512
```

To boot clean, exit Windows, place the bootable floppy disk in drive A (if it isn't still there), and then reboot. You'll see an A:\> prompt instead of the usual C:\> prompt.

TECHNO NERD TEACHES...

AUTOEXEC.BAT and CONFIG.SYS are important configuration files that DOS looks for each time you start or reboot your computer. The ones DOS normally uses are found in the root drive (i.e., C:\) of your hard drive. Later in this chapter (and in some of the chapters to come), I may ask you to edit these files. They're simple text files, so you can do it in any text editor. The easiest method, though, is to pull down Program Manager's or File Manager's **F**ile menu, select **R**un, enter **SYSEDIT** in the Run dialog box, and then select **OK**. The System Configuration Editor window that appears displays both AUTOEXEC.BAT and CONFIG.SYS (as well as WIN.INI and SYSTEM.INI). See Chapter 9, "Learning to Love Those Strange INI Files," for more info on SysEdit.

Investigating Installation Irritations

Windows, being the complex creation that it is, is no stranger to installation woes. This section eyeballs some of the more common problems that arise when you run Windows' Setup program.

Your Computer Hangs While Installing Windows

One of the most exasperating installation problems is when your system *hangs* (i.e., it stops dead in its tracks, and no amount of coaxing, gesticulating, or verbal coercion will make it start again). The temptation is to insert any handy object through your display. I've found this to be a good last resort but, in the meantime, here are a few possible solutions.

> **TECHNO NERD TEACHES...**
>
> The following solutions also apply if Setup pops you out to the DOS prompt before the installation is complete.

Remove all memory-resident programs. By far the most common cause of installation hangups is a clash between Setup and a TSR. Try starting the installation with the command **setup /t**. This tells Setup to check for conflicting TSRs. If conflicts are found, Setup will give you instructions on how to proceed. If no conflicts are reported, you're not out of the woods yet because Setup may have missed something. Try a clean boot and then run Setup again.

Turn off Setup's hardware-detection scheme. If TSRs aren't the problem, Setup may be choking during its "auto-detection" phase. During this phase, the program tries to save you some time by automatically detecting the type of hardware on your system. Unfortunately, if Setup makes a mistake, your computer will hang. (This is especially true if Setup chooses the wrong driver for your video display.) To turn off auto-detection, use the command **setup /i** when you begin the installation, and Setup displays a standard configuration, as shown in the following figure. Select the settings appropriate for your computer, and then continue with the installation.

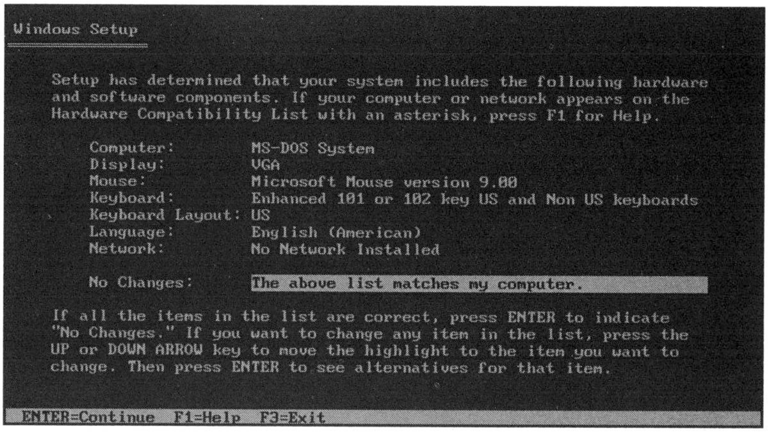

Without auto-detection, Setup displays a standard configuration.

If Setup always hangs when it switches to Windows Mode, try a different display driver. Setup is actually two programs in one. The first program (called DOS Mode Setup) analyzes your system and installs the files you need to start Windows. The second program (Windows Mode Setup) actually runs in Windows, and it installs the rest of the Windows files and configures applications (such as Program Manager).

If Setup fails when switching from DOS Mode to Windows Mode, it's likely that the display driver that Setup is using is incorrect. Use the command **setup /i** to prevent Setup from automatically selecting a display driver. When Setup displays the system settings (as described earlier), select the correct display option for your system. If you're not sure about this, select a generic driver (such as VGA or EGA). If the problem persists, contact the manufacturer of the video board and ask them about it. They may need to send you a new video driver that is compatible with Windows 3.1.

You Have Hardware Problems During Installation

Windows has to work with an incredible variety of hardware. There are, literally, dozens of video displays, mice, keyboards, and printers. And of course, as users, we expect Windows to work no matter what bizarre combination we've cobbled together. That's a tall order for any software, and it's a testament to the Microsoft programmers that Windows works as well as it does. This is no comfort, however, if you are having hardware problems—so here are a few things to look for:

Turn off Setup's hardware detection scheme and select the options yourself. Setup tries to detect the hardware on your system automatically. Although it's usually pretty good at it, mistakes can happen. To bypass this scheme, run Setup with the command **setup /i**, and select your own hardware settings as described earlier in this chapter.

If you can't find a setting appropriate for your hardware, contact either the manufacturer or Microsoft for a driver. Windows communicates with your hardware using a small piece of software called a *device driver*. If your hardware doesn't appear in the Setup lists, you need to get the appropriate driver. The best source to contact is the manufacturer of the device. Otherwise, Microsoft themselves maintain an extensive device driver library. While you're waiting for the driver to arrive, you may still be able to install Windows by selecting generic devices from the hardware lists in Setup. Here are some suggestions:

Computer	MS-DOS System
Display	VGA or EGA
Mouse	Microsoft
Keyboard	Enhanced 101 or 102 key US
Printer	Generic/Text

If you're upgrading from 3.0 to 3.1, you may need to upgrade your drivers as well. Many device drivers that worked fine with Windows 3.0 are incompatible with version 3.1. Contact the manufacturer or Microsoft for a replacement.

Miscellaneous Installation Problems

This section lists a few of the more common questions and problems that crop up during Windows installation.

You want to install a minimal version of Windows on a system with limited hard disk space. Fully installed, Windows takes up over 10 megabytes of precious hard disk real estate. If you can't afford to give up that much space, you can simply leave off a few of Windows' accessories and options. To do this, follow these steps:

1. Type **setup**, press **Enter**, and follow the on-screen prompts.

2. When Setup asks you which method you want to use, select the **Custom Setup** option.
3. When Setup switches to Windows Mode, you'll eventually see a dialog box called Windows Setup that lists the five Windows components: Readme **F**iles, **A**ccessories, **G**ames, Screen **S**avers, and **W**allpapers, Misc.
4. To prevent Setup from installing an entire component, simply deselect its check box. To remove only selected files, click on the appropriate **Files** button. In the dialog box that appears, highlight the files you want to remove, and then select the **R**emove button. Select **OK** to return to the Windows Setup dialog box.
5. Repeat step 4 for each of the components.
6. Select C**o**ntinue to proceed with the installation.

You copied a file from the installation disks to your hard drive and it doesn't work. The files on the installation disks are stored in a "compressed" format to save space. You need to use the Expand utility that comes with Windows to decompress a file for normal use. (Windows does this automatically when you perform a normal installation.) The general format to use is

expand *CompressedName DecompressedName*

Here, *CompressedName* is the name of the file on the installation disk (including the drive letter), and *DecompressedName* is the name you want to give the file (including the drive and directory). The *CompressedName* always ends with an underscore character (_). In the following steps, I'll show you how to expand the file MOUSE.CO_ from install disk 4 to the file MOUSE.COM. (MOUSE.COM is used as part of a solution in Chapter 25, "Relieving Hardware Headaches").

1. Exit Windows, if necessary.
2. Type **cd\windows** to change to the Windows directory.
3. Place the installation disk containing the file MOUSE.CO_ in drive A (substitute drive B for A, if needed).
4. Type **expand a:mouse.co_ c:\windows\mouse.com** and press **Enter**. Expand decompresses the file.

Solving Startup Snags

Have you ever had problems starting your car? If so, you know only too well the subsequent emotional roller coaster ride: basic shock is the first to hit ("Oh no!"), then comes denial ("This *can't* be happening."), then anger ("@#$*&!"), and finally frustration ("Why me?"). To make matters worse, this only seems to happen on the coldest mornings, when you're late for work (chalk up another one for Murphy's Law).

Windows startup problems can be equally frustrating. With a deadline looming or an in-basket full of paper, the last thing you need is for your operating system to refuse to run. This section discusses several of the most common Windows startup problems and their solutions.

Windows Reports an Error on Startup

When Windows won't load, you'll often find that the program at least has the common decency to tell you what happened. This section looks at a few of the error messages you're likely to see.

Windows reports an "Out of Environment Space" message on startup. The *environment space* is a small section of your computer's memory that DOS uses to store certain kinds of information. DOS normally reserves 256 bytes for the environment (160 bytes if you're using DOS 4 or earlier) where a *byte* is the equivalent of a single character. This is usually more than enough for most situations, but some programs (such as Windows) add their own environment information. If too much is added, you'll see the **Out of environment space** message. The solution is to simply increase the size of the environment space. Here are the steps to follow:

1. At the DOS prompt, type **cd** and press **Enter** to move to your hard disk's root directory.
2. Start up your favorite text editor and load the CONFIG.SYS file. (If you don't have a favorite text editor, but you do have at least DOS 5, you can load CONFIG.SYS by typing **edit config.sys** and pressing **Enter**.)

3. Look for a line that begins with **SHELL=**. Add or edit the line so that it reads as follows:

   SHELL=C:\DOS\COMMAND.COM C:\DOS /E:512 /P

4. Save the file, exit to DOS, and then reboot your computer.

In step 3, the /E:512 part changes the size of the environment space to 512 bytes. If this is still not enough, keep increasing the size of the environment in increments of 256 (the maximum size is a whopping 32,768 bytes).

Windows reports a "Group File Error: Cannot open program-group file *filename*" message (where *filename* is the name of a group file such as MAIN.GRP). Windows stores the details of your Program Manager program groups in special *group files* on your hard drive. The "Group File Error" occurs when Windows tries to load a group file that has been corrupted or accidentally deleted. If you're using Windows 3.1, the program asks if you want to attempt to load this group in the future. Simply select the No button, and the problem is solved. If you're still using 3.0, the solution takes a little more legwork. You should first try to restore the group file from a backup disk if you have one. If you don't, you need to tell Program Manager not to try to load the group during subsequent startups. Here are the necessary steps:

1. Using Notepad or some other text editor, open the file PROGMAN.INI (you'll find it in your main Windows directory) and look for the section titled [Groups] (see the picture below).

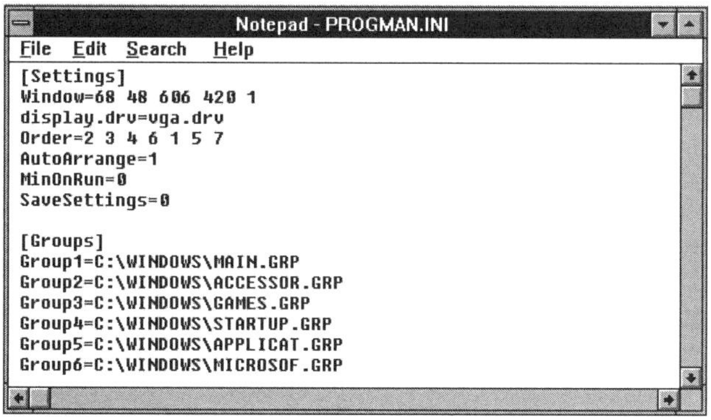

Program Manager tracks your groups by using PROGMAN.INI's [Groups] section.

2. You should see a line in the [Groups] section that includes the name of the group file that caused the error (for example, **Group1=C:\WINDOWS\MAIN.GRP**). Delete the line.
3. Save the file, exit the text editor, and then exit and restart Windows.

Windows reports an "Internal stack overflow" message. A *stack* is a temporary storage location used by programs (much like a stack of trays in a cafeteria). If the stack area is too small, it "overflows," and you get the above message. To fix the problem, edit CONFIG.SYS to include the line **STACKS=9,256**. (If you're using MS-DOS 3.2, use the line **STACKS=9,192.**)

Windows Won't Start in 386 Enhanced Mode

Windows 3.1 uses two different modes: standard and 386 enhanced. Standard mode is fine if you're just using Windows applications. But if you want to multitask DOS applications or run them in a window, you need to use 386 enhanced mode. Sometimes, however, Windows won't start in one mode or the other. If Windows won't start in 386 enhanced mode, try these solutions.

Make sure you have a system capable of handling 386 enhanced mode. 386 enhanced mode is very sophisticated, and it requires equally sophisticated hardware. Specifically, you need a 386 or better computer with at least 2 megabytes of total memory and at least 1 megabyte of extended memory. If your system doesn't have this minimum configuration, you're out of luck.

Make adjustments to your CONFIG.SYS file. For Windows 3.1 to run in 386 enhanced mode, you need to make sure the following lines are in your CONFIG.SYS file:

DEVICE=C:\WINDOWS\HIMEM.SYS
FILES=30
BUFFERS=20

Try some different startup methods. Start Windows with the command **win /d:v**. If Windows starts okay, add the following line to the [386Enh] section of the file SYSTEM.INI:

VirtualHDIRQ=Off

If Windows still doesn't start, try the command **win /d:x**. If Windows loads now, you need to add the following line to SYSTEM.INI's [386Enh] section:

SystemROMBreakPoint=Off

Windows Hangs During Startup

If Windows is bailing out whenever you try to start it, try these solutions.

Increase the FILES setting in CONFIG.SYS. When Windows is cranking itself up to speed, it tends to open up a lot of files in the process. However, the FILES setting in CONFIG.SYS sets a limit to the number of files (or, technically, file handles) that can be open at any time. If Windows bumps up against that ceiling, it'll hang. To remedy this, edit your CONFIG.SYS file to set FILES=30. Don't be afraid to try a higher number if this doesn't work. Settings of 50 or 60 are not at all unusual.

Don't use your keyboard while Windows is loading. Some users have reported that Windows will hang occasionally if they start typing before the program is completely loaded. To be safe, wait until you see the Program Manager window before you touch your keyboard.

Use the /B switch to track down the problem. If you start Windows with the command **win /b**, the program logs the progress of the startup and stores the information in a text file called BOOTLOG.TXT in your main Windows directory. If Windows fails to boot, BOOTLOG.TXT should tell you why. Look for a line that begins **LoadFail**; this will tell you which file Windows choked on. You can sometimes recover by expanding the appropriate file from your original Windows disks (as described earlier in this chapter). More often, you'll need to report the error to Microsoft Technical Support.

The Least You Need to Know

This chapter examined a number of solutions for installation and startup headaches. Here's a rehash of the main events:

- To get a clean boot in DOS 6, press **F5** when you see the **Starting MS-DOS** message. For earlier versions of DOS, create a bootable floppy disk and create clean AUTOEXEC.BAT and CONFIG.SYS files.
- If your computer hangs during installation, try running Setup after a clean boot, or try turning off hardware detection using the command **setup /i**.
- To install a minimal version of Windows, select the **Custom Setup** option, and then deselect the Windows options you don't need.
- If Windows hangs during startup, try using a higher FILES setting in CONFIG.SYS and avoid touching the keyboard until Windows is fully loaded. If all else fails, start Windows with the command **win /b** to create BOOTLOG.TXT.

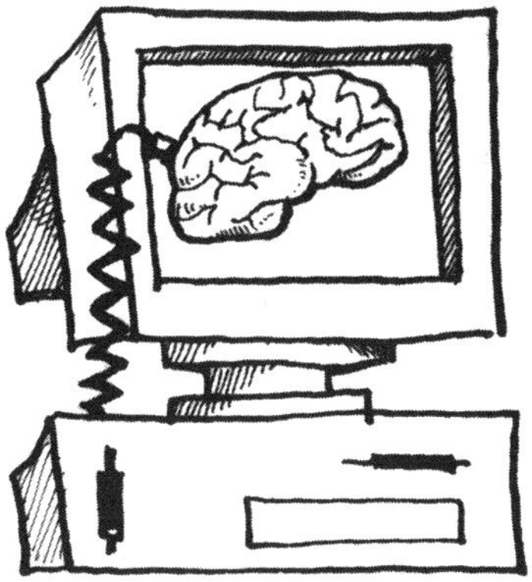

Chapter 22
Maneuvering the Memory Maze

In This Chapter

- A short, relatively painless memory primer
- How to get more memory for Windows applications
- How to get more memory for DOS applications
- Using MemMaker to squeeze out every last bit of memory
- Mondo memory machinations that'll have you singing "Thanks for the Memory"

Entire books can be (and have been) written about the relationship between Windows and memory. What it all boils down to, though, is quite simple: the more memory you have, the happier Windows is. However, not all of us can afford to throw 64 megabytes of memory at our problems. We have to make do with less, and that, in essence, is what this chapter is all about. I'll show you some ways to fight back if a lack of memory is causing your applications to run slowly (or not at all).

If you're looking for info on SmartDrive or swap files, head on down the road to Chapter 23, "From Slowpoke to Speed Demon: Making Windows Fly," to get the scoop on these important features.

A Brief History of Memory

Your computer's memory is arguably its most important component, yet few people seem to understand what it is or what it does. So we'll begin with a brief, non-technical explanation of some basic memory concepts.

Hard Disks Versus Memory

To begin with, let's talk about the difference between your *hard disk* and your *memory*. Many people confuse these two terms because the storage capacity of both is measured in megabytes. There's a big difference, however, and to see it, try thinking of your computer as a carpenter's workshop. A typical workshop is divided into two basic areas: storage space and work space. During a project, the carpenter will take materials and tools from the storage area and manipulate them in the work area. This is exactly what happens in your computer. Your applications and data files are stored on your hard disk and when you need to work with them, they're copied into memory.

SPEAK LIKE A GEEK

A **byte** is a single character of information. A **kilobyte** (abbreviated as K or KB) is 1,024 bytes, and a **megabyte** (abbreviated as either M or MB) is 1,024 kilobytes.

The problem is that most hard disks can store dozens or even hundreds of megabytes of data, whereas the memory capacity of a typical computer is limited to only a few megabytes or so. This means that your computer's "work space" is much smaller than its "storage space." For a carpenter, a small work space limits the number of tools and materials he can use at any one time. For a computer, it limits the number of programs and data files that you can load.

The "640K Barrier"

The first restriction placed on your computer's work space is the so-called "640K barrier." This means that the maximum amount of memory that DOS can use to run your programs and data files is 640K (this area is also called *conventional memory*). "Now hold on a minute," I hear you saying. "Why the heck have I got all these megabytes of memory in my computer if all I can use is 640K?" Don't worry, there are ways around the 640K barrier that I'll talk about a little later on.

TECHNO NERD TEACHES...

Why 640K? Why not 650K or 6,400K? Well, 640K was the maximum amount of memory available to programs on the original IBM PC. And since that became the standard, so did 640K. The IBM PC was actually capable of working with a full 1MB (1,024K) of memory, but the engineers usurped 384K for hardware uses.

Why is the 640K barrier a problem? Well, there was a time when it seemed impossible that programs would ever come close to using up 640K. In fact, the first IBM PCs shipped with only 16K of memory! However, as programs grew more complex and sophisticated, their size increased correspondingly. Not only that, but people began using more *TSR* (terminate-and-stay-resident) software. These programs, such as mouse drivers and productivity enhancers like SideKick, stay available in memory and so use up portions of the 640K area. Before long, programmers and users were bumping their heads on the 640K ceiling, and new methods were needed to get around this limitation. The fact that you now routinely see programs with files that are as large as two or three *megabytes* shows that they succeeded.

Expanded Versus Extended Memory

To get around the 640K limit, the world's computer geniuses came up with two solutions: *expanded memory* and *extended memory*. These concepts are almost universally confused and misunderstood, so let's take a minute to see if we can knock some sense into them.

As a carpenter, you can increase your work space in two ways: you can *expand* the total area by erecting a separate building, or you can *extend* the existing work space itself with an addition. This is the principal difference between expanded memory and extended memory. Expanded memory usually comes in the form of a separate piece of equipment (called a *memory board*) that you have to install. You get extended memory, on the other hand, just by plugging memory chips directly into your computer's main circuit board (provided you have an 80286 or better computer).

How does this extra memory help? Well, your applications still have to stay within the 640K region, but there are small programs (called *memory managers*) that shuffle bits of program code and data files between the 640K area and the expanded or extended memory.

For example, suppose you're in your workshop and you need to use a lathe, but you haven't got the room. No problem. Your assistant (the memory manager) knows that the lathe is either outside in the tool shed (expanded memory) or in an adjacent area (extended memory). He makes room by grabbing something you don't need for now (a band saw, for instance), takes it to the expanded or extended memory area, exchanges it for the lathe, and then brings the lathe to your workshop.

What Kind of Memory Does Windows Prefer?

Windows and Windows applications use only extended memory. However, if you use DOS applications that require expanded memory (such as Lotus 1-2-3 version 3.1), you have two options:

- Run Windows in 386 enhanced mode. In this mode, Windows automatically simulates expanded memory from your system's extended memory for any DOS application that needs it.
- Run Windows in Standard mode and use an *expanded memory manager*. An expanded memory manager (such as the EMM386 program that comes with Windows) uses extended memory to simulate expanded memory.

Dealing with "Insufficient Memory" Problems

Now that you're thoroughly confused, we can talk about some solutions to that most vexing of Windows problems: the "Insufficient Memory" message. From the discussion above, we can conclude that there are two basic approaches we can take to solving this problem:

- Optimize your use of conventional memory (the first 640K).
- Optimize your use of extended memory (or expanded memory, if it's needed by your DOS applications).

Solutions for Both Windows and DOS Applications

The solutions presented in this section are applicable to both Windows and DOS applications.

If you have other applications running, close them one at a time until your application will start. This, I suppose, is the most obvious (but the least convenient) solution. If you have any running applications that you really don't need, shut them down. The bigger the application, the more memory you'll save. Other memory-stealers are the TSR programs you may have loaded before starting Windows. You may need to examine your AUTOEXEC.BAT and CONFIG.SYS files (or get a nearby computer guru to do it for you) to see if you really need everything that's being loaded.

Delete the contents of the Clipboard. When you cut or copy a selection in a Windows application, the program stores the data in an area of memory called the Clipboard. If you're working with only a few lines of text, this area remains fairly small. However, cutting or copying a graphic image can increase the size of the Clipboard to several hundred kilobytes or more. If you've run out of memory, a large Clipboard may be the problem. To release this memory, try one of the following methods:

- If you have an application running, highlight a small section of text (a single character will do), pull down the Edit menu, and select the Copy command. This replaces the current Clipboard with a much smaller one.
- In Program Manager, select the **Clipboard Viewer** icon from the **Main** group. When the Clipboard Viewer window appears, pull down the Edit menu and select the Delete command.

Release some "system resources." *System resources* are two small (64K) chunks of memory that Windows uses to keep track of things like the position and size of open windows, dialog boxes, and your desktop configuration (wallpaper and so on). You can have megabytes of free memory but you'll still get **Insufficient Memory** errors if you run out of system resources! (In fact, I've heard it estimated that low system resources are the culprit in up to 90% of these errors; ask any Windows guru about his or her pet peeve, and you'll probably receive an almost unanimous response: "those @#$%&*! system resources!")

How can you tell if your system resources are getting low? In Program Manager, select the **H**elp menu's About Program Manager command. In the About Program Manager dialog box that appears, check out the System Resources line at the bottom. This tells you what percentage of the system resource areas is still available. Problems develop when this number drops below 20%. (The number Windows shows for "Memory" may be a bit confusing: it's actually a combination of the memory you have free and the size of your swap file. See Chapter 23 to learn what the heck a "swap file" is.)

Here are a few tips for preserving your system resources:

- In Program Manager, don't open any program groups you don't need. In fact, many people reduce their total number of program groups to one or two.
- When working with Windows applications, don't leave open any unnecessary document windows. Also, turn off such features as status bars, rulers, and toolbars if you don't use them.
- When working with DOS applications, run them full screen instead of in a window.
- Turn off the wallpaper on your desktop.
- Upgrade to Windows 3.1 if you haven't done so already. The new version uses system resources more intelligently than previous versions.

TECHNO NERD TEACHES...

For an easier way to keep an eye peeled on your system resources, check out Memory Monitor on the disk that accompanies this book. This little program lets you keep an eye on your system resources without your having to run the About Program Manager command.

Load larger applications first. Because of the way Windows uses memory, you can often start more programs if you load your larger Windows applications before your smaller ones.

Run MemMaker if you have DOS 6. DOS 6 includes an important new tool called MemMaker that makes it easy to configure your system to get the most out of your memory. To try it out, follow these steps:

1. Exit Windows.
2. Type **memmaker** and press **Enter**. DOS displays the Welcome to MemMaker screen.
3. Press **Enter**. DOS asks if you want to use Express or Custom Setup (see below).

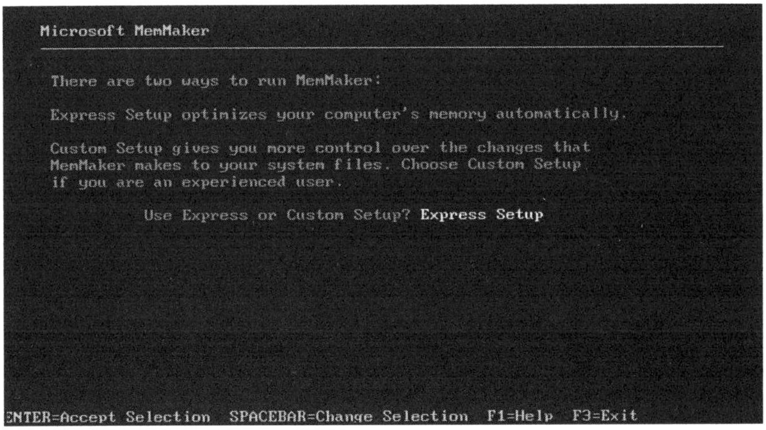

For a no-brainer MemMaker operation, choose the Express Setup.

4. Make sure **Express Setup** is displayed (if not, press the **Spacebar**), and then press **Enter**. MemMaker asks if you have any programs that use expanded memory.
5. Unless you're sure you have programs that need expanded memory, select **No** and press **Enter**. MemMaker warns you that it's about to reboot your computer.
6. Remove any floppy disks from your drives and press **Enter**. MemMaker reboots and then tries out various memory configurations. When it finds the best one, it lets you know.
7. Press **Enter** to reboot your computer for a second time. MemMaker asks if your computer seems to be working properly.
8. Select **Yes** if all is well; otherwise, select **No**, and then press **Enter** three times to have MemMaker undo its changes.

9. If you selected **Yes**, MemMaker displays some statistics showing how much memory you've gained. When your head starts to hurt too much, press **Enter** to return to DOS.

Edit CONFIG.SYS and AUTOEXEC.BAT if you have DOS 5. If you're using DOS 5, you can still get more memory, but I'm afraid you have to make the appropriate changes to CONFIG.SYS and AUTOEXEC.BAT by hand.

For starters, here's a summary of the changes you need to make for CONFIG.SYS:

- At the top of the file, add the following two lines:

  DEVICE=C:\WINDOWS\HIMEM.SYS
  DOS=HIGH

- If you have at least a 386 computer, add the following lines below the HIMEM.SYS line you added previously:

  DEVICE=C:\WINDOWS\EMM386.EXE NOEMS
  DOS=UMB

  If you have programs that require expanded memory, change the NOEMS part of the EMM386.EXE line to **RAM**.

- For each device driver loaded in CONFIG.SYS (i.e., every line that begins with the word DEVICE—except for the HIMEM.SYS and EMM386.EXE lines you've just added), change DEVICE to DEVICEHIGH. For example, consider the following simple CONFIG.SYS file:

  FILES=30
  BUFFERS=20
  DEVICE=C:\DOS\ANSI.SYS

  After the changes suggested above, the same file would now look like this:

  DEVICE=C:\WINDOWS\HIMEM.SYS
  DEVICE=C:\WINDOWS\EMM386.EXE NOEMS
  DOS=UMB

```
DOS=HIGH
FILES=30
BUFFERS=20
DEVICEHIGH=C:\DOS\ANSI.SYS
```

For AUTOEXEC.BAT, you need only precede each line that loads a memory-resident program with the word LOADHIGH, as in the following example:

```
PROMPT $P$G
PATH C:\WINDOWS;C:\DOS
SET TEMP=C:\WINDOWS\TEMP
LOADHIGH C:\WINDOWS\MOUSE.COM
LOADHIGH C:\DOS\DOSKEY.COM
```

TECHNO NERD TEACHES...

What's going on here with all this UMB, DEVICEHIGH, and LOADHIGH stuff? Well, what you're actually doing is taking advantage of the third solution for hurdling the 640K barrier (besides extended and expanded memory). Remember when I told you that the designers of the original IBM PC absconded with 384K for hardware? This is called the *upper memory area*, and it turns out that it's full of holes! Specifically, it has all these little pockets of unused memory called *upper memory blocks*. The HIMEM.SYS program can reclaim these UMBs, as they're called, and use them to store programs that would otherwise take up valuable space in conventional memory. That's what the DEVICEHIGH and LOADHIGH statements are doing: they load programs into upper memory.

Buy more memory. The ultimate way to beat the low-memory blues, of course, is simply to add more memory to your system. (Although, as you've seen, you still need to watch that your system resources don't get too low.) Unfortunately, memory prices have risen over the past couple of years, so it may not be possible to add more than a couple of megabytes without breaking your budget. Contact your computer manufacturer to find out the best kind of memory to add to your system.

Solutions for DOS Applications

This section outlines solutions to out-of-memory problems that apply only to DOS applications running under Windows.

Load DOS programs before Windows applications. Because of the way Windows applications use memory, you can often load more applications if you load DOS programs before you load any Windows applications.

Edit the application's PIF memory settings. If you run out of memory trying to load a DOS application, you can try modifying a couple of settings in its PIF. Open the appropriate PIF (see Chapter 5, "Taming the DOS Beast," for the PIF particulars) and change the KB **R**equired setting to –1. This forces Windows to give the application all the available conventional memory. Also, if you're running Windows in 386 enhanced mode, make sure the KB **D**esired box is also set to –1.

Change the application's PIF so that it loads through COMMAND.COM. COMMAND.COM is the DOS program that executes DOS commands and loads DOS applications. You may be able to eke out a little more memory for an application if you change its PIF so that it loads a copy of COMMAND.COM and *then* loads the application. Here are the steps to follow:

1. In the PIF Editor, load the application's PIF.
2. Change the **P**rogram Filename to **COMMAND.COM**.
3. In the **O**ptional Parameters field, enter /C followed by the name of the file that starts the application, including the proper drive and directory (you need to leave a space after /C). The following picture shows an example PIF that loads WordPerfect.

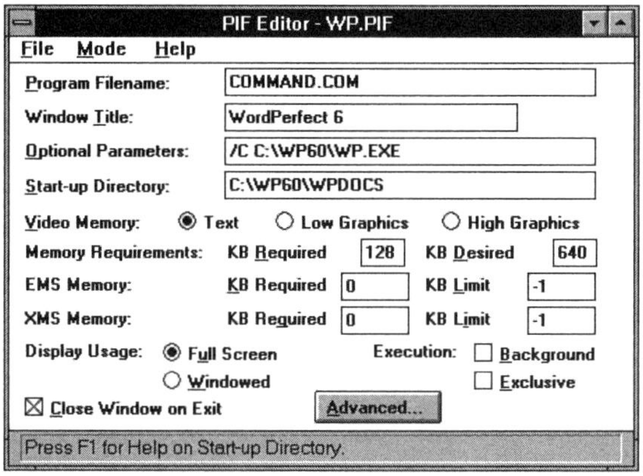

A PIF that loads WordPerfect via COMMAND.COM.

4. Use the File Save As command to save the new PIF to a different name.

The Least You Need to Know

This chapter showed you a number of techniques for dealing with **Out of memory** errors. Here's a summary of just a few of the tricks you learned:

- If your hard disk is like a carpenter's storage area, your computer's memory would be like the work area.
- Because of the 640K barrier, programmers came up with expanded memory and extended memory as workarounds. Expanded memory usually comes as a separate piece of equipment (called a *memory board*); you get extended memory just by plugging memory chips directly into your computer's main circuit board.
- To get more memory for your Windows applications, shut down existing applications, delete the Clipboard contents, or release some system resources.

continues

continued

- If you have DOS 6, you can get more memory just by running a program called MemMaker. If you're still using DOS 5, you can achieve similar results by adding a few lines to your CONFIG.SYS and AUTOEXEC.BAT files.
- To get more memory for DOS applications under Windows, try loading the DOS program first, or else make modifications to the program's PIF.

Chapter 23
From Slowpoke to Speed Demon: Making Windows Fly

In This Chapter

- Making your hard drive howl
- Faster application loading
- Improving printer performance
- Getting your video up to speed
- A fistful of ways to avoid the dreaded hourglass icon

Your applications have all the zip of a wet sponge, but that's the reality of working in Windows, right? Wrong! Unless your system is extremely old or has extremely slow hardware (especially the hard disk and video card), there's plenty you can do to rev up Windows to a respectable pace. And I'm not talking about upgrading to blazing Pentium machines with humongous hard disks and scads of memory. This chapter shows you how to soup up Windows using only the programs and features that come built right into either Windows or DOS. It all comes free of charge, and you'll be surprised at what a difference it makes.

Hot Rod Hard Disk Access

By far the biggest bottleneck on your system is your hard disk. Windows spends much of its life hauling data from the hard disk to memory, and then sending it back again. If its transportation routes are clogged or are too chaotic, even the fastest hard disk will run like a dachshund through cheese dip.

To help you avoid such a fate, the next few sections offer some helpful techniques that'll ensure your hard disk works as hard as it can.

Caching In on SmartDrive

In Chapter 22, "Maneuvering the Memory Maze," I used the analogy of a carpenter's workshop to describe the difference between a hard disk and memory. When you start a program, portions of the code are retrieved from the hard disk (the storage area) and are loaded into memory (the work space). As you work with different parts of the program, different chunks of code are swapped between memory and the hard drive. This is analogous to a carpenter swapping different tools and materials between the work area and the storage area.

For example, suppose the carpenter is using a screwdriver and wants to switch to a drill. Well, he could return the screwdriver to the storage area and grab the drill at the same time. However, suppose there's a possibility that the carpenter may need the screwdriver again soon. Wouldn't it make sense to keep it handy, just in case? For these situations, he could establish a temporary storage area for tools and materials that may be needed in the short term.

The computer equivalent to this temporary storage location is a chunk of memory called a *disk cache* (it's pronounced *cash*), and it's monitored by a disk cache program. Portions of your applications and their data files are stored in the cache, and if they're needed again, they're retrieved from memory instead of the hard disk. Since memory is many times faster than a hard drive, this results in a noticeable improvement in speed.

Windows 3.1 comes with its own disk caching program called SmartDrive. To use it, add the following line to the beginning of your AUTOEXEC.BAT file:

c:\windows\smartdrv.exe

(As a reminder, the easiest way to get to your AUTOEXEC.BAT file is to pull down Program Manager's or File Manager's **F**ile menu, select **R**un, type **SYSEDIT**, and then select **OK**. When the System Configuration Editor appears, select the **C:\AUTOEXEC.BAT** window. Remember also that to put your changes into effect, you have to exit Windows and reboot your machine.)

DOS 6 comes with a new, improved version of SmartDrive. If you're using DOS 6, the SmartDrive line in your AUTOEXEC.BAT file should read as follows:

c:\dos\smartdrv.exe

Putting Your Hard Disk Affairs in Order with DOS 6's Defrag

If you have DOS 6, you can use the new Defrag utility to *defragment* the files on your hard disk and greatly improve performance. Defragmenting sounds pretty serious, but it's just DOS' way of tidying up a messy hard disk. It puts your files in order and does a few other neat-freak chores. (Don't worry though: Defrag doesn't touch the contents of the files, and they still appear in the same places when you look for them in File Manager.)

TECHNO NERD TEACHES...

So just how do files get fragmented, anyway? Well, to be blunt, DOS is a slob. When it writes files back to the hard drive, it often just throws them anywhere it can find space. This is a simple way to work (DOS is a bit dim, so it likes to keep its life as simple as possible), but it often means that pieces of your files get scattered willy nilly around your hard disk. And the more pieces there are, the longer it'll take to load the file next time. After a while, this can get so bad that your hard drive is slowed to a crawl.

Before using Defrag, you need to do a little preparation yourself:

- As described in Chapter 13, "Fiddling Around with File Manager," you should delete from your hard disk any files you don't need. Defragmenting junk files only slows down the whole process.
- Exit Windows and make sure there are no other programs running. (Ideally, you should perform a "clean boot" before running DEFRAG. See Chapter 20, "An Ounce of Prevention: Avoiding Trouble," to learn about clean booting.)
- Check for hard disk errors by running DOS 6's ScanDisk utility (again, see Chapter 20 for details).

When you're ready, follow these steps to use Defrag:

1. At the DOS prompt, type **defrag** and press **Enter**. Defrag asks you to select the drive you want to "optimize" (optimizing is the same as defragmenting).
2. Use the up or down arrow keys to highlight the drive you want to optimize, and then select **OK**. Defrag reads the information from the disk and displays its recommended optimization method, as shown below.

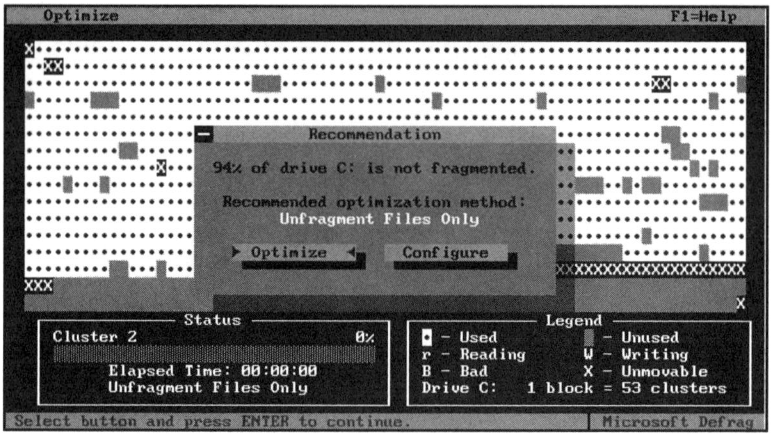

Defrag recommends an optimization method.

3. Press **Enter** to accept Defrag's recommendation. Defrag then begins optimizing the disk. The Status area in the lower left corner keeps you posted on the progress of the operation. The large area in the middle of the screen is a map of the drive you selected. Keep an eye on this area to watch Defrag moving files around. Depending on how badly fragmented your files are, this could take anywhere from a few seconds to a few minutes.
4. When Defrag finishes its chores, you'll hear a beep, and a dialog box will appear to tell you the program has **Finished condensing**. Select **OK**, then select **Exit DEFRAG** from the dialog box that appears.

How often you defragment your hard disk depends on how often you use your computer. If you use it every day, you should run Defrag about once a week. If your computer doesn't get heavy use, you'll probably only need to run Defrag about once a month or so.

A Windows Swap Meet: Creating a Permanent Swap File

When Windows is running in 386 enhanced mode, it frees up memory by "swapping" chunks of program code and data files to a special file on your hard disk called a *swap file*. This file can be either *temporary* or *permanent*. The one advantage of a temporary swap file is that it saves hard disk space because it gets deleted every time you exit Windows. (Of course, if you do most of your work within Windows this is of small benefit.) However, a permanent swap file will usually give you better performance because Windows can access it faster. Follow these steps to set up a permanent swap file:

1. Start the Control Panel and select the **386 Enhanced** icon, or pull down the **S**ettings menu and select the 386 Enhanced command. The 386 Enhanced dialog box appears.
2. Select the **V**irtual Memory button. Control Panel displays the Virtual Memory dialog box.
3. Select the **C**hange button to expand the dialog box to the one shown in the following figure.

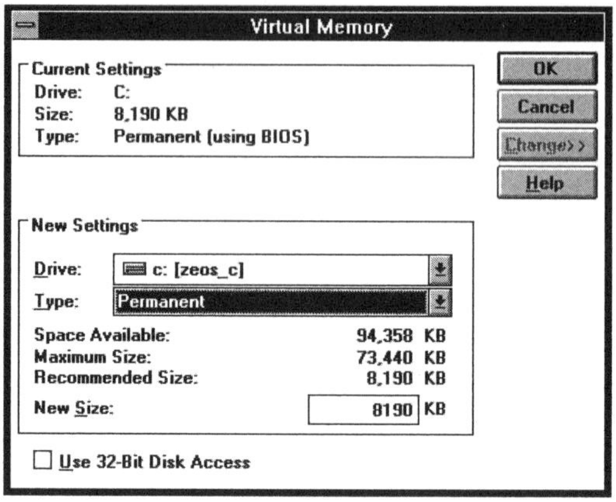

Use this version of the Virtual Memory dialog box to create a permanent swap file.

4. In the **New Settings** group, select **Permanent** from the **Type** drop-down list box.
5. Select **OK**. Control Panel asks if you're sure you want to change the settings.
6. Select **Yes**. Control Panel asks if you want to restart Windows.
7. Select the **R**estart Windows button.

TECHNO NERD TEACHES...

Even though a permanent swap file is faster than a temporary one, it operates at a snail's pace compared to your computer's memory chips. So the more memory you have, the less often Windows will need to use the hard drive to get the files it needs. Although you can run Windows with as little as 2MB of memory, 4MB is better, and 8MB will make your head spin. If you can't afford extra memory right now, make sure you read Chapter 22, "Maneuvering the Memory Maze," to find out how to maximize what you've got.

Using Windows 3.1's FastDisk Feature

If you have the proper type of hard disk, you can take advantage of a nifty new feature of Windows 3.1 called FastDisk. What does FastDisk do? Well, a technical discussion of this utility is beyond the scope of this book (and not terribly exciting). All you need to know is that it can greatly increase the speed at which Windows accesses your hard disk. If you're using a swap file (if you're not, you should be; see the previous section), this can really speed up your applications (and allow you to open more of them at the same time).

To use FastDisk, follow the instructions given in the previous section to display the expanded Virtual Memory dialog box (the one shown earlier). Activate the Use 32-Bit Disk Access check box at the bottom of the dialog box, and select **OK**. Follow the on-screen prompts to save the new setting and restart Windows.

Lowering Your Loading Times

One way to speed up your work is to actually get to work faster. You do this in Windows by reducing the time it takes to load both Windows itself and your Windows applications. Here are a few tips to help you do just that.

Remove junk you don't need from your Startup group. Every icon you've stuffed into your Startup group is loaded every time you start Windows. If you've got some applications in there that you rarely use, delete them to give Windows a few less errands to run during loading.

> E-Z
>
> If you don't need any of your Startup group stuff for a particular Windows session, hold down the **Shift** key while Windows is loading to prevent it from running the Startup group icons.

Keep WIN.INI lean and mean. One of Windows' major startup chores involves reading WIN.INI line by line. So, generally speaking, the smaller WIN.INI is, the faster Windows will load. In particular, remove any fonts you don't need (as described in Chapter 7, "Flexing Your Font Muscles"). Also, you should periodically check WIN.INI to make sure there are no extraneous lines floating around from applications you've deleted. (To make sure this doesn't happen, see Chapter 19, "How to Uninstall a Windows Application.")

Launch applications and documents simultaneously. If you have a document you use regularly, you should create an icon for the document in Program Manager (check out Chapter 12, "Let's Do Launch:

Interesting Ways to Start Applications," to learn how it's done). Opening its application first and then opening the document by hand takes about twice as long as launching the document directly.

Launch regular documents at startup. If you have several documents from several applications that you use all the time, be sure to add icons for the documents into your Startup group. Yes, Windows itself will take much longer to load, but your total load time will be much faster than if you started each document separately.

Keep your PostScript fonts to a minimum. If you prefer to use Adobe Type 1 PostScript fonts instead of TrueType, you should know that having too many of them in your system can bring a loading application down to its knees. Going from 200 fonts down to about 50 or so can cut loading time in half.

Don't load extraneous application modules. Many Windows applications have extra modules that you can load separately. In Excel, for example, you can load an Analysis Toolpack that gives the program all kinds of sophisticated math capabilities. The problem is that most of these modules take forever to crank themselves up to speed. If you don't need 'em, don't load 'em.

Tips for Printing Promptly

If your print jobs are quite large or if they include graphics, you may as well watch the paint peel while you wait for Windows to wheeze out your pages. In fairness, Windows 3.1 does a better job than 3.0 does, but there's still room for improvement. This section shows you a few ways to increase Windows' printing speed.

Change Print Manager's printing priority. When you print, Windows divides its time between processing the print job and running your application. To speed up printing, you can tell Windows to spend more time on the print job. This will slow down your application, but at least your printing speed will improve. To try it out, select the **Print Manager** icon from Program Manager's **Main** group, pull down Print Manager's **O**ptions menu, and then select the **H**igh Priority command.

Use TrueType fonts. Microsoft went to great lengths to design TrueType to work well with popular printers such as the Hewlett-Packard LaserJet series. This means that TrueType fonts such as Arial and Times New Roman will print noticeably faster than similar non-TrueType fonts.

> Even with Print Manager's priority set to High, you can speed up a print job even more by simply leaving your computer alone while the job prints. Any input—whether from a mouse or keyboard—will take time away from the printing process.

Use a RAM disk to store Print Manager's temporary files. If you've got plenty of memory (5 megabytes or more), you can give a big boost to Windows printing speed by setting up a *RAM drive*. A RAM drive ("RAM" is short for Random Access Memory) is simply a section of extended memory that is set up to work just like a disk drive. It has its own drive letter, and you can do all the things you'd normally do on a regular disk drive, such as copying files, creating directories, and so on.

Therefore, using a RAM drive is an advantage because the computer can access files in memory many times faster than it can access files on a hard drive. So you can improve Windows printing speed by telling Print Manager to send its temporary files to a RAM drive. To set this up, you need to do the following:

- In your CONFIG.SYS file, add the following line:

  DEVICE=C:\WINDOWS\RAMDRIVE.SYS 2048 /E

- In your AUTOEXEC.BAT file, change the SET TEMP line to read:

  SET TEMP=D:

(I'm assuming here that your RAM drive is drive D; DOS assigns the first unused drive letter to the RAM drive.) Reboot your computer (be sure to exit Windows first, of course) to put these changes into effect.

If you're not printing graphics, change your laser printer's resolution to 150 dots per inch (dpi). Using a lower resolution on your laser printer has no effect on text, but it will speed up the print job. To change the resolution, first start Control Panel and select the **Printers** icon. Select the **S**etup button from the Printers dialog box and, in the dialog box that appears (see the example below), select **150 dots per inch** from the **R**esolution drop-down list box.

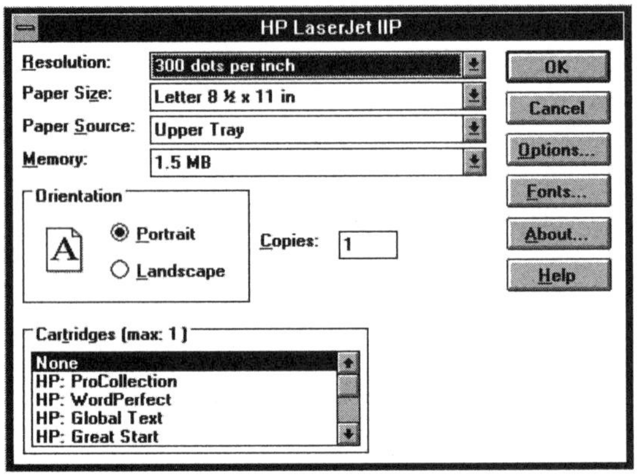

*Use the **Resolution** list to select 150 dots per inch.*

If you're using a LaserJet printer, you can get a further speed boost for documents that contain only text. Select the **O**ptions button and, in the Options dialog box, make sure the Print TrueType as **G**raphics check box is deactivated. Select **OK** and exit the remaining dialog boxes.

Pass on Print Manager for short documents. If you mostly work with short documents (say, fewer than 10 pages), you can print faster if you tell Windows to bypass Print Manager. You won't be able to do anything else while the print job is running, but your printouts will be quicker. Start Control Panel and select the **Printers** icon. In the Printers dialog box, deactivate the **U**se Print Manager check box, then select **Close**.

Upgrade your printer driver. You can often get a substantial speed boost simply by upgrading the printer driver that shipped with Windows. Most drivers are constantly being improved, so you should always try to use the latest versions. You can get the new file either from the manufacturer or from Microsoft's download service. (Trudge back to Chapter 17 "Getting Wired with Terminal," to learn how to dial into the Microsoft BBS.)

Putting the Whip to Windows Video

With several hundred thousand pixels to keep up with (and, in some cases, several hundred colors as well) today's video adapters can put a strain on even the most muscular CPU. If you find yourself constantly waiting for screens to be updated, the following tips may help.

Don't use 256 colors if you don't have to. Unless you need them to do graphics, using 256 colors will only slow you down unnecessarily. To instantly make your display several times faster, switch to a 16-color driver. (Not sure how to switch video drivers? No problem-o. Chapter 3, "Tweaking Windows with Setup," tells you everything you need to know.) If you really don't care what your screen looks like, you'll get the best performance with a monochrome mode.

Try different display drivers. Many video adapters come with several drivers for each mode. Try different drivers to see if any of them gives you better performance. Also, video manufacturers are constantly tweaking their drivers to get improved performance. See if you can get the latest upgrade.

If your adapter can switch between 8-bit and 16-bit operation, make sure it's set for 16-bit mode. A 16-bit VGA board processes display data at about twice the speed of an 8-bit adapter. Some adapters allow you to switch between these two modes for compatibility reasons. If yours does, refer to the manual and make sure you're operating in 16-bit mode.

If you're considering upgrading your adapter beyond Super VGA, look into boards with accelerators or coprocessors. Many of the newer high resolution video adapters come with extra chips (or, in some cases, full-fledged microprocessors) that assume much of the graphics processing donkey work. This improves performance for two reasons:

- The routines on the boards that process the graphics data are highly optimized for these tasks. They can handle basic tasks such as drawing lines much faster than your normal system.
- They free up your computer's main processing unit for other tasks.

These boards are a little more expensive, but they may be worth the extra cash for video that's three to five times faster.

Use TrueType fonts. Windows can render TrueType fonts much faster than any other kind. So even something as simple as scrolling through a document is noticeably faster if the document includes TrueType fonts exclusively.

The Least You Need to Know

This chapter showed you some ways to transform Windows performance from pokey to perky. Here's a checklist to run through to make sure Windows is running at top speed:

- To get the fastest hard disk access, make sure you're running SmartDrive.
- If you have DOS 6, use the Defrag program to defragment your hard disk and force DOS to clean up its room.
- Setting up a permanent swap file and enabling the FastDisk feature are great ways to make sure Windows is making the most of your hard disk.
- To improve load times, keep your Startup group and WIN.INI clean, and create icons for your frequently used documents.
- For faster printing, set Print Manager's priority to High, use TrueType fonts, and try setting up a RAM disk for the temporary files.
- You'll get faster video performance if you avoid 256-color video drivers, make sure your adapter is in 16-bit mode, and use the latest and greatest driver available from the manufacturer.

Chapter 24
Applications That Won't Applicate

In This Chapter

- Surviving Windows' annoying General Protection Faults
- Interpreting Windows' arcane error messages
- What to do when your printer won't print
- A miscellany of Windows application problems
- More snappy solutions to common computer complaints

Let's face facts: most of us use Windows not because of Windows itself, but because it allows us to run some of the coolest applications on the planet. But no matter how great we think these applications are, it only takes a single inexplicable error or unrecoverable lockup to make us start cursing their very existence. To help you avoid these frustrations, this chapter looks at some of the most common problems that plague Windows applications and, of course, offers a fistful of solutions.

Dealing with the Dreaded General Protection Fault

I often wonder if monitor repair shops increased their business after Microsoft released Windows 3.0. Why? Well, I know I myself was tempted on more than one occasion to stick my fist or some other handy object through my screen because of 3.0's ubiquitous *Unrecoverable Application Errors* (UAEs).

What is a UAE? Well, in layman's terms, it means simply that an application has stuck its nose where it doesn't belong. Windows divides up your system's memory and assigns chunks of it to your loaded applications. While an application is running, its area of memory is its own private property. If another application trespasses on this area, Windows intercepts it and declares a UAE.

The good news is that Windows 3.1 has eliminated the UAE. The bad news is that they replaced it with a new error: the *General Protection Fault* (GPF). Happily, Windows is much better at recovering from these errors. In 3.0, Windows simply shut down the offending application—no questions asked. In 3.1, you often get to close the application yourself (and, most importantly, save your work before doing so).

What Happens When a GPF Occurs?

When Windows detects a General Protection Fault, all sorts of internal bells and alarms go off and, depending on how badly things are messed up, one of three things will happen:

- You'll see a dialog box telling you that a GPF has occurred. In some cases, this dialog box only has a **Close** button. When you select this button, Windows nixes the clumsy oaf of an application that caused the problem. If you're lucky, the dialog box will have both a **Close** and an **Ignore** button. In this case, try selecting **Ignore** a few times to get back into the application. If you're successful, immediately save your work and get the heck out of there.

- If your system locks up, press **Ctrl+Alt+Delete** and wait a few seconds. If the problem isn't too severe, you'll see the following message:

  System has either become busy or has become unstable
  -Press any key to return to Windows and wait
  -Press CTRL+ALT+DEL again to restart your computer (all unsaved information will be lost)

You can sometimes press any key and wait things out. But more often than not, you'll have to bail out altogether (by pressing **Ctrl+Alt+Delete** to display the above message, and then pressing **Ctrl+Alt+Delete** again to reboot).

- If your system locks up with a particularly ugly GPF, pressing **Ctrl+Alt+Delete** brings up the following message:

  This Windows application has stopped responding to the system
  -Press ESC to cancel and return to Windows
  -Press ENTER to close this application (all unsaved information will be lost)
  -Press CTRL+ALT+DEL again to restart your computer (all unsaved information will be lost)

> **OOPS!**
> Even if you manage to recover from a GPF, you're not out of the woods yet. Your system is probably unstable, so you should exit Windows and reboot your machine. Once you've rebooted, run either DOS 6's ScanDisk utility (as described back in Chapter 20, "An Ounce of Prevention: Avoiding Trouble") or the **CHKDSK /F** command to fix any disk errors that might have occurred.

- If Windows managed to intercept the rogue program in time, you can usually press **Esc** to return to the application, save your work, and then exit. Otherwise, press **Enter** to shut down the application. As a last resort, you can press **Ctrl+Alt+Delete** to reboot and start over again.

Troubleshooting Those Nasty GPFs

This section looks at a number of ways to prevent GPFs (or UAEs if you're still using Windows 3.0) from happening.

Upgrade your DOS version. GPFs can result from using the wrong version of DOS. You need to check two things:

- Are you using the version of DOS that was designed for your computer? Some companies (such as IBM and Compaq) remake DOS in their own image, so to speak, for use on their machines. If you have such a system, make sure you're using the appropriate DOS version.

- If your computer uses generic DOS, you need at least version 3.1 (although version 3.3 is a more realistic minimum). If you're using version 4, I'd strongly suggest moving up to a later version (preferably version 6.2).

> To find out which version of DOS you're using, open a DOS window, type **ver**, and press **Enter**.

Check to see if Windows was set up for the wrong computer type. Part of the Windows setup involves specifying the computer type. (This may have been done automatically by the Setup program if you chose the Express installation.) You may need to rerun the Setup program to change this setting. If you do, here are the steps to follow:

1. Exit Windows.
2. In the WINDOWS directory, type **setup** and press **Enter**.
3. Use the up arrow key to highlight the **Computer** setting, and then press **Enter**. Setup displays a list of computers (see below).

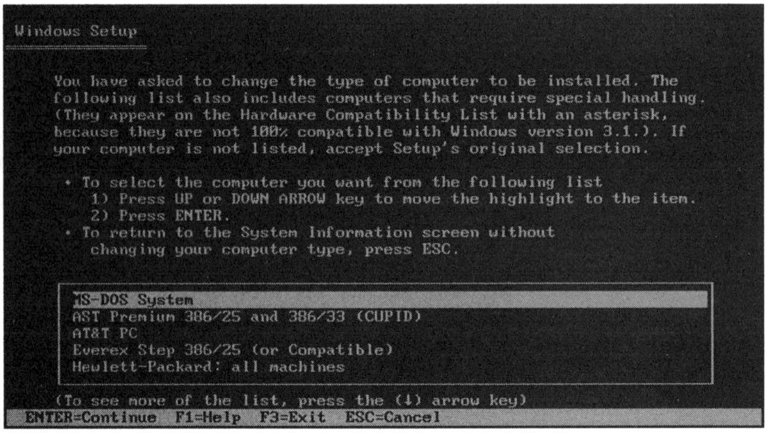

*When you select the **Computer** setting, Setup displays a list of computers that are 100% compatible with Windows.*

4. If applicable, select your computer type from the list and press **Enter**. Otherwise, press **F3** twice to exit Setup.
5. Press **Enter** to accept the new configuration, then follow the on-screen prompts.

If you're running an application written for Windows version 2, upgrade to a newer version. Programs designed to run under Windows version 2 will not run properly in versions 3.0 or 3.1. Upgrade to a newer version of the program, if possible.

Use ScanDisk or Chkdsk to weed out disk errors. Corrupted or damaged files on your hard disk are another common source of GPFs. To check for (and fix) these problems, exit to DOS, type **scandisk /autofix /nosave** (if you have DOS 6) or **chkdsk /f** (if you have an earlier version of DOS), and then press **Enter**. In the latter case, if DOS asks if you want to save some files, press **N** to select No.

Keep an eye on your system resources. You can bet your bottom dollar that a GPF is just around the corner if your system resources (I explained what these were back in Chapter 22, "Maneuvering the Memory Maze") drop below the 20% mark. Keep an eye on them if you're working with large applications. (Simply pull down Program Manager's **H**elp menu and select About Program Manager; or, better yet, use the Memory Monitor program on this book's disk.) When the percentage gets too low, exit all your applications, and then exit and restart Windows.

Make adjustments to your CONFIG.SYS file. Some GPFs are caused by too few file handles and a too small environment space (Chapter 21, "Ignition Trouble: Installation and Startup Woes," explained what this stuff means). To fix these problems, edit your CONFIG.SYS file so it has the following lines:

```
FILES=50
SHELL=C:\DOS\COMMAND.COM C:\DOS /E:1024 /P
```

Use Dr. Watson to see if a single application is causing the problem. Many GPFs are the result of bug-ridden applications that have run amok. If you have one of these sloppily programmed rogues, complain long and loud to the developer and demand a (bug-free) upgrade.

How can you tell if a single program is causing all your GPFs? Well, if Windows always crashes while you're performing the same operation in the same application, you can pretty well narrow down the cause. If the crashes seem to be more random, you need to do a little more legwork.

Fortunately, Microsoft has made tracking down the source of GPFs much easier by including a utility called Dr. Watson with Windows 3.1.

Dr. Watson is a memory-resident utility that only kicks into life when a GPF occurs. Dr. Watson creates a text file (it's called DRWATSON.LOG, and you'll find it in your main Windows directory) that records all the technical details about Windows' state at the time of the crash. It will also ask you what you were doing when the crash occurred and will add this to the log. Although the information recorded by Dr. Watson is way too technical for our purposes, the good people in your application's tech support department will know what to do with it.

The best way to use Dr. Watson is to have it running in memory at all times. Therefore, most people create an icon for Dr. Watson in their Startup group. When you create your Dr. Watson program item, you need to enter **drwatson.exe** in the Command Line text box of the Program Item Properties dialog box.

Nasty Windows Error Messages

Although GPFs (or UAEs in version 3.0) are the most common problem with Windows applications, they're by no means the only ones. Windows has, unfortunately, all kinds of error messages that may pop up on your screen from time to time. This section looks at a few of the most common ones.

Windows reports that an application has "violated system integrity." This error is a more serious version of the General Protection Fault. In this case, your only option is to reboot and start over. Use the solutions described earlier. In particular, make sure you check your hard disk for file errors (by running ScanDisk or Chkdsk).

If a Windows applet violates system integrity, it may mean that its executable file (the file that starts the program) has been corrupted. Use Windows' Expand utility (as explained in Chapter 21, "Ignition Trouble: Installation and Startup Woes") to copy the appropriate file from your original Windows disks. Look for a file with the extension EX_ (for example, NOTEPAD.EX_ or PBRUSH.EX_), and expand it to your Windows directory. Make sure you give the expanded file the extension EXE.

Windows tells you it "Cannot find file *x* or one of its components." You'll usually see this message when you try to start an application, and it means that Windows can't find the file you specified as the command to load the program. You need to check two things:

- If you're trying to run the application from a Program Manager icon, check the icon's properties to make sure the Command Line is correct. You likely need to adjust (or add) the drive and directory where the file is located.
- If the application is being loaded from WIN.INI, open this file and check the drive and directory specified in either the Load= or the Run= line.

Windows says its "permanent swap file is corrupted." As explained in Chapter 23, "From Slowpoke to Speed Demon: Making Windows Fly," permanent swap files can really improve Windows' performance. If they get messed up, though, Windows will get all huffy. To put Windows back in a good mood, simply recreate the swap file (using the steps outlined in Chapter 23).

You get a "stack overflow" error. I covered this one back in Chapter 21. To fix it, edit your CONFIG.SYS file so it contains the following line:

```
STACKS=9,256
```

Notepad tells you it has "Insufficient memory for this operation." This message is a bit misleading, to say the least. It doesn't mean your system is low on memory; instead, it means the file you're trying to load into Notepad is too big. Notepad, you see, is the 90-pound weakling of text editors; it can only view files as large as 50K, and it can only edit files up to 45K. If your text files are bumping their heads on these ceilings, you'll have to switch to a more powerful editor.

> **OOPS!**
>
> Write can easily handle larger files. One caveat, though: if you're working with pure text files, make sure Write doesn't convert them to its native format.

Perturbing Printing Problems

When you consider the number of applications that print and the variety of printers they can print to, it's no wonder that Windows printing can sometimes be a real nightmare. This section looks at some general printing problems you may run into.

Before trying any of the solutions in this section, you should first check to see if you can print properly from DOS. If you can't, it's not a Windows printing problem, and you need to contact the printer manufacturer. To test DOS printing, make sure your printer is ready to go, and then open a DOS session by selecting the **MS-DOS Prompt** icon from Program Manager's **Main** group. When you have the C:\> prompt, type **dir > lpt1** and press **Enter**. (If your printer is attached to a port other than LPT1, substitute the appropriate port.) This should send a directory listing to your printer.

If you have a PostScript printer, you need to use a different test. At the C:\> prompt, enter the following command:

copy c:\windows\system\testps.txt lpt1

Again, substitute the appropriate port for LPT1, if necessary.

Print Manager Reports the Printer Is "Offline or Not Selected"

This error message indicates that Print Manager can't communicate with your printer. Here are some possible solutions.

Check the printer itself. Before starting any print jobs, make sure of the following:

- Your printer is powered up.
- It's on-line (this means that it's ready to receive output). Most printers have an "Online" button you can select.
- The cable connections are secure.
- There's paper in the printer.
- There's no paper jam.

Increase the "transmission retry" value. If all is well with the printer, you can try increasing the amount of time that Windows waits before displaying the message. Depending on the print job, some printers will take an extra long time to process the data that Windows sends. If they take *too* long, Windows will assume that the printer is "offline," and you'll get an error. To fix this, follow these steps:

1. Load Control Panel and select the **Printers** icon. Control Panel displays the Printers dialog box.
2. Select the Connect button to display the Connect dialog box shown below.

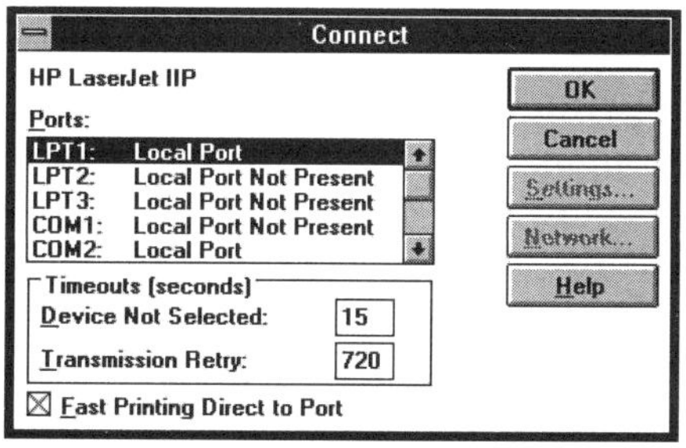

Use the Connect dialog box to increase the Transmission Retry value.

3. Increase the number in the Transmission Retry box (the maximum value is 999 seconds).
4. Select **OK** to return to the Printers dialog box, and then select **Close**.

You Can't Print from a Windows Application

If a Windows application won't let you print anything, try these solutions.

Install a printer driver. Most Windows applications that can print include a Print command in their File menu. If this command is "dimmed" (if it appears in a light gray text and you can't highlight it), it means you have no printer driver installed. Follow the steps outlined way back in Chapter 6, "Hard Copy Hijinks: Getting the Most Out of Windows Printing," to install a printer driver.

Select a different printer. Most Windows applications have a Print Setup command in their File menu. When you select this command, you should see a list of your installed printers. If a printer other than the one you want is highlighted, select the appropriate printer and choose **OK**.

> **TECHNO NERD TEACHES...**
>
> Instead of constantly selecting the correct printer in all your applications, you should set up the printer as the Windows default printer. Chapter 6 tells you everything you need to know.

Reinstall a corrupted printer driver. Alternatively, your printer driver may have gotten all mangled somehow. You need to remove the driver from your system and then reinstall it. To remove the driver, follow these steps:

1. In Control Panel's Printers dialog box, highlight your printer in the Installed Printers list, and then select the Remove button. Control Panel asks if you're sure you want to remove it from the list.
2. Select Yes. Control Panel removes the printer.
3. Switch back to Program Manager and load File Manager.
4. Select the WINDOWS\SYSTEM directory, highlight the printer driver file (look for a file with the extension DRV, such as EPSON.DRV or PSCRIPT.DRV), and delete it.
5. Exit File Manager, return to Control Panel, and reinstall the driver. If the problem persists, you may need to contact the printer manufacturer for an updated driver.

Make sure the printer is set up for the correct port. If you can't get Windows to print, it may be trying to print to the wrong port. To check this, open Control Panel's Printers dialog box and find your printer in the Installed Printers list. The listing will show your printer's name followed by "on *port*" where *port* is the port to which Windows thinks your printer is connected. If this isn't correct, select the Connect button and choose the proper port from the Ports list in the Connect dialog box.

Try using the LPT1.DOS (or LPT1.OS2) port. One common printing problem occurs when a Windows printer driver is not fully compatible with your printer. You can often get around this problem by telling Windows to print to a port called LPT1.DOS. This overrides Windows printing and prints directly through DOS. You'll find this port in the Ports list of the Connect dialog box (see the steps in the previous solution).

Make sure your AUTOEXEC.BAT file contains a SET TEMP command. As explained back in Chapter 6, when you try to print a document, Print Manager doesn't print the actual file, but instead copies (or "spools") it to a temporary file. This temporary file then prints in the background while you continue working.

For this whole process to work properly, Print Manager must know where (i.e., in which directory) to create its temporary files. This is determined by a SET TEMP command in your AUTOEXEC.BAT file (for example, SET TEMP = C:\WINDOWS\TEMP). You need to check two things:

- Is there a SET TEMP command in your AUTOEXEC.BAT file? If not, add one.
- Does the SET TEMP command point to an existing directory? If not, change the directory or use File Manager to create it.

OOPS!

Make sure that the drive you use in the SET TEMP command has at least 2 megabytes of available disk space. Anything less can cause problems.

Miscellaneous Bad Things

Here's a list of a few more common Windows glitches:

The icon or window title bar of an application is flashing. When you see a flashing icon or title bar, it means that an application running in the background has some sort of message for you. It may be reporting on the status of an operation, or it may be an error. Select the application to check out the message.

You've lost some or all of your Program Manager groups. If Windows crashes, it may take a few innocent bystanders down with it. Some common victims include your Program Manager groups. If you have backup copies of the GRP files that contain the group info, restore them to your Windows directory. Otherwise, pull down Program Manager's File menu and select Run. In the Run dialog box, enter **setup /p** and select **OK**. This command tells Setup to recreate your original program groups.

File Manager won't let you write files to, delete files from, or format a floppy disk. If you're trying to copy files to a floppy disk, the disk may be full; in this case, delete some files from the disk or try another.

Alternatively, the disk may be *write-protected*, which means you can't copy or move files to the disk, delete or rename files on the disk, or format the disk. Here's how to tell whether or not a disk is write-protected:

- When a 5 1/4-inch disk is *not* write-protected, you'll see a small notch in the side of the disk. If the notch is covered with tape, simply remove the tape to disable the write-protection.
- For a 3 1/2-inch disk, the write-protection is controlled by a small, movable tab on the back of the disk. If the tab is toward the edge of the disk, the disk is write-protected. To disable the write-protection, slide the tab away from the edge of the disk.

Your Windows applications really bog down while you're printing. Print Manager's printing priority is probably set to High. This means that Windows devotes more resources to printing than to anything else. You can speed up your applications a notch or two by starting Print Manager, pulling down its Options menu, and selecting either Medium Priority or Low Priority.

Your fonts print differently than they appear on your screen. You'll either need to reinstall your printer driver (as explained earlier in this chapter), or you'll need to reinstall the font (Chapter 7, "Flexing Your Font Muscles," has the details).

The Least You Need to Know

This chapter showed you how to solve problems related to Windows applications. Here's a recap of some of the trouble-shooting techniques you learned:

- General Protection Faults (or Unrecoverable Application Errors in Windows 3.0) are caused by badly behaved programs trespassing on another application's turf.
- When a GPF occurs, follow the instructions on-screen. If possible, try to return to your application to save your work. In any case, always exit Windows and reboot your computer after a GPF.
- You can often eliminate GPFs by upgrading either your DOS version or the version of the application you're using. Also, make sure your system resources never drop below 20%. If the problem won't go away, have Dr. Watson make a house call to keep an eye on things.
- If you're having printer problems, make sure the printer is fired up, has plenty of paper, and so on. Otherwise, you may need to install (or reinstall) a printer driver.
- To restore your original Program Manager groups, enter **setup /p** in the Run dialog box.
- If File Manager gags on a floppy disk, check to see if the disk is write-protected.

Chapter 25 Relieving Hardware Headaches

In This Chapter

- Solving mouse problems
- Fixing keyboard complaints
- Tackling video woes
- Lots of helpful hints for overcoming hardware hitches

So far, most of the problems we've looked at have been of the software variety. Unfortunately, hardware is often just as flaky, and it's usually even trickier to fix. In most cases, you're dealing with a defective part that needs to be replaced, so no amount of fiddling will get you back up and running. Sometimes, though, you can solve a hardware glitch with some simple tweaks. This chapter takes a look at these more tractable hardware headaches.

Mending Your Mouse

One of the advantages of the Windows environment is that you can use a mouse to "point-and-click" whenever you want to select a command or start an application. You lose this advantage, however, whenever your mouse doesn't operate properly. This section outlines a few of the things that can go wrong with your mouse.

Your Mouse Pointer Moves Erratically

You'll sometimes find that you move your mouse on its pad, and the darn pointer either stays where it is, or it heads off into oblivion or some other equally inconvenient spot. When this happens, try out the following solutions.

Make sure the mouse is attached to your computer. This may seem somewhat obvious, but the number one rule when troubleshooting any device is to first ask "Is it plugged in?" You'd be surprised how often the answer is a sheepish "No."

Clean the inside of the mouse. If your mouse is behaving erratically, it may simply need to be cleaned inside. A well-used mouse can take in quite a collection of dust, crumbs, and other alien substances, so you should clean yours regularly. Your mouse documentation should tell you the proper cleaning procedure. If your mouse has a roller ball, you can also follow these steps:

1. Remove the cover on the bottom of the mouse.
2. Remove the roller ball.
3. Using a cotton swab dipped lightly in isopropyl alcohol or water, clean the rollers and other contact areas.
4. Wipe off any excess liquid, and then replace the ball and cover.

Try a firmer mouse pad. If your mouse pad's too soft, the roller ball sinks down too far when you move the mouse. This can cause the roller to stick, and so create erratic pointer movements. Try one of the firmer varieties of mouse pad.

Exit and restart Windows. When you restart Windows, the program reinitializes the mouse, which is often enough to get the thing going again. If this still doesn't work, try exiting Windows and rebooting your computer.

Change the mouse driver. Windows provides you with a list of mouse drivers, each of which is designed to be used with a specific type of mouse. If you're using the wrong driver, the pointer may not move at all or it may do some crazy things. To remedy this, you need to use Windows' Setup program to change the driver. Check out Chapter 3, "Tweaking Windows with Setup," to find out how this is done.

If you have a Logitech mouse, make sure you use the Logitech driver even if your mouse is "Microsoft Mouse-compatible."

Change the port Windows expects your mouse to be attached to. The physical connection that you use to attach your mouse is called a *port.* If your mouse is attached to one port and Windows is looking for it on another, nothing much is going to happen.

To fix this, take a look at the back of your computer and see which port your mouse is using. (The ports, hopefully, will be labeled COM1, COM2, and so on. If not, you may need to refer to your computer's documentation.) Then, using Notepad, open MOUSE.INI from your main Windows directory and change the MouseType= line to one of the values in the following table:

Port	Line
COM1	MouseType=Serial1
COM2	MouseType=Serial2
PS/2-style	MouseType=PS2
Bus	MouseType=Bus

Windows Hangs Whenever You Move Your Mouse

If Windows freezes when you try to move the mouse pointer, you likely need to adjust a line in your CONFIG.SYS file. Load CONFIG.SYS and look for a STACKS= line. If you don't see one, add the following line:

STACKS=9,256

If the STACKS= line does exist, make sure it equals the above value. If moving your mouse still hangs Windows, try increasing the value to 12,128 or 12,256.

Windows Doesn't Always Recognize Your Double-Clicks

One of the things that a mouse-aware program must do is distinguish between two consecutive single-clicks and a double-click. For example, if you click once, wait five seconds, and then click again, that would qualify as two single-clicks in most people's books. But what if there's only a second between clicks? Or half a second? This threshold is called the *double-click speed*: anything faster is considered a double-click. If you find Windows doesn't recognize some of your double-clicks, you need to try one of the following solutions.

Set a slower double-click speed. The slower the double-click speed, the greater the chance that Windows will recognize your double-clicks. Chapter 2, "Dressing Windows for Success: Customization Fun," showed you how to set the double-click speed for the new Microsoft Mouse. If you're still using the old one (or some other mouse), here's what you do:

1. Start Control Panel and select the **Mouse** icon. The Mouse dialog box appears, as shown below.

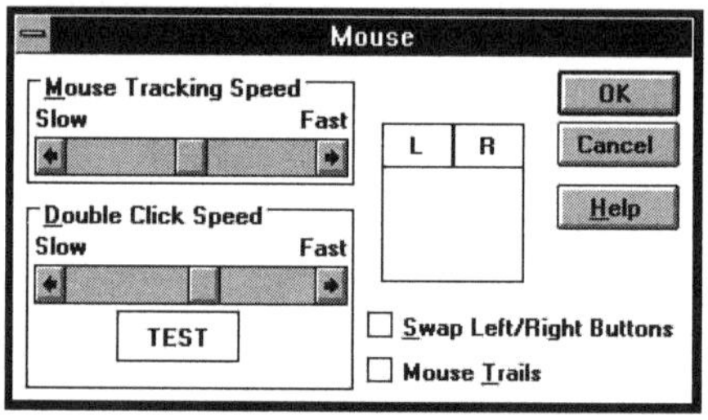

Use the Mouse dialog box to adjust the double-click speed.

2. Move the Double Click Speed slider to the left (slower).
3. Double-click on the TEST area. It'll reverse colors if Windows recognized your double-click.
4. Repeat steps 2 and 3 until Windows recognizes your double-clicks consistently.
5. Select **OK** to return to the Control Panel.

Adjust WIN.INI. Alternatively, Windows may not recognize a double-click if you move your mouse too much between the first and second clicks. To give yourself a little more room to maneuver, add the following lines to the [Windows] section of your WIN.INI file:

DoubleClickHeight=10
DoubleClickWidth=10

You Have Trouble Seeing the Mouse Pointer

If you use a laptop or if your eyesight isn't what it used to be, you may be having trouble keeping track of the little mouse pointer. There are a number of third-party products on the market that will solve this problem, but before you spend your hard-earned money on these utilities, there's an easy solution that comes with Windows 3.1: *mouse trails*. This feature leaves a trail of mouse pointers as you move the mouse, which makes it much easier to find the little guy. See Chapter 2 to learn how to set up this option (as well as some other features that make the pointer easier to spot) with the new Microsoft Mouse. For other rodents, try the following steps:

> **OOPS!**
>
> Not all mouse drivers support this feature. If you don't see a Mouse Trails option in your Mouse dialog box, your driver can't display trails.

1. Start Control Panel and select the **Mouse** icon to display the Mouse dialog box.
2. Activate the Mouse Trails check box.
3. Select **OK** to return to the Control Panel.

The Mouse Pointer Moves Too Slowly or Too Quickly

When you move the mouse on its pad, Windows translates this movement and tracks the mouse pointer accordingly. If you find your pointer is either leaping across the screen at the merest touch, or crawling across the screen no matter how furiously you shake the mouse, you can adjust the tracking speed by following these steps. (Once again, see Chapter 2 for instructions on adjusting the new Microsoft Mouse.)

1. Start Control Panel and select the **Mouse** icon to display the Mouse dialog box.
2. Move the Mouse Tracking Speed slider to the left (slower) or to the right (faster).
3. Move your mouse to test the tracking speed.
4. Repeat steps 2 and 3 until you're comfortable with the speed you've set.
5. Select **OK** to return to the Control Panel.

Your Mouse Doesn't Work in DOS Applications

In case you've forgotten, I'll remind you that a *device driver* is a software program that acts as a go-between for your programs and a physical device such as a mouse. Windows comes with its own mouse driver, but it works only for Windows and Windows applications. Any mouse-aware DOS applications that you run within Windows can't use the Windows driver. Instead, you need to load a separate driver *before* you start Windows. Here are the required steps:

> **TECHNO NERD TEACHES...**
>
> These steps assume you're using a mouse that's Microsoft Mouse-compatible. If not, replace MOUSE.COM with the appropriate driver supplied by your mouse manufacturer. If you have either a Logitech or Hewlett-Packard mouse, use Windows' LMOUSE.COM or MOUSEHP.COM files, respectively.

1. Load your AUTOEXEC.BAT file and add the following line:

    C:\WINDOWS\MOUSE.COM

2. Exit Windows and use the Expand utility (see Chapter 21, "Ignition Trouble: Installation and Startup Woes," to learn how to use Expand) to decompress the MOUSE.CO_ file from your installation disks to the MOUSE.COM file in your WINDOWS directory.
3. Reboot your computer and restart Windows.

Correcting Keyboard Kinks

Although Windows' interface is generally easier to use with a mouse, a keyboard is still a necessity. And while the vast majority of keyboard problems are hardware-related, there are a few problems you can take care of yourself.

Your Keyboard Is Too Slow

When you press and hold a letter on your keyboard, you notice two things: first, once you press the key, there's a slight *delay* before the second letter appears; second, the subsequent letters appear at a constant rate (called the *repeat rate*). If your keyboard feels slow, you either have your delay set too long or your repeat rate set too slow (or both). The good news is that Windows allows you to change both of these values. Here's how:

1. Start Control Panel and select the **Keyboard** icon. The Keyboard dialog box appears, as shown below.

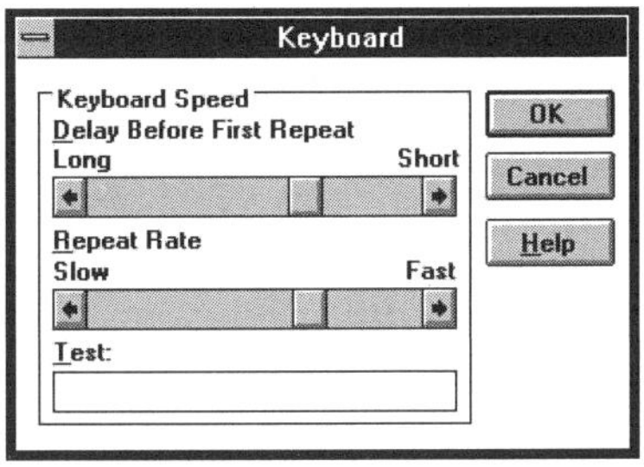

Use the Keyboard dialog box to adjust the delay and repeat rate.

2. For a shorter delay, move the **D**elay Before First Repeat slider to the right.
3. For a faster repeat rate, move the **R**epeat Rate slider to the right.
4. To check your new settings, move the cursor to the **T**est box, and then press and hold down a key.
5. Repeat steps 3–5 until the keyboard speed is set the way you want.
6. Select **OK** to return to the Control Panel.

Your Keyboard's F11 and F12 Keys Don't Work

If Windows is set up with a keyboard driver for an "AT-style" or "XT-style" (84- or 86-key) keyboard, you won't be able to use the F11 and F12 keys. To fix this, crank up Windows Setup program and select the appropriate 101- or 102-key driver. (See Chapter 3, "Tweaking Windows with Setup," to get the details on using Setup.)

Your Numeric Keypad Numbers Don't Work

Most of the keys on a numeric keypad have two types of characters: a number and a navigation symbol (the arrow keys, Home, End, Page Up, and Page Down). The Num Lock key is used to toggle a numeric keypad between these two types. If you can't get any numbers, simply press Num Lock to activate them. Most keyboards also have a NUM LOCK indicator that lights up when Num Lock is turned on.

A Windows Shortcut Key Doesn't Work in a DOS Program

In a Program Information File (PIF), Windows allows you to reserve some of its shortcut keys for use within an application. For example, if you like to use the "Cool Switch" (i.e., pressing **Alt+Tab** to move between applications) and you find it doesn't work in a DOS program, the Alt+Tab key combination is probably reserved in the program's PIF. Follow these steps to fix this problem:

1. Open the program's PIF (you'll need to read Chapter 5, "Taming the DOS Beast," to learn about PIFs and the PIF Editor).
2. Click on the Advanced button. The Advanced Options dialog box appears (see below).

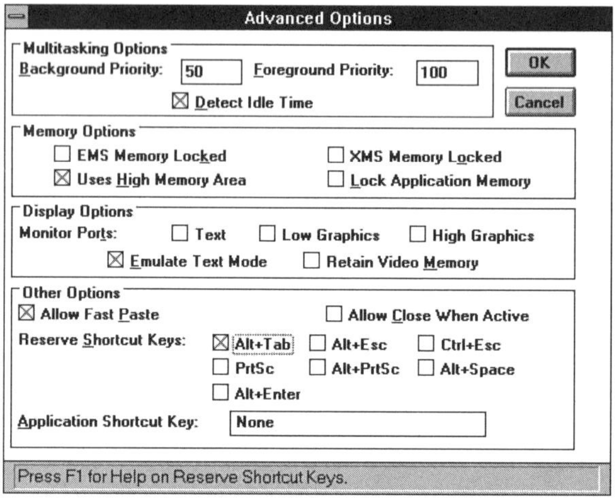

Use the Advanced Options dialog box to fix a DOS program that doesn't respond to Windows' shortcut keys.

3. In the Reserve Shortcut Keys area, deactivate the key combination that you want to use.
4. Select **OK**.
5. Exit the PIF Editor and save your changes when prompted.

You Lose Characters When Typing

If you type faster than Windows can process your keystrokes, it places the characters it can't deal with just yet in a special memory area called a *keyboard buffer*. If you're *really* fast, you may fill up the buffer and end up losing characters. If this happens, you need to increase the size of the buffer so Windows can handle what you throw at it. To do this, open WIN.INI, find the [Desktop] section, and enter the following line:

TypeAhead=1024

If the problem persists, increase the TypeAhead value (the max is 2,047).

Curing Video Ills

Your video display may be the most important component of your system since you're forced to look at it for hours on end every day. This is especially true for us Windows users since one of Windows' most appealing features is its good-looking graphical interface. But the fanciest interface in the world isn't worth a hill of beans if your display is displaying garbage. If you're having video trouble, the following sections show you how to adjust your set.

Dealing with Distorted Displays

If your display goes snaky on you, try any of these solutions to bring things back to normal.

Reinstall the video driver. One of the most common causes of display problems is a corrupt video driver. You can usually fix the problem by reinstalling the driver. Since your display is distorted, you can't use the Setup program within Windows itself. Instead, press **Alt+F4** and then **Enter** to exit Windows (you may need to do this several times if you have any applications running) and change to your main Windows directory. (You do this by typing **cd\windows** and pressing **Enter**.) Then run the DOS version of Setup as explained in Chapter 3, "Tweaking Windows with Setup."

Switch to a lower resolution driver. If you're having problems with, say, a Super VGA driver, use Setup (the DOS version) to switch to a VGA driver. If your display is okay with the lower resolution driver, you need to contact the manufacturer for an updated driver for the higher resolution.

Exit and restart Windows. Sometimes a display problem is nothing more than a temporary mental lapse on Windows' part. Try exiting Windows (press **Alt+F4** and **Enter**) and restarting.

Turn off your screen saver. Some screen savers can cause video problems. To prevent a screen saver from loading when you start Windows, try either of these methods:

- If the screen saver loads from your Startup group, hold down **Shift** while Windows starts in order to prevent the screen saver (and anything else in the Startup group) from loading. Once you're safely in Program Manager, remove the screen saver from your Startup group.
- Open WIN.INI and, in the [Windows] section, remove the screen saver from the Load= line.

Your VGA Adapter Doesn't Display Properly

There are lots of VGA adapters on the market, and most manufacturers have modified the basic VGA design to get improved features and enhanced performance. Unfortunately, these modifications can also cause strange behavior under Windows. If you have a VGA board that doesn't display properly, try these solutions on for size.

Reinstall the VGA driver. The VGA driver on your hard disk may have become corrupted. Reinstall the driver from the original disk that came with the adapter. If the problem persists, you may need to contact the manufacturer for an updated driver.

Use Windows' VGA driver. Windows comes with its own VGA driver that should work with most VGA adapters. Use the Setup program to reconfigure Windows. Be sure to select **VGA** from the list of drivers.

Turn off the adapter's "auto-switch" feature. Some VGA adapters switch modes automatically. Windows, though, doesn't like this behavior (it prefers to tell the adapter to switch modes itself). Check the manual that came with the adapter to see if it has this "auto-switch" capability (it may also be called "auto-emulation") and disable it, if possible.

Check for memory conflicts. Try starting Windows with the command **win /d:x**. If your adapter works now, the problem is a memory conflict in Windows' 386 enhanced mode. Open SYSTEM.INI and, in the [386Enh] section, add the following line:

EMMExclude=A000-CFFF

This tells Windows not to use a section of memory that is commonly utilized by VGA adapters.

Your Super VGA Adapter Doesn't Display Properly

Given a choice between VGA and Super VGA, most people would pick the latter. It's no wonder: with over 50% more pixels on the screen, you get a sharper picture and a larger screen area. Unfortunately, until recently the Super VGA "standard" hasn't been much of a standard at all. With the variety of Super VGA adapters on the market, troubles are inevitable. Here are some solutions:

Reinstall the Super VGA driver. The Super VGA driver on your hard disk may have become corrupted. Reinstall the driver from the original disk that came with the adapter. If the problem persists, you may need to contact the manufacturer for an updated driver.

Use Windows' Super VGA driver. As with VGA, Windows comes with its own Super VGA driver that is a good starting point if you're having trouble with a third-party driver. Use the Setup program to reconfigure Windows. Be sure to select **Super VGA** from the list of drivers.

Check for memory conflicts. The same memory conflicts that can occur with VGA adapters can also occur with Super VGA. Use the techniques outlined in the VGA section to resolve these memory conflicts.

The Least You Need to Know

This chapter completed our crash course (no pun intended) in Windows troubleshooting with a look at some common hardware hindrances. Here's a recap of the day's top stories:

- If your mouse is acting up, first make sure it's properly connected. You should also clean the little guy regularly. Otherwise, you can try reinstalling the mouse driver or changing the port that Windows thinks the mouse is attached to.
- Use Control Panel's Mouse icon to change the double-click speed, set up mouse trails for easier viewing, and adjust the tracking speed.
- If your keyboard is too slow, use Control Panel's Keyboard icon to adjust the delay and repeat rate.
- Most video conundrums are caused by problems with the video driver. In most cases, you can remedy the situation by reinstalling the driver, installing a new driver, or switching to a lower video mode.

Speak Like a Geek: The Complete Archive

286, 386, 486 These are the aficionado's cool short forms for the *80286*, *80386*, and *80486* microprocessors. The microprocessor is the head honcho chip inside your computer that controls the whole shebang. Most people describe it as the "brain" of the computer, so you can think of these numbers as your computer's IQ. In that sense, a 386 machine is "smarter" than a 286, but a 486 is the genius of the group. To get the most out of DOS programs in Windows, you really should have a 386 or better computer. See *386 enhanced mode*.

386 enhanced mode Fancy-schmancy mode that lets Windows do things like DOS multitasking, running DOS programs in a window, and more. Windows runs in this mode automatically if you have a 386 or better computer.

accessory One of the mini-applications that comes free with Windows.

active window The window you're currently slaving away in. You can tell a window is active by looking at its title bar: if the bar shows white letters on a dark background the window is active. (Inactive windows show dark letters on a white background, unless you changed your colors.)

application Software that accomplishes a specific, practical task. It's the same thing as a program.

application window A window containing a running application, such as Program Manager or Write.

AUTOEXEC.BAT A text file containing commands run by DOS each time you fire up your computer.

background mode A mode where a program continues performing a task "behind the scenes." Typical background tasks are spreadsheet recalculations, document printing, and modem file transfers.

batch file A special text file that holds multiple DOS commands and performs them all in one fell swoop.

boot Computer geeks won't tell you to start your computer, they'll tell you to *boot* it. This doesn't mean you should punt your monitor across the room. The term *booting* comes from the phrase "pulling oneself up by one's own bootstraps," which just means that your computer can load everything it needs to operate properly without any help from the likes of you and me.

byte Computerese for a single character of information. So, for example, the phrase *This phrase is 28 bytes long* is, yes, 28 bytes long (you count the spaces, too).

byte-bonding When computer users talk about stuff that non-computer users don't understand. See also *geeking out.*

cascade A cool way of arranging windows so that they overlap each other but you can still see each window's title bar.

cascade menu A menu that appears when you select certain pull-down menu commands.

character spacing The amount of space that a font reserves for each character. In a *monospace font,* every character gets the same amount of space regardless of its true width. In a *proportional font,* the space allotted to each letter varies according to the width of the letter.

check box A square-shaped switch that toggles a dialog box option on or off. The option is toggled on when an X appears in the box.

child directory The *subdirectory* one level below the current *directory*. See also *parent directory*.

clean boot To *boot* your computer without loading any *device drivers* or *memory-resident software*.

click To quickly press and release the left mouse button.

Clipboard A storage location in memory that holds data temporarily during cut and paste operations.

command button A rectangular doohickey (usually found in dialog boxes) that, when chosen, runs whatever command is spelled out on its label.

COMMAND.COM The DOS command interpreter. It takes the commands you enter at the DOS prompt and translates them into computer language.

CONFIG.SYS A text file that DOS uses to configure your computer each time you start it up.

Control menu A menu common to every Windows window that you use to manipulate various features of the window. You activate the Control menu by clicking on the *Control-menu box* in the upper left corner of the window or by pressing **Alt+Spacebar** (for an application window) or **Alt+hyphen** (for a document window).

Control-menu box The icon for the Control menu. It appears as a square in the upper left corner of a window.

conventional memory The first 640K of your computer's memory. See also *upper memory*, *extended memory*, and *expanded memory*.

cutout In Paintbrush, an area of a drawing that has been selected using either the Scissors or Pick tool.

data files The files used by you or your programs. See also *program files*.

defragment To rearrange the files on your hard disk so they aren't scattered in small chunks all over your hard drive. If you have DOS 6, use the DEFRAG program to defragment your hard disk.

delay The amount of time it takes for a second character to appear when you press and hold down a key.

desktop A metaphor for the Windows screen. Starting a Windows application is similar to putting a folder full of papers (the application window) on your desk. To do some work, you pull some papers out of the folder (the document windows) and place them on the desktop.

device driver A small program that translates signals from a hardware device (such as a mouse) so they can be understood by software (such as Windows).

dialog boxes Ubiquitous windows that pop up on the screen to ask you for information or to seek confirmation of an action you requested (or sometimes just to say "Hi").

directory A storage location on your hard disk for keeping related files together. If your hard disk is like a house, a directory is like a room inside the house. See also *subdirectory*.

directory window A File Manager window.

document window A window opened within an application. Document windows hold whatever you're working on in the application.

double-click To quickly press and release the left mouse button *twice* in succession.

double-click speed The maximum amount of time between mouse clicks that Windows will allow for a double-click to be registered.

drag To press and hold down the left mouse button and then move the mouse.

drag-and-drop A technique that lets you run File Manager commands (such as Copy) or applications simply by dragging files or icons to strategic screen areas.

drop-down list box A list box that normally shows only a single item but, when selected, displays a list of options.

expanded memory Memory, usually in the form of an add-on card, outside the normal memory installed on your computer's main circuit board.

extended memory Memory, in the form of extra chips on your computer's main circuit board, over and above one megabyte.

extension The three-character ending to a DOS file name. The extension is separated from the main name by a period.

FAWOMPT Frequently Argued Waste of My Precious Time. See also *holy war*.

file An organized unit of information inside your computer. If you think of your hard disk as a house, files can be either servants (your applications) or things (data used by you or by a program).

file name The name of a file (duh). File names are made up of three parts: the primary name, followed by a period, followed by an *extension*. The primary name must be no longer than 8 characters.

floppy disk A portable storage medium that consists of a flexible disk protected by a plastic case. Floppy disks are available in a variety of sizes and capacities.

focus The window that has the attention of the operating system (that is, Windows).

font A character set of a specific typeface, type style, and type size.

font management program A software program that automatically scales font characters to the size you select.

formatting The process of setting up a disk so that it can read and write information.

fritterware Any software that causes you to fritter away time fiddling with its various bells and whistles.

geeking out When people who are *byte-bonding* actually start playing with a computer during an otherwise non-technical social event.

group A window within Program Manager that contains a collection of program items.

hard disk The main storage area inside your computer. In the computer house analogy, the hard disk is equivalent to the inside of the house.

holy war A never-ending debate on the merits of one thing versus another, where people use the same arguments over and over, and nobody's opinion ever budges even the slightest one way or the other. DOS versus Windows is the classic holy war. See also *FAWOMPT*.

icons The little pictures that Windows uses to represent programs and files.

INI file An initialization file. INI files are text files that contain various settings that Windows and Windows programs use to set themselves up. The most common INI files are WIN.INI and SYSTEM.INI.

insertion point cursor The blinking vertical bar you see inside a text box and a word processing application, such as Write. It tells you where the next character you type will appear.

kilobyte 1,024 bytes. To be cool, always abbreviate this as "K."

list box A small window that displays a list of items such as file names or directories.

macro Any recorded sequence of mouse clicks or keystrokes. You record macros using Windows' Recorder accessory. See Chapter 18, "Windows Robotics: Recording Recorder Macros."

maximize To increase the size of a window to its largest extent. A maximized application window fills the entire screen. A maximized document window fills the entire application window.

megabyte 1,024 kilobytes or 1,048,576 bytes. The cognoscenti write this as "M" or "MB" and pronounce it "meg."

memory resident program A program that stays in memory once it is loaded and works "behind the scenes." The program normally responds only to a specific event (such as the deletion of a file) or a key combination. Also called terminate-and-stay-resident (TSR) programs.

menu bar The horizontal bar on the second line of an application window. The menu bar contains the application's pull-down menus.

microprocessor See *286, 386, 486.*

minimizewindows To reduce a window to an icon.

mouse potato The computer equivalent of a couch potato. It applies to anyone who spends lots of time in front of his or her computer screen.

multitasking The capability to run several programs at the same time. It simply means that Windows, unlike some people you may know, can walk and chew gum at the same time.

option buttons Dialog box options that appear as small circles in groups of two or more. You can choose only one option from a group.

parent directory The directory one level above the current directory. See also *child directory.*

point To move the mouse pointer so that it rests on a specific screen location.

port The connection that you use to plug in the cable from a device, such as a mouse or printer.

program files The files that run your programs. See also *data files.*

program group See *group.*

program item An application icon within a program group.

pull-down menus Hidden menus that you open from an application's menu bar to access the commands and features of the application.

RAM Stands for random-access memory. The memory in your computer that DOS uses to run your programs.

raster fonts Fonts in which each character is represented by a pattern of dots.

repeat rate After the initial delay, the rate at which characters appear when you press and hold down a key.

root directory The topmost directory on a drive. It is designated by the slash (\). For example, the root directory of drive C: is C:\.

scalable font A font in which each character exists as an outline that is scaled to different sizes. Examples of scalable fonts that come with Windows are Arial, Courier New, and Times New Roman. Scalable fonts require a software program called a *type manager* to do the scaling. Windows 3.1 comes with its own type manager: TrueType.

scroll bar A bar that appears at the bottom or on the right of a window whenever the window is too small to display all of its contents. Some dialog boxes also use scroll bars as controls for entering values.

shell An application, such as Program Manager, that insulates you from the inner workings of your computer.

spinner A dialog box control for entering numbers. You click the upward-pointing arrow to increase the number; you click the downward-pointing arrow to decrease the number.

subdirectory A directory within a directory.

system resources Two small (64K) memory areas that Windows uses to keep track of things like the position and size of open windows, dialog boxes, and your desktop configuration (wallpaper and so on).

text box A screen area you use to type in text information, such as a description or a file name.

text editor A program that lets you edit files that are text only. The Windows text editor is called Notepad.

title bar The area on the top line of a window that displays the window's title.

tracking speed How quickly the mouse pointer moves across the screen when you move the mouse on its pad.

TrueType A *font management program* that comes with Windows 3.1.

type size A measure of the height of a font. Type size is measured in *points*, where there are 72 points in an inch.

type style Character attributes, such as regular, bold, and italic. Other type styles (often called type *effects*) are underlining and strikeout characters.

typeface A distinctive graphic design of letters, numbers, and other symbols.

upper memory The area between 640K (*conventional memory*) and one megabyte.

vector fonts Fonts that are created from an obscenely complex mathematical model that defines an outline for each character (which is then filled in with whatever the current text color is).

window A rectangular screen area in which Windows displays applications and documents.

write-protection Floppy disk safeguard that prevents you from changing any information on the disk. The 5 1/4-inch disks normally have a small notch on the side of the disk. If the notch is covered with tape, the disk is write-protected. Simply remove the tape to disable the write-protection. For a 3 1/2-inch disk, the write-protection is controlled by a small movable tab on the back of the disk. If the tab is toward the edge of the disk, the disk is write-protected. To disable the write-protection, slide the tab away from the edge of the disk.

What's on the Freebies Disk

The programs included on the disk range from the ridiculous to the sublime (and just about everything in between). They're all *freeware*, which means you pay a grand total of *nothing* for the whole lot. That's right: zero, zilch, zip, nada, nought, gratis. Ah, I can hear the skeptics in the crowd mumbling something about getting what you pay for. Hey, you'd be surprised! These programs only sacrifice quantity, not quality. They're all compact little programs that, in most cases, do one thing and do it well. Who says there's no such thing as a free lunch?

Installing the Disk

The Freebies disk comes with its own installation program (called Setup) that lets you choose which programs and files you want to install. Here are the steps to follow to install the disk:

1. Place the Freebies disk in drive A or drive B.
2. In Program Manager, select the **F**ile menu's **R**un command to display the Run dialog box.
3. Type **a:setup** or **b:setup** (depending on which drive the disk is in), and then select **OK**. Setup takes a few seconds to pull itself up by its own bootstraps and then displays the Setup dialog box.
4. If you want the Freebies files copied to a drive or directory other than the one shown, make your changes in the **Install To** text box. Select **C**ontinue to proceed with the installation. The Setup Options dialog box appears, as shown in the following figure.

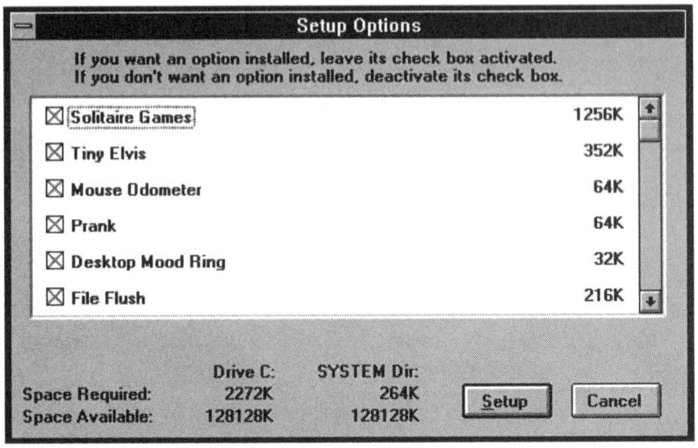

Use the Setup Options dialog box to select which files you want to install.

5. In the list of options, deactivate the check boxes for those you don't want, and leave the check boxes activated for those you do.
6. Select the **S**etup button. Setup copies the selected files, creates a Freebies group, and inserts icons for the programs you selected.

Fun Stuff

Since, as they say, all work and no play makes Jack (and Jill, too, I suppose) a dull boy (and girl), the Freebies disk includes a few fun, silly, and just plain dumb programs. Here's the rundown:

Solitaire Games This is a collection of three games: Golf Solitaire, Pyramid Solitaire, and a version of Acey-Ducey. Each game is pretty straightforward, and they all include Help files in case you get stuck. The files are installed in two places: the FREEBIES\GAMES directory and the WINDOWS\RLZRUN10 directory.

Tiny Elvis Elvis himself appears as an icon at the bottom of your screen. Every few minutes or so, he stands up and says something like "Man, look at that window. Whoa, that sucker's huge!" He then does a little dance and sits back down. To configure Tiny Elvis, click on the icon, select Configura**t**ion from the menu that appears, and then enter your choices in the Tiny Elvis Configuration dialog box.

Mouse Odometer This program also appears on your desktop as an icon. The icon label tells you how far your mouse has traveled. To set up Mouse Odometer, click on the icon, and then select **P**references from the menu. In the Preferences dialog box, you can set how often Mouse Odometer updates itself, the unit of measurement, and more.

Prank When you start this little program, a fake DOS prompt suddenly appears, and then a workman drags the Windows desktop onto the screen. For a cheap April Fool's joke, plant this program in a friend's Startup group.

Desktop Mood Ring An electronic version of the famous Lucky Mood Ring. Move the mouse pointer over the ring icon, and then hold down the right mouse button. After a few seconds, the ring's color stops changing; the color you end up with will be a reflection of your mood. To find out what each color signifies, click on the icon and select Guide to Your Moods from the menu. The dialog box that appears interprets your color.

File Flush When you select the **File Flush** icon from the **Freebies** group, a toilet bowl icon appears on the desktop. If you drag a file from File Manager and drop it onto the icon, the file is deleted, and you hear a splash(!). In reality, File Flush has moved the file to a directory named FLUSH. Double-clicking the File Flush icon presents a window with two buttons: Flush and Restore. If you select Flush, File Flush removes the files from the FLUSH directory (accompanied, of course, by the requisite flushing sounds). If you select Restore, the Restore File(s) dialog box appears. You can use this dialog box to select which files you want to restore. Setup installs three File Flush program files in the WINDOWS directory: FLUSH.EXE, FLUSH.WAV, and SPLASH.WAV.

Flying Screen Savers These are variations on the Flying Windows screen saver. There are six altogether: Flying Flakes (i.e., snowflakes; SSFLYFLA.SCR), Flying Flowers (SSFLYFLO.SCR), Flying Hands (SSFLYHND.SCR), Flying Stars (SSFLYSTR.SCR), Flying Suns (SSFLYSUN.SCR), and Flying Yin-Yangs (SSFLYYIN.SCR). All six files are copied to your WINDOWS directory, so they're immediately available as screen savers. If you'd like to try your hand at creating your own "flying" screen savers (it's easy!), select the **Flying Screen Savers Instructions** icon from the **Freebies** group.

Decay This is one of the wildest screen savers I've ever seen. Your screen actually seems to melt before your very eyes! Too cool (or should I say too hot) for words. Again, the screen saver file (DECAY.SCR) is copied directly to your WINDOWS directory. In the Screen Saver Name list, select **Let the screen decay**, and then sit back and watch the show.

Totally Tubular Screen Saver This screen saver shows a tube-like structure bouncing around your screen. It's pretty simple, but it can be downright hypnotic (if, since I created the darn thing, I do say so myself). The file is called TUBULAR.SCR, and it requires that the file VBRUN300.DLL be in your Windows SYSTEM subdirectory (Setup copies this file to SYSTEM automatically).

Serious Stuff

Because there are times when you have to stop playing around and get down to work, the Freebies disk contains a few programs that can help you be more productive. Here's a summary:

Memory Monitor This is a utility that keeps an eye on your system resources and free memory (the total of your system's extended memory and swap file size). If you minimize Memory Monitor, it just shows the system resources. By default, Memory Monitor probes these values every five seconds. If you don't want to keep such a close tab on things, use the Monitor Interval drop-down list to select a longer interval (10 seconds, 30 seconds, or 60 seconds). If you'd like to keep memory monitor on-screen at all times, pull down the **M**onitor menu and activate the Always on Top command. If you notice your system resources getting dangerously low (say, below 20%), select the **R**estart Windows button. (Memory Monitor requires that the file VBRUN300.DLL be in your Windows SYSTEM subdirectory.)

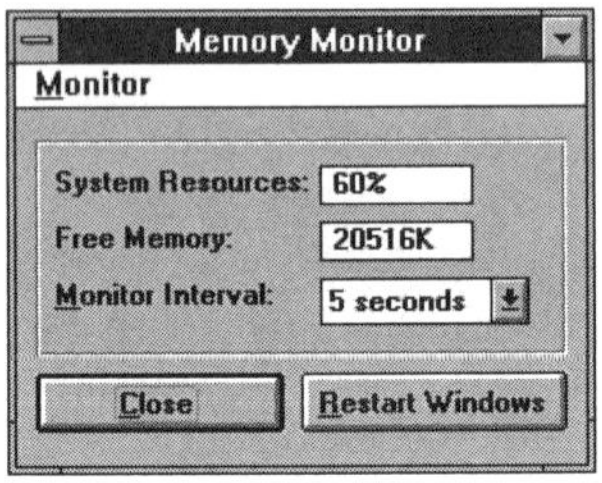

The Memory Monitor window.

Mortgage Minder This program lets you calculate the monthly payment for a mortgage, and it'll even take into account an extra principal payment each month. To use it, first fill in the following text boxes:

House Price   The full price for the house.

Down Payment   The down payment you plan to make.

Annual Interest Rate   The yearly mortgage interest rate.

Term   The term of the mortgage, in years.

Extra Principal/Mth   The extra principal payment you plan to pay each month (enter a negative amount).

Start Date   The starting date for the mortgage (enter the date in MM-YY format).

When you're ready, select the Calculate button. Mortgage Minder fills in the Regular Payment fields and, if you entered a value in the Extra Principal/Mth box, the With Extra Payment fields.

If you'd like to see an amortization schedule (showing, for each month in the term, the date, the current balance, the interest paid, and the principal paid), select the Amortization Table button. In the Save Amortization Table As dialog box, enter a name and destination for the text file containing the table, and then select **OK**. Mortgage Minder calculates the table and then displays it in Notepad.

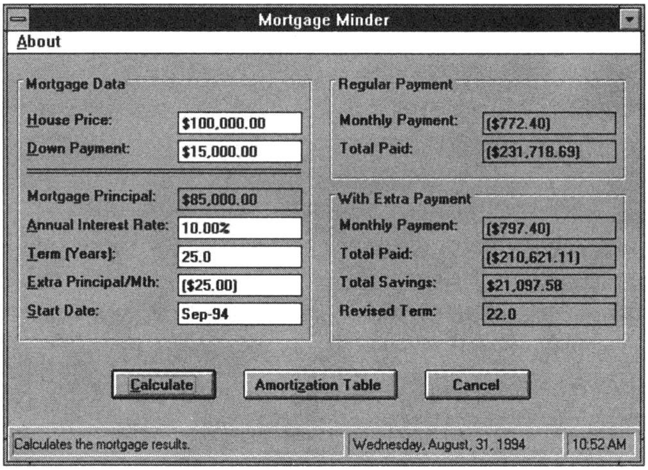

The Mortgage Minder window.

ALLINI   I introduced INI files in Chapter 9, "Learning to Love Those Strange INI Files," and then we used them in various other chapters to make Windows work the way we wanted it to. INI files are clearly important, but they can be a pain to edit because it's often hard to find the sections and settings you need. ALLINI changes all that. It's an INI file editor that works by showing you the section names in a given INI file. You can then easily select the section you need and edit its settings.

The ALLINI window.

100 Letters This is a collection of 100 pre-fab business letters that handle everything from a résumé cover letter to a layoff notice. Each letter is a straight text file that can be modified to suit your needs. The files are installed in compressed format in the FREEBIES\LETTERS directory. To decompress the files, pull down Program Manager's **File** menu, select **Run**, type **C:\FREEBIES\LETTERS\LETTERS.EXE**, and then select **OK**. You'll find it's hard to tell what each file contains by its file name. (For example, what do you suppose the file 1SLPYBS.TXT is all about?) To get a translation, open the document FILES388.TXT.

RecStop In Chapter 18, "Windows Robotics: Recording Recorder Macros," I showed you how to create Program Manager icons for your macros. These icons have two quirks that can make them frustrating: they don't work properly if Recorder is already running, and they leave Recorder open when they're done. This means that, after running one macro icon, you can't run another until you switch to Recorder and shut it down. To save this hassle, I created RecStop, a little utility that does one thing only: it checks to see if Recorder is running, and closes it if it is. The next time you record a macro that you'll be using as an icon, finish the macro by running RecStop. (The easiest way to do this would be to press **Alt+Tab** to get to Program Manager, select the **F**ile menu's **R**un command, type **C:\FREEBIES\RECSTOP\RECSTOP.EXE**, and press **Enter**; alternatively, assign a shortcut key to the **RecStop** icon in the **Freebies** group, and then press the key combination in your macro.) Recorder will ask if you want to save your changes; select **Y**es. When you run the icon, RecStop will kick in at the end and close Recorder automatically.

Index

Symbols

A

B

C

D

E

F

G

H

I

K-L

M

N-O

P

Q-R

S

T